OUTDOORS

D1026865

TAKE A HIKE
BOSTON

JACQUELINE TOURVILLE

Hilliard Branch
15821 CR 108
Hilliard, FL 32046

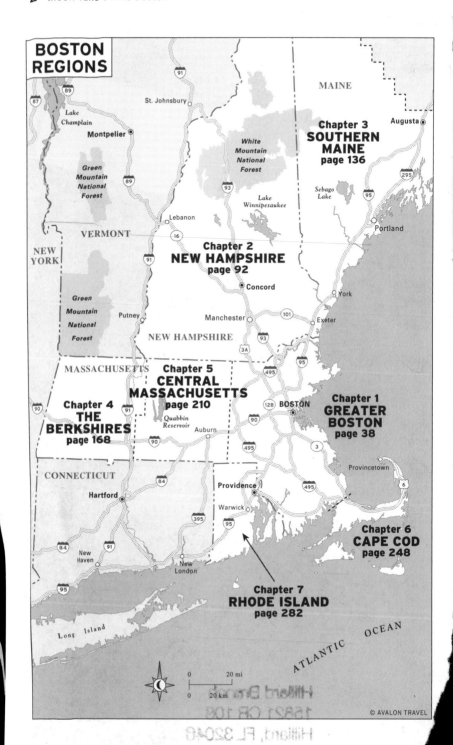

BOSTON REGIONS

MAINE

Chapter 3 SOUTHERN MAINE page 136

Lake Champlain

Montpelier

St. Johnsbury

Augusta

White Mountain National Forest

Green Mountain National Forest

Sebago Lake

Lake Winnipesaukee

Portland

Lebanon

VERMONT

Chapter 2 NEW HAMPSHIRE page 92

NEW YORK

Concord

York

Green Mountain National Forest

Putney

Manchester

Exeter

NEW HAMPSHIRE

MASSACHUSETTS

Chapter 5 CENTRAL MASSACHUSETTS page 210

Chapter 1 GREATER BOSTON page 38

Chapter 4 THE BERKSHIRES page 168

Quabbin Reservoir

Auburn

BOSTON

CONNECTICUT

Provincetown

Hartford

Providence

Warwick

Chapter 6 CAPE COD page 248

New Haven

New London

Chapter 7 RHODE ISLAND page 282

Long Island

ATLANTIC OCEAN

0   20 mi

0   20 km

© AVALON TRAVEL

Contents

How to Use This Book

ABOUT THE MAPS

This book is divided into chapters based on regions that are within close reach of the city; an overview map of these regions precedes the table of contents. Each chapter begins with a region map that shows the locations and numbers of the trails listed in that chapter.

Each trail profile is also accompanied by a detailed trail map that shows the hike route.

Map Symbols

-------	Featured Trail	(80)	Interstate Freeway	○	City/Town
-- -- -- -- -	Other Trail	(101)	U.S. Highway	✗ ✈	Airfield/Airport
▫▫▫▫▫▫▫▫	Expressway	(21)	State Highway	⚲	Golf Course
———	Primary Road	[66]	County Highway	⬝	Waterfall
———	Secondary Road	★	Point of Interest	⬛	Swamp
▫ ▫ ▫ ▫ ▫	Unpaved Road	▣	Parking Area	▲	Mountain
·············	Ferry	⬛	Trailhead	⬥	Park
——·——·	National Border	▲	Campground	)(	Pass
——··——	State Border	▪	Other Location	✦	Unique Natural Feature

ABOUT THE TRAIL PROFILES

Each profile includes a narrative description of the trail's setting and terrain. This description also typically includes mile-by-mile hiking directions, as well as information about the trail's highlights and unique attributes.

The trails marked by the **BEST** ◖ symbol are highlighted in the author's Best Hikes list.

Options

If alternative routes are available, this section is used to provide information on side trips or note how to shorten or lengthen the hike.

Directions

This section provides detailed driving directions to the trailhead from the city center or from the intersection of major highways. When public transportation is available, instructions will be noted here.

Information and Contact

This section provides information on fees, facilities, and access restrictions for the trail. It also includes the name of the land management agency or organization that oversees the trail, as well as an address, phone number, and website if available.

ABOUT THE ICONS

The icons in this book are designed to provide at-a-glance information on special features for each trail.

- 🔲 The trail climbs to a high overlook with wide views.
- 🔲 The trail offers an opportunity for wildlife-watching.
- 🔲 The trail offers an opportunity for bird-watching
- 🔲 The trail features wildflower displays in spring.
- 🔲 The trail visits a beach.

- 🔲 The trail travels to a waterfall.
- 🔲 The trail visits a historical site.
- 🔲 The trail is open to snowshoers in winter.
- 🔲 Dogs are allowed.
- 🔲 The trail is appropriate for children.
- 🔲 The trail is wheelchair accessible.
- 🔲 The trailhead can be accessed via public transportation.

ABOUT THE DIFFICULTY RATING

Each profile also includes a difficulty rating. The ratings are defined as follows:

Easy: Easy hikes are 5 miles or less round-trip and have less than 700 feet of elevation gain (nearly level). They are generally suitable for families with small children and hikers seeking a mellow stroll.

Easy/Moderate: Easy/Moderate hikes are between 4 and 8 miles round-trip and have 500 1,200 feet of elevation gain. They are generally suitable for families with active children above the age of six and hikers who are reasonably fit.

Moderate: Moderate hikes are between 5 and 9 miles round-trip and have 1,000 2,000 feet of elevation gain. They are generally suitable for adults and children who are fit.

Strenuous: Strenuous hikes are between 5 and 10 miles round-trip and have 1,800 2,800 feet of elevation gain. They are suitable for very fit hikers who are seeking a workout.

Butt-kicker: Butt-kicker hikes are between 7 and 14 miles round-trip and have 3,000 feet or more of elevation gain. These hikes are suitable only for advanced hikers who are very physically fit.

The level of difficulty for any trail can change considerably due to weather or trail conditions. Always phone ahead to check on current trail and weather conditions.

INTRODUCTION

Author's Note

What keeps me calm when my commute comes to a grinding halt in Boston traffic? Thinking about my hiking gear stored neatly in the trunk, ready for another weekend away from the urban hustle and bustle. From beginner-friendly, low terrain treks to alpine adventures in New England's higher elevations, my Saturday escapes have given me the chance to explore just about every peak and valley found within a few hours drive of Boston.

From the sand dunes of Cape Cod and the craggy coast of Maine to the famous White Mountains of New Hampshire and the rolling hills of the The Berkshires, the diversity of hiking terrain surrounding Boston is nothing short of amazing. Throughout the New England area—and within the pages of this book—you will find hikes that readily accommodate the young and old, the physically challenged, the most expert of hikers, and the novice.

Where to start? For those new to hiking, or new to the Boston area, get to know the "wild side" of the metro area by exploring trails closest to the city. Walden Pond in nearby Concord is accessible by public transportation and is a chance to explore the pond and woods made famous by Henry David Thoreau. Head to the North Shore to explore the rocky woods of Dogtown in Gloucester or spend the day on the South Shore exploring such local gems as World's End in Hingham or the pine forest of Myles Standish State Forest. More advanced hikers may be surprised to find that just minutes from downtown Boston, trails in the Blue Hills Reservation and Middlesex Fells offer challenge, plenty of elevation gain, and lots of rewarding views.

Outside the Hub, interesting and inspiring destinations abound. In southern Maine, there's the urban destination of Portland, Maine and the Eastern Promenade, the city's scenic recreation path along Casco Bay. Also found in Maine's southern tier are hikes that take you deep into towering evergreen forests, up scenic mountain peaks, and out along the rocky Maine coast—a true microcosm of what makes the Pine Tree State a can't-miss for hikers. In neighboring New Hampshire, climb to the top of Mount Lafayette along the Franconia Ridge in the White Mountains or wander through lush woods on the way to hidden ponds and waterfalls. Mount Monadnock in the southern part of the Granite State is one of the most frequently climbed summits in the world and you will see why after a trip to the top reveals mountain views unrivaled anywhere in region.

Back in Massachusetts, Cape Cod beckons with unforgettable hikes that take you along the crashing surf of the National Seashore, through salt marshes and swamps, and arguably to some of the most beautiful natural scenery found anywhere on earth. (Yes, I am biased, but hiking to the tip of Great Island to watch the sunset over Cape Cod Bay is something you won't soon forget.)

Pushing west from Boston brings you to the uplands of central Massachusetts and finally to the The Berkshires, where the state's best mountain hikes are found. Mount Greylock, the highest peak in the state is here (though technically part of the Taconic Range), as are satisfying climbs up Monument Mountain, Mount Toby, and Mount Tom, part of the volcanic steprock Metacomet Ridge that stretches along the Connecticut River Valley. Autumn foliage in the deciduous-heavy forests of western Massachusetts burns bright, making trails in the area a good pick for a colorful fall outing.

Finally, just a quick trip south on I-95 brings you to Rhode Island. Don't let its small size fool you. "Rhody" is home to nothing short of a stellar number of quality, lower elevation hiking trails and walking paths, many of them tucked away in surprisingly large wildlife and nature preserves. In Newport, the famous Cliff Walk, a seaside hike in the shadow of sprawling Gilded Age mansions, has no equal in New England. Elsewhere in the Ocean State, opportunity abounds for bird-watching, coastal walks, and long rambles through quiet patches of woods. And just 13 miles off the mainland coast is Block Island, named by The Nature Conservancy as one of "The Last Great Places" in the western hemisphere. Though it's one of Rhode Island's most popular summer tourist destinations, roughly 20 percent of the island has been set aside for conservation, preserving Block's wild, lonesome feel.

The hikes found within the pages of this book are each among my favorite. I hope you find, as I have, that these are trails you want to explore and visit again and again. Craggy summits, ethereal forests, glacier-carved lakes, kid-friendly walking paths, wheelchair accessible trails, waterfalls, and even a bit of true wilderness adventure await you. So come on Boston, pick a hike and pack your gear!

Best Hikes

❰ Best for Bird-Watching
Dike Trail, Greater Boston, page 52
Mount Agamenticus, Southern Maine, page 153
Mount Tom, The Berkshires, page 201
Quabbin Reservoir, Central Massachusetts, page 237
Norman Bird Sanctuary, Rhode Island, page 269
Ninigret National Wildlife Refuge, Rhode Island, page 308

❰ Best Butt-Kickers
Blue Hills Skyline Trail, Greater Boston, page 78
Mount Lafayette, New Hampshire, page 105
Mount Greylock, The Berkshires, page 170
Mount Toby, The Berkshires, page 181

❰ Best Coastal Hikes
Spectacle Island and Georges Island, Greater Boston, page 67
Ogunquit Cliff Walk, Southern Maine, page 156
Province Lands Trail, Cape Cod, page 250
Great Island Trail, Cape Cod, page 256
Newport Cliff Walk, Rhode Island, page 299

❰ Best for Fall Foliage
Welch and Dickey, New Hampshire, page 107
Mount Monadnock, New Hampshire, page 126
Fire Tower Hike, The Berkshires, page 176
South Sugarloaf Mountain, The Berkshires, page 178
Crow Hills, Central Massachusetts, page 221

❰ Best Historical Hikes
Dogtown Trail, Greater Boston, page 49
Battle Road Trail, Great Boston, page 55
Walden Pond Trail, Greater Boston, page 58
Mohawk Trail, The Berkshires, page 173
Rattlesnake Knob and the Horse Caves, Central Massachusetts, page 234

◖ Best Kid-Friendly Hikes
Battle Road Trail, Greater Boston, page 55
Drumlin Farm, Greater Boston, page 61
Spectacle Island and Georges Island, Greater Boston, page 67
Beaver Brook Trail, New Hampshire, page 129
Mohawk Trail, The Berkshires, page 173

◖ Best by Public Transportation
Battle Road Trail, Greater Boston, page 55
Walden Pond Trail, Greater Boston, page 58
Skyline Trail, Greater Boston, page 64
Spectacle Island and Georges Island, Greater Boston, page 67
Blue Hills Skyline Trail, Greater Boston, page 78

◖ Best for Solitude
Noanet Peak, Greater Boston, page 72
Pine Barrens and Ponds Loop, Greater Boston, page 86
Hubbard River Trail, The Berkshires, page 204
Willard Brook, Central Massachusetts, page 219

◖ Best Summit Views
Mount Lafayette, New Hampshire, page 105
Mount Monadnock, New Hampshire, page 126
South Sugarloaf Mountain, The Berkshires, page 178
Monument Mountain, The Berkshires, page 190
Crag Mountain, Central Massachusetts, page 214

◖ Best for Wheelchair Access
Battle Road Trail, Greater Boston, page 55
Back Cove Trail and Eastern Promenade, Southern Maine, page 144
Tranquility Trail, The Berkshires, page 184
Norwottuck Trail, The Berkshires, page 199
Cape Cod Rail Trail, Cape Cod, page 268

Hiking Tips

It doesn't require much more than a little wilderness knowledge and a backpack's worth of key items to ensure your day hike in New England is a safe and fun adventure. Here are some tips to make the most out of your hikes.

HIKING ESSENTIALS

Much could be written about how to outfit oneself for hiking in a region like New England, with its significant range of elevations and latitudes, alpine zones, huge seasonal temperature swings, and fairly wet climate.

Don't leave your clothing, gear, and other equipment choices to chance. Boston and the greater New England region are packed with plenty of friendly, locally-owned stores that offer quality, outdoor clothing and footwear options (and knowledgeable staff to help you). Or, take part in the venerable Yankee tradition of the swap meet. Many of New England's mountain clubs hold semi-annual or seasonal meets, giving hikers the irresistible chance to scoop up quality used gear at a very frugal price. Swap meets are also a fun and easy way to meet others in the hiking community.

Clothing

Clothes protect you against the elements and also help to regulate body temperature. What you wear when you go hiking should keep you dry and comfortable, no matter what the weather and season. From underwear to outerwear, pick garments that offer good "breathability." Wool blends and the new breed of synthetic microfibers do a good job at wicking moisture away from the skin. Shirts and pants made from microfiber polyesters are also extra light and stretchy, allowing for maximum range of movement.

You will also want to dress in layers: underwear, one or more intermediate layers, and, finally, an outer layer. Wearing multiple layers of clothing offers you lots of flexibility for regulating body temperature and exposure. Test your clothing at different temperatures and levels of activity to find out what works best for you.

EXTRA CLOTHING

At lower elevations amid the protection of trees or on a warm day, you may elect to bring no extra clothing for an hour-long outing, or no more than a light jacket for a few hours or more. The exception to this is in the Seacoast region, where hikes are more exposed to cool wind. In addition, the higher elevations, especially in the high peaks of New Hampshire, get much colder than the valleys—about three degrees Fahrenheit per thousand feet—and winds can grow much stronger. Even in the southern fringes of the White Mountains, a warm fall day at the trailhead can still yield snowy conditions at the summit.

Insulating layers, a jacket that protects against wind and precipitation, a warm hat, gloves, a rain poncho, and extra socks are always a good idea to bring along when out on a long hike. Even on a shorter trek, stowing a jacket, hat, and extra pair of socks in your backpack is always a good idea.

Shoes and Socks
HIKING BOOTS
The most important piece of gear may be well-fitting, comfortable, supportive shoes or boots. Finding the right footwear requires trying on various models and walking around in them in the store before deciding. Everyone's feet are different, and shoes or boots that feel great on your friend won't necessarily fit you well. Deciding how heavy your footwear should be depends on variables like how often you hike, whether you easily injure feet or ankles, and how much weight you'll carry. My general recommendation is to hike in the most lightweight footwear that you find comfortable and adequately supportive.

There are three basic types of hiking boots. Sneaker-like trail shoes are adequate when you are hiking in a dry climate and on well-established paths. Traditional hiking boots, sometimes called trail hikers or trail boots, are constructed with a higher cut and slightly stiffer sole to provide support on steep inclines and muddy paths. Mountaineering boots are for those who might need to attach crampons for a better grip on glaciers or hard-packed snow on mountain hikes and rock or ice climbing. Mountaineering boots are built with a very stiff sole to give your feet and ankles support and protection as you climb more challenging terrain.

The hiking boot experts at L.L. Bean, New England's premier shopping destination for outdoor gear and equipment, recommend hikers consider the various advantages of fabric-and-leather boots and all-leather boots. Fabric-and-leather boots are lighter and easier to break in, but all-leather boots offer added protection and durability in rigorous terrain, as well as being water resistant and breathable. Quality boots can be found in either style.

Try boots on at the end of the day when your feet are more swollen and wear the socks you plan to wear on the trail. Boots should feel snug but comfortable, so you can still wiggle your toes. Most hiking boots won't feel as instantly comfortable as sneakers, but they shouldn't pinch, cause hot spots, or constrict circulation. They should fit securely around your ankle and instep. Try walking down an incline at the store. Your feet should not slide forward, nor should your toenails scrape against the front of your boot. If your foot slides forward, the boot could be too wide. If the back of your heel moves around, your boots might not be laced up tight enough.

Once you purchase a pair of boots, break them in slowly with short hikes. Leather boots in particular take a while to break in, so take a couple of two- or three-hour hikes before your big trip or wear them around the house. If you find any sharp pressure points, use leather conditioner to soften the leather.

Socks

With exertion, one foot can sweat up to two pints of vapor/fluid per day. That's why wicking technology in hiking socks is so important. Without it, bacteria and fungus can become a problem. The best hiking socks are made from 100 percent wool or a wool blend of at least 50 percent wool. Unlike most synthetic fibers, which have to wait for moisture to condense into a liquid before wicking it away from your skin, wool socks absorb and transfer moisture in its vapor state, before it condenses. When it's hot, this creates a mini air-conditioning unit next to your feet, releasing heat through your socks and boots. And when it's cold, wicking keeps bone-chilling moisture at bay.

Some newer synthetics and synthetic blends are engineered to wick moisture; read the package label carefully and ask the store clerk for recommendations. The one fiber to stay away from is cotton, which absorbs water and perspiration and holds it next to your skin. If you are hiking with wet feet and the temperature drops below freezing, you risk getting frostbite. A good sock system combined with good hiking boots reduce that possibility.

For comfort and maximum circulation, look for socks that won't bind your feet and avoid those made with excessive stitching or a scratchy knit that could lead to chafing. Terry woven socks are a good pick to distribute pressure and support your natural posture. And thicker isn't always better. Depending on the fit of your boots and the climate you'll be hiking in, a medium-weight wool sock that fits to mid-calf is often your best bet.

Rain Gear

Coastal currents smashing up against weather fronts dropping south from Canada give New England its famously fickle weather. Especially in summer, a sunny late morning start to your hike could mean a return trip in a raging rainstorm, often with very little warning time. No matter where you go or how long you expect to be out on the trail, bring along rain gear. It doesn't need to be elaborate: a vinyl foul-weather poncho left in its packaging until needed is a compact addition to your pack.

If you do end up getting caught in a thunderstorm or sudden downpour, move away from high ground and tall trees immediately. Take shelter in a low spot, ravine, or thin place in the woods, cover up with your poncho, and wait for the storm to pass. Also, look carefully at your surroundings, making sure you are not standing in a dry riverbed or wash while waiting, in case of flash floods.

Being out in rainy weather is also a concern for your feet and legs. Brushing up against wet ferns or low-lying plants can make for uncomfortably damp pant legs and soaked socks and boots. In case you do get stuck in the rain, another good piece of equipment to have on hand is a pair of gaiters, leggings made of Gore-Tex or other water-repellent materials. Gaiters are held in place under each boot with a stirrup and extend over your pants to just below the knee.

Water and Food

Like any physical activity, hiking increases your body's fluid needs by a factor of two or more. Take along water even on the shortest of treks. For hikes of more than a few miles, a good rule of thumb is two liters of water per person, but even that could leave you mildly dehydrated (especially if the weather is warm or the hike requires great physical exertion), so carry a third liter if you can. Dehydration can lead to other, more serious, problems, like heat exhaustion, hypothermia, frostbite, and injury. If you're well hydrated, you will urinate frequently and your urine will be clear. The darker your urine, the greater your level of dehydration. If you feel thirsty, dehydration has already commenced. In short: Drink a lot.

Streams and brooks run everywhere in New England. If you're out for more than a day in the backcountry, finding water is rarely a problem (except on ridge tops and summits). But microscopic organisms *Giardia lamblia* and *Cryptosporidium* are common in backcountry water sources and can cause a litany of terrible gastrointestinal problems in humans. Assume you should always treat water from backcountry sources, whether by using a filter or iodine tablets, boiling, or another proven method to eliminate giardiasis and other harmful bacteria. Day hikers will usually find it more convenient to simply carry enough water from home for the hike.

Similarly, your body consumes a phenomenal amount of calories walking up and down a mountain. Feed it frequently. Carbohydrate-rich foods such as bread, chocolate, dried fruit, fig bars, snack bars, fresh vegetables, and energy bars are all good sources for a quick burst of energy. Fats contain about twice the calories per pound than carbs or protein, and provide the slow-burning fuel that keeps you going all day and keeps you warm through the night if you're sleeping outside; sate your need for fats by eating cheese, chocolate, canned meats or fish, pepperoni, sausage, or nuts.

On hot days, "refrigerate" your water and perishables such as cheese and chocolate:

Fill a water bottle (the collapsible kind works best) with very cold water, and ice cubes if possible. Wrap it and your perishables in a thick, insulating fleece and bury it inside your pack. Or the night before, fill a water bottle halfway and freeze it, then fill the remainder with water in the morning before you leave for the hike.

Navigational Tools

At some point, almost every hiker becomes lost. Missing trail signs, trail detours, faded blazes, and snow, fog, and other conditions can make staying the course very rough going. First, take every step to prevent becoming lost. Before you hike, study a map of the area to become familiar with the trails, nearby roads, streams, mountains and other features. Leave a trip plan with family or friends and sign in at the trailhead register or nearby ranger cabin, if a hiker registry is available.

Always hike with a map and compass. And as you ramble along the trail, observe the topography around you (ridges, recognizable summits, rivers, etc.). They serve as good reference points, particularly when you are above the tree line. Some hikers leave small piles of rocks spaced at regular intervals to help them navigate treeless, alpine areas. Should you become disoriented, stop, pull out your map and look at the countryside for familiar landmarks.

Few people remain truly lost after consulting a map and calmly studying the terrain for five minutes. If you still need help orienting yourself, you may want to head to a ridge or high ground so you can identify hills or streams that are marked on your topographical map. Lay your map on the ground and put your compass on top to orient north. Another helpful gadget is an altimeter, which can tell you

GLOBAL POSITIONING SYSTEM (GPS) DEVICES

Working with a system of orbiting satellites, GPS receivers are able to accurately pinpoint your position, elevation, and time anywhere on the face of the earth. Out on the trail, GPS devices can help you navigate from point to point, indicating bearings and the distance remaining to reach your destination. It can also help should you become lost.

Despite these advances, GPS technology is not a replacement for the old standby of a compass and paper topographical map. GPS units are not yet able to provide an adequately detailed view of the surrounding landscape, batteries typically wear out in less than a day, and some landscape conditions can interfere with signal strength. Still, when used in concert with a topographical maps, a GPS device is an extremely useful addition to your navigational toolbox.

Every hike in this book lists GPS coordinates for the hike's trailhead. Use these for better road navigation on the drive to your destination. Inputting the trailhead GPS coordinates before leaving on your hike will also help you retrace your steps if you become lost.

your approximate elevation; you can then pinpoint this elevation on a topographic map. Until you have your bearings, don't wander too far from your original route. If you told family members or fellow hikers where you plan to hike, that area is where rescuers will start searching for you.

Should you continue to be lost, STOP (stop, think, observe, plan). And don't panic. Not only does it cloud your judgment, you will be using up energy that you may need later on. Stay put and, if you carry a whistle, blow it at timed intervals to signal rescuers or other hikers (yelling also works).

TRAIL MAPS

A map of the park, preserve, or public land you are visiting is essential. Even if you have hiked a trail a hundred times, carry a map. Unexpected trail closures, an injury requiring a shorter route, bad weather, or an animal encounter can all result in a sudden change of plans that require map assistance. Some may believe a GPS device takes the place of a map, but this isn't always true. If you get lost, a detailed trail map showing lakes, rivers, ridge lines, trail junctions, and other landmarks is still the most reliable way to get back on the trail.

Many land agencies provide free paper maps at the trailhead, though be aware that some state parks and land agencies are much more vigilant about restocking than others. Check the agency's website to see if maps can be printed out beforehand or call to request a map be sent to you. The Appalachian Mountain Club and the Appalachian Trail Conservancy also publish a number of New England hiking maps.

BLAZES AND CAIRNS

New England's forests abound with blazes—slashes of paint on trees used to mark trails. Although not all trails are well blazed, popular and well-maintained trails usually are—you'll see a colored slash of paint at frequent intervals at about eye level on tree trunks. Double slashes are sometimes used to indicate a sharp turn in the trail. Trails are blazed in both directions, so whenever you suspect

Rock cairns (small piles of rocks) can act as directional signs to keep you from getting lost.

© SABRINA YOUNG

you may have lost the trail, turn around to see whether you can find a blaze facing in the opposite direction; if so, you'll know you're still on the trail.

Above tree line or in places where tree blazes may be ineffective, trails may be marked either with blazes painted on rock or with cairns, which are piles of stones constructed at regular intervals. Care may be needed to discern artificially constructed cairns from the landscape surrounding them, but cairns in rocky areas are usually built higher and are obviously constructed by people.

Flashlight

Carrying a flashlight in your pack is a must, even when your hike is planned to end well before dusk. Emergencies happen, and being stuck on the trail after dark without a flashlight only compounds the situation. Plus, if you have ever been in New England right before a thunderstorm, you know fast moving cloud cover can turn the landscape pitch dark in seconds. Micro flashlights with alloy skins, xenon bulbs, and a battery life of eight hours on two AA batteries provide ample illumination and won't add much weight to your pack. Throw in some spare batteries and an extra light—or just pack two flashlights to always be covered. A reliable, compact, and waterproof micro flashlight can typically be purchased for under $20.

Sunscreen and Sunglasses

Who wants to ruin a beautiful day on the trail by ending it with a serious sunburn? Applying sunscreen or sunblock to exposed skin and wearing a baseball cap or wide-brimmed hat can easily prevent overexposure to sun. SPF strengths vary, but applying sunscreen at least a half-hour before heading out gives the lotion or spray enough time to take effect. When deciding which sunscreen to buy, look for a fragrance-free formula; strongly scented lotions and sprays may attract mosquitoes. And don't forget your sunglasses. Squinting into the sun for hours on end is not only bad for the delicate skin around your eyes, it's almost a certain way to develop a bad case of eye strain. Look for sunglasses with lenses that provide 100 percent UVA and UVB protection.

Backpack

When just out for the day, a roomy backpack will do to hold your belongings; toting an oversized metal frame pack is not necessary unless you plan on camping overnight and need to bring along camp stove, bed roll, tent, and other extra gear. Shoulder straps should be foam padded for comfort. Look for backpacks made of water-resistant nylon. And just like clothes or shoes, try the pack on to make sure it has the fit you want.

Trekking Poles

For hikers who need a little extra physical support, trekking poles or walking sticks relieve feet and legs of tens of thousands of pounds of pressure over the course of an all-day hike. They are particularly useful in helping prevent knee and back pain from rigorous hiking. If you find a good walking stick along your journey, before heading back to your car, leave the stick in an obvious spot for another weary hiker to stumble upon. It warmed my heart one day to find at least a dozen walking sticks leaning against a trailhead signpost, free for anyone to use.

using trekking poles on a steep hike

First-Aid

New England's most rugged trails—and even parts of its more moderate paths—can be very rocky and steep. Uneven terrain is often a major contributor to falls resulting in serious, acute injury. Most of us have a fairly reliable self-preservation instinct—and you should trust it. If something strikes you as dangerous or beyond your abilities, don't try it, or simply wait until you think you're ready for it.

An injury far from a road also means it may be hours before the victim reaches a hospital. Basic training in wilderness first aid is beneficial to anyone who frequents the mountains, even recreational hikers. New England happens to have two highly respected sources for such training, and the basic course requires just one weekend. Contact SOLO (Conway, NH, 603/447-6711, www.soloschools.com) or Wilderness Medical Associates (Scarborough, ME, 207/730-7331, www.wildmed.com) for information.

First-Aid Kit

It's wise to carry a compact and lightweight first-aid kit for emergencies, especially in the backcountry, where an ambulance and hospital are often hours, rather than minutes, away. Prepare any first-aid kit with attention to the type of trip, the destination, and the needs of people hiking (for example, children or people with medical conditions).

A basic first-aid kit consists of:
- aspirin or an anti-inflammatory
- four four-by-four-inch gauze pads
- knife or scissors
- moleskin or blister pads
- one roll of one-inch athletic tape
- one six-inch Ace bandage
- paper and pencil
- safety pins
- SAM splint (a versatile and lightweight splinting device available at many drug stores)
- several alcohol wipes
- several one-inch adhesive bandages
- tube of povidone iodine ointment (for wound care)
- two large handkerchiefs
- two large gauze pads

Pack everything into a thick, clear plastic resealable bag. And remember, merely carrying a first-aid kit does not make you safe; knowing how to use what's in it does.

FOOTCARE

At an Appalachian Mountain Club hiking seminar, one instructor wisely noted that, besides the brain, "Your feet are the most important part of your body." Hurt any other body part and we might conceivably still make it home under our own power. Hurt our feet, and we're in trouble.

Take care of your feet. Wear clean socks that wick moisture from your skin while staying dry. Make sure your shoes or boots fit properly, are laced properly, and are broken in if they require it. Wear the appropriate footwear for the type of hiking you plan to do. If you anticipate your socks getting wet from perspiration or water, bring extra socks. On hot days, roll your socks down over your boot tops to create what shoe manufacturers call "the chimney effect," cooling your feet by forcing air into your boots as you walk.

On longer treks, whenever you stop for a short rest on the trail—even if only for 5 or 10 minutes—sit down, pull off your boots and socks, and let them and your feet dry out. If you feel any hot spots developing, intervene before they progress into blisters. A slightly red or tender hot spot can be protected from developing into a blister with an adhesive bandage, tape, or a square of moleskin.

If a blister has formed, clean the area around it thoroughly to avoid infection. Sterilize a needle or knife in a flame, then pop and drain the blister to promote faster healing.

Put an antiseptic ointment on the blister. Cut a piece of moleskin or other blister pad (these should have a soft side and a sticky side with a peel-off backing) large enough to overlap the blistered area. Cut a hole as large as the blister out of the center of the moleskin, then place the moleskin over the blister so that the blister is visible through the hole. If done properly, you should be able to walk without aggravating it.

HEAT STROKE

Our bodies produce a tremendous amount of internal heat. Under normal conditions, we cool ourselves by sweating and radiating heat through the skin. However, in certain circumstances, such as extreme heat, high humidity, or vigorous activity in the hot sun, this cooling system may begin to fail, allowing heat to build up to dangerous levels.

If a person becomes dehydrated and cannot sweat enough to cool their body, their internal temperature may rise to dangerously high levels, causing heat stroke. Symptoms include headache, mental confusion, and cramps throughout the entire body. If you have these symptoms, or notice them in a member of your hiking party, take immediate action to lower the body's core temperature. Get out of the sun and move to a shadier location. Pour water over the victim and fan the skin to stimulate sweating; sit in a nearby stream, if possible. Encourage the victim to drink liquids and rest. If symptoms are severe or don't improve within a few minutes of starting first aid, do not hesitate to call for help.

Probably the most effective way to cut risk for heat stroke is to stay adequately hydrated. When the temperatures soar on a New England summer day, stop frequently on the trail for water and rest breaks.

HYPOTHERMIA

In humans and other warm-blooded animals, core body temperature is maintained near a constant level through internal temperature regulation. When the body is over-exposed to cold, however, internal mechanisms may be unable to replenish excessive heat loss. Hypothermia is defined as any body temperature below 95°F (35°C). Despite its association with winter, hypothermia can occur even when the air temperature is in the 50s. Often the victim has gotten wet or overexerted themself on the trail. Hypothermia is a leading cause of death in the outdoors.

Symptoms of hypothermia include uncontrollable shivering, weakness, loss of coordination, confusion, cold skin, drowsiness, frost bite, and slowed breathing or heart rate. If a member of your hiking party demonstrates one or more of these symptoms, send a call out for help and take action immediately. Get out of the wind and cold and seek shelter in a warm, dry environment. Help the victim change into windproof, waterproof clothes and wrap up in a blanket, if one is available; start a fire to add extra warmth. Encourage the victim to eat candy, energy bars, and other high-sugar foods to boost energy. Do not offer alcohol, it only makes heat loss worse.

Victims of mild to moderate hypothermia may be suffering from impaired judgment and not be making rational decisions. They might try to resist help; be persistent.

Sprains and Breaks

For any sprain or strain, remember RICE: rest, ice, compression, elevation. First, have the patient rest by lying down on the ground or nearest flat surface. Next, reduce swelling by gently placing a plastic freezer bag filled with cold water on the injury. To compress the ankle, snugly wrap the injury in an ACE bandage. (First-aid tape will also work.) The wrap should cover the entire foot except for the heel and end several inches above the ankle. Most compression wraps are self-fastening or come with clip fasteners—or use tape to secure the end. If toes become purplish or blue, cool to the touch, or feel numb or tingly according to the patient, the wrap is too tight and should be loosened.

Keep the leg elevated until swelling is visibly reduced. When you or someone you are with suffers a sprained ankle or other minor injury on the trail, keep an open mind about finishing the hike. Because it's always more enjoyable when everyone can fully participate, it might be best to cut your losses and come back another time.

ON THE TRAIL
Climate

With New England's mountains, hills, and flatlands, as well as an ocean moderating the Seacoast climate, this region's fair-weather hikers can find a trail to explore virtually year-round. But the wildly varied character of hiking opportunities here also demands some basic knowledge of and preparation for hitting the trails.

The ocean generally keeps coastal areas a little warmer in winter and cooler in summer than inland areas. Otherwise, any time of year, average temperatures typically grow cooler as you gain elevation or move northward.

The Boston area's prime hiking season stretches for several months from spring through fall, with the season's length depending on the region. In general, summer high temperatures range 60°F–90°F with lows from 50°F to around 32°F at higher elevations. Days are often humid in the forests and lower elevations and windy on the mountaintops. July and August see occasional thunderstorms, but July through September is the driest period. August is usually the best month for finding ripe wild blueberries along many trails in southern Maine and New Hampshire.

September is often the best month for hiking, with dry, comfortable days, cool nights, and few bugs. If you want to hike on Cape Cod, September is a good month for avoiding tourist crowds. Fall foliage colors peak anywhere from mid-September or early October in northern New England to early or mid-October in the south; by choosing your destinations well and moving north to south, you can hike through vibrant foliage for three or four successive weekends. The period from mid-October into November offers cool days, cold nights, no bugs, few people, and often little snow.

In the smaller hills and flatlands of central and southern New England, the snow-free hiking season often begins by early spring and lasts into late autumn. Some of these trails are even occasionally free of snow during the winter, or offer opportunities for snowshoeing or cross-country skiing in woods protected from strong winds, with warmer temperatures than you'll find on the bigger peaks up north. Many Seacoast trails, even in Maine, rarely stay snow-covered all winter, though they can get occasional heavy snowfall and be very icy in cold weather.

In the White Mountains, winter conditions set in by mid-November and can

CROSS-COUNTRY SKIING AND SNOWSHOEING

Many hikes in this book are great for cross-country skiing or snowshoeing in winter. But added precaution is needed for this. Days are short and the temperature may start to plummet by mid-afternoon, so carry the right clothing and don't overestimate how far you can travel in winter. Depending on snow conditions and your own fitness level and experience with either snowshoes or skis, a winter outing can take much longer than anticipated — and certainly much longer than a trip of similar distance on groomed trails at a cross-country ski resort. Breaking your own trail through fresh snow can also be very exhausting — take turns leading and conserve energy by following the leader's tracks, which also serve as a good return trail.

The proper clothing becomes essential in winter, especially the farther you wander from roads. Wear a base layer that wicks moisture from your skin and dries quickly, middle layers that insulate and do not retain moisture, and a windproof shell that breathes well and is waterproof or water-resistant (the latter type of garment usually breathes much better than something that's completely waterproof). Size boots to fit over a thin, synthetic liner sock and a thicker, heavyweight synthetic-blend sock. For your hands, often the most versatile system consists of gloves and/or mittens that also can be layered, with an outer layer that's waterproof and windproof and preferably also breathable.

Most importantly, don't overdress. Remove layers if you're getting too hot. Avoid becoming wet with perspiration, which can lead to too much cooling. Drink plenty of fluids and eat snacks frequently to maintain your energy level; feeling tired or cold on a winter outing may be an indication of dehydration or hunger.

As long as you're safe, cautious, and aware, winter is a great time to explore New England's trails. Have fun out there.

become very severe, even life threatening. Going above the tree line in winter is considered a mountaineering experience by many (though these mountains lack glacier travel and high altitude), so be prepared for harsh cold and strong winds. Spring trails are muddy at low elevations—some are closed to hiking during the April/May "mud season." For more information about weather-related trail conditions, refer to the individual hike listings.

Health and Safety

FITNESS

Few of us would consider hiking a high-risk activity. But like any physical activity, it does pose certain risks, and it's up to us to minimize them. For starters, make sure your physical condition is adequate for your objective—the quickest route to injury is overextending either your skills or your physical abilities. You wouldn't presume that you could rock climb a 1,000-foot cliff if you've never climbed before; don't assume you're ready for one of New England's hardest hikes if you've never—or not very recently—done anything nearly as difficult.

Build up your fitness level by gradually increasing your workouts and the length of your hikes. Beyond strengthening muscles, you must strengthen the soft connective tissue in joints like knees and ankles that are too easily strained and take weeks or months to heal from injury. Staying active in a variety of activities—hiking, running, bicycling, Nordic skiing—helps develop good overall fitness and decreases the likelihood of an overuse injury. Most importantly, stretch muscles before and after a workout to reduce the chance of injury.

HIKING SOLO

For safety's sake, hiking with a partner is always best. If you do decide to take to the trail alone, take some basic precautions. Regardless of whether the hike you plan to take is short or long, tell a friend or family member about your plans—when you plan to depart from the trailhead, your basic route, and the anticipated time you expect to return. Stick to daylight hikes and always plan to return before dark. If there is a hiker log book at the trailhead, sign in, noting the time you are starting out. In state forests, duck your head in at the ranger station to grab a trail map and say hello. The more people who know of your presence, the better.

Bringing your cell phone along for added security? New England is one of the country's most wired regions, but still be aware that cell reception can be iffy in spots, especially western Masschusetts and northern New Hampshire.

HUNTING SEASON

Some of the trails listed in this book do cross through lands open to hunters;

hunting season varies by state and region, but generally runs from fall through early winter. During hunting season, nonhunters should wear blaze orange, or an equally bright, conspicuous color. Hunting accidents with hikers are almost unheard of in New England and the hunters you may come across on the trail are usually responsible and friendly and deserve like treatment.

Trail Etiquette

One of the great things about hiking is the quality of the people you meet on the trail. Hikers generally do not need an explanation of the value of courtesy, and one hopes this will always ring true. Still, with the popularity of hiking on the increase, and thousands of new hikers taking to the trails of New England every year, it's a good idea to brush up on some etiquette basics.

As a general rule and a friendly favor to other hikers, yield the trail to others whether you're going uphill or down. All trail users should yield to horses by stepping aside for the safety of everyone present. Likewise, horseback riders should, whenever possible, avoid situations where their animals are forced to push past hikers on very narrow trails. Mountain bikers should yield to hikers, announce their approach, and pass nonbikers slowly.

Many of us enjoy the woods and mountains for the quiet, and we should keep that in mind on the trail, at summits, or backcountry campsites. Many of us share the belief that things like cell phones, radios, and CD players do not belong in the mountains. High tech devices may also pose serious safety risks when used on the trail. Texting while hiking? Not a good idea when you should be watching out for exposed tree roots and rocky footing. Likewise, listening to music or audiobooks through headphones could prevent you from hearing another hiker alerting you to dangers ahead.

New England has seen some conflict between hikers and mountain bikers, but it's important to remember that solutions to those issues are never reached through hostility and rudeness. Much more is accomplished when we begin from a foundation of mutual respect and courtesy. After all, we're all interested in preserving and enjoying our trails.

Large groups have a disproportionate impact on backcountry campsites and on the experience of other people. Be aware of and respect any restrictions on group size. Even where no regulation exists, keep your group size to no more than 10 people.

Tips for Avoiding Crowds

Even on some of the Boston area's most popular hikes, it is still possible to beat the crowds and have the trail all—or mostly—to yourself. Timing is everything. For hikes of less than six or seven miles round-trip, try to arrive at the trailhead early in the morning. Start your hike by 8 or 9 A.M. on a sunny Saturday morning and you will probably be returning to your car just as the weekend crush is arriving. For very short hikes, waiting until late afternoon or early evening before hitting the trail almost always ensures low boot traffic. But keep these late day hikes short and to destinations with easy footing just in case you're still out on the trail when night falls.

For very long hikes of nine miles round-trip or more, this early-bird strategy will not work, since early morning is the normal start time for most longer hikes. To still salvage a little solitude on your journey, you might want to consider breaking high mileage hikes into a two-day trek with an overnight stay at a shelter or backcountry campground. Start out on the trail later in the day and aim to camp at least halfway to the summit (within a mile of the summit is ideal). As early as you can the next day, finish the climb and enjoy the peaceful stillness.

Another way to avoid the crowds is to hike during the work week, when even the busiest of New England's trailheads are almost empty. If it felt as though you were part of a conga line climbing to the top of Great Blue Hill on a warm, sunny Sunday afternoon, come back on Wednesday and find almost no one around. Similarly, time your hikes according to the seasons. With the exception of a few places in northern New England that tend to stay muddy and even icy well into late spring, June is often the best month for encountering light boot traffic. Birds chirp, the air is fresh, wildflowers bloom in the meadows, and the throngs of summer tourists—and swarms of mosquitoes—have yet to arrive. Similarly, the week after Labor Day weekend is often quiet on the trail, with family vacationers gone back to school and the fall foliage season not yet underway.

HIKING WITH CHILDREN

Exploring the great outdoors with kids is one of life's great rewards. Starting from a very young age, a baby can be placed in a carrier and taken out on almost any trail where the walking is flat and the environment serene; the rhythmic pace of hiking tends to lull even the fussiest of infants right to sleep. Backpack carriers are a good way to tote toddlers on-trail and, depending on the model, can accommodate a child of up to 35 pounds. When hiking with a child-carrier pack, keep a small mirror in your pocket so you can frequently check on your passenger without having to stop and remove the pack.

Around age three, kids are ready to hit the trail along with the rest of the family. But, little legs don't travel very far. Make your family outings kid-centric by picking short hikes that lead to exciting features such as waterfalls, duck-filled ponds, giant glacial erratics, huge gnarled tree trunks, beaver dams, and small hills with big views. Even if the hike is under a half mile in total length, plan extra time for rest stops and lots of un-fettered exploration. Most children love the grown-up feel of having their own lightweight backpack; fill the pack with a water bottle and snack treats.

When a child reaches school age, physical ability rises dramatically. And so does his or her responsibility as a hiker. Teach your children how to read maps, how to use a compass, and what to do if lost. Show by example how to be courteous to the other hikers you encounter on the trail. Your efforts will be appreciated.

Hiking with Pets

Dogs are great trail companions and generally love the adventure of hiking every bit as much as their owners do. But dogs can create unnecessary friction in

Hiking with kids can be fun and enjoyable for all.

the backcountry. Dog owners should respect any regulations and not presume that strangers are eager to meet their pet. Keep your pet under physical control whenever other people are approaching. And for your dog's protection, always bring a leash along, even if regulations don't call for one.

Due to their focus on wildlife conservation, several bird refuges and Audubon sanctuaries prohibit pets of any kind, including dogs. Call ahead to these and other destinations to find out trail regulations for pets.

Leave No Trace

Many of the Boston area trails receive heavy use, making it imperative that we all understand how to minimize our physical impact on the land. The nonprofit organization Leave No Trace (LNT) advocates a set of principles for low-impact backcountry use that are summarized in these basic guidelines:

• Be considerate of other visitors.
• Dispose of waste properly.
• Leave what you find.
• Minimize campfire impact.
• Plan ahead and prepare.
• Respect wildlife.
• Travel and camp on durable surfaces.

LNT offers more in-depth guidelines for low-impact camping and hiking on its website www.lnt.org. You can also contact them by mail or phone: Leave No Trace Inc., P.O. Box 997, Boulder, CO 80306, 303/442-8222 or 800/332-4100.

Camping

The following are more recommendations that apply to many backcountry areas in New England:

- Avoid building campfires; cook with a backpacking stove. If you do build a campfire, use only wood found locally as a way to prevent the spread of destructive forest pests introduced from areas outside New England. In all six states, campers are encouraged not to move firewood more than 50 miles from its original source. Store-bought, packaged firewood is usually okay, as long as it is labeled "kiln dried" or "USDA Certified." Wood that is kiln dried is generally free of pests, although if the wood is not heated to a certain temperature, insects can survive.
- Avoid trails that are very muddy in spring; that's when they are most susceptible to erosion.
- Bury human waste beneath six inches of soil at least 200 feet from any water source.
- Burn and bury, or carry out, used toilet paper.
- Carry out everything you carry in.
- Choose a campsite at least 200 feet from trails and water sources, unless you're using a designated site. Make sure your site bears no evidence of your stay when you leave.
- Do not leave any food behind, even buried, as animals will dig it up. Learn how to hang food appropriately to keep it from bears. Black bears have spread their range over much of New England in recent years, and problems have arisen in isolated backcountry areas where human use is heavy.
- Even biodegradable soap is harmful to the environment, so simply wash your cooking gear with water away from any streams or ponds.
- Last but not least, know and follow any regulations for the area you will be visiting.

Wildlife

The remarkable recovery of New England's mountains and forests during the past century from the abuses of the logging industry has spawned a boom in the populations of many wild animals, from increased numbers of black bears and moose to the triumphant return of the bald eagle and peregrine falcon. For the most part, you don't have to worry about your safety in the backcountry when it comes to wildlife encounters. It's typical for hikers to see lots of scat and a traffic jam of prints on the trail without ever actually spotting the animals that left this evidence behind.

Still, a few sensible precautions are in order. If you're camping in the backcountry, know how to hang or store your food properly to keep it from bears and smaller animals like mice, which are more likely to be a problem. You certainly should never approach the region's two largest mammals: moose, which you may see in northern New England, and bear, which you may never see. These creatures are wild and unpredictable; a moose can weigh several hundred pounds and put the hurt on a much smaller human. The greatest danger posed by moose is that of hitting one while driving on dark back roads at night; hundreds of collisions occur in Maine and New Hampshire every year, often wrecking vehicles and injuring people. At night, drive more slowly than you would during daylight. As one forest ranger warns, "the most dangerous part of hiking in the mountains is the drive to the trailhead."

Plants

From fern-choked forest floors to fields filled with wild blueberries, plant life in New England is varied and diverse. And luckily, there are only a few poisonous plant species to be wary of: poison ivy, poison oak, and poison sumac. The three plants contain urushiol, an oil that causes an allergic reaction and rash in humans. According to the American Academy of Dermatology, humans typically come in contact with urushiol by brushing up against or touching the plants, touching an object or animal that has come in contact with the oil, or breathing in urushiol particles if a poison plant is burned in a campfire.

Urushiol penetrates the skin in minutes, but the rash usually takes 12–72 hours to appear, followed quickly by severe itching, redness, swelling, and even blisters. When the rash develops, streaks or lines often reveal where the plant brushed against the skin. A rash triggered by urushiol does not spread and is not contagious.

Recognizing Poisonous Plants

Hikers' best protection against the itchy rash caused by urushiol is learning how to identify the plants that contain the oil.

Poison Ivy: Leaves of three, let them be. Poison ivy grows as vines or low shrubs almost everywhere in New England and true to that famous phrase from summer camp, the plant consists of three pointed leaflets; the middle leaflet has a much longer stalk than the two side ones. Leaflets are reddish when they bud in spring, turn green during the summer, and then become various shades of yellow, orange, or red in the autumn. Small greenish flowers grow in bunches attached to the main stem close to where each leaf joins it. Later in the season, clusters of poisonous berries form. They are whitish, with a waxy look.

Poison Oak: There are two main species of poison oak, but the species commonly found in New England is the Atlantic poison oak, a vine plant or bush. Poison oak leaves grow in clusters of three leaves; the lobed appearance of each leaf resembles the white oak. Plants put out berries in spring that are white or yellowish-green in color and leaflets change color with the seasons. Poison oak tends to grow in sandy soils.

Poison Sumac: Though it is one of New England's native tree species, poison sumac is the rarest of the urushiol-containing plants. Sumac can be identified

poison ivy

by its row of paired leaflets that contains an additional leaflet at the end. Often the leaves have spots that resemble blotches of black enamel paint. These spots are actually urushiol, which when exposed to air turn brownish black. Poison sumac tends to grow near wet areas and bogs.

TREATING POISON IVY, POISON OAK, AND POISON SUMAC

When an allergic reaction develops, the skin should be washed well with lukewarm water and soap. All clothing should be laundered, and everything else that may be contaminated with urushiol should be washed thoroughly. Urushiol can remain active for a long time. For mild cases, cool showers and an over-the-counter product that eases itching can be effective. Oatmeal baths and baking-soda mixtures also can soothe the discomfort. When a severe reaction develops contact a dermatologist immediately, or go to an emergency room. Prescription medication may be needed to reduce the swelling and itch.

Insects

Black flies, or mayflies, emerge by late April or early May and pester hikers until late June or early July, while mosquitoes come out in late spring and dissipate (but do not disappear) by midsummer. No-see-ums (tiny biting flies that live up to their name) plague some wooded areas in summer. Of particular concern in

LYME DISEASE

Deer ticks are often carriers of the bacteria that causes Lyme disease. Hundreds of cases of the disease – most mild and treatable with antibiotics – are diagnosed in New England each year. The easiest way to avoid tick bites is to wear socks, long pants, and a long-sleeve shirt whenever you hike, and especially when you hike in areas with tall grass and/or large deer populations. Tucking your pant legs into your socks prevents the best protection against the tiny ticks, but never fail to check your skin thoroughly at the end of a hike. Most tick bites cause a sharp sting, but some may go unnoticed.

If you do find a tick, don't panic. Take a pair of tweezers and place them around the tick as close to your skin as possible. Gently pull the tick straight out to avoid parts of it breaking off still attached to the skin. The majority of tick bites are no more of a nuisance than a mosquito or black fly bite. If you do notice a rash spreading out from around the bite within a week of finding the tick, it may be an early sign of Lyme disease. Other symptoms are similar to the flu – headache, fever, muscle soreness, neck stiffness, or nausea – and may appear anywhere from a few days to a week or so after being bitten. If you do notice any symptoms, seek medical help immediately. When caught in its early stages, Lyme disease is easily treated with antibiotics; left untreated, the disease can be debilitating.

recent years has been the small, but growing number of cases of eastern equine encephalitis (EEE) in humans, spread by EEE-infected mosquitoes. It's still very rare, but cases of EEE tend to emerge each year at the end of summer and early fall. Mosquitoes acquire EEE through contact with diseased birds.

You will want to have some kind of bug repellent with you no matter where your hike takes you. (Even the windswept coast isn't free of insects; New England's swarms of black flies first appear on the coast and then move inland.) There is much debate about the health effects of wearing sprays containing the chemical DEET; some may prefer ointments made with essential oils and herbs believed to deter bugs. Or skip the sprays and salves and wear a lightweight jacket made of head-to-waist (or head-to-toe) mosquito netting. These unusual creations are made by Bug Baffler, a New Hampshire–based company, and sold online (www.bugbaffler.com).

HIKING GEAR CHECKLIST

Long-distance backpackers need to worry about hauling along camping and cooking equipment, but besides good boots, comfortable clothes, water, food, and a trusty map, it doesn't take much to have all the gear you need for a day hike. Here are some must-haves for your next outing. And, of course, bring along your hiking guide!

In Case of Emergency

- Altimeter
- Compass
- Extra clothes
- First-aid kit
- Lightweight (or mylar) blanket
- Pen or pencil and paper
- Swiss Army-style knife
- Waterproof matches

Creature Comforts

- Binoculars
- Bird, wildlife, and tree or flower identification guides
- Bug spray and sunscreen
- Camera
- Face cloths
- Fishing pole and fishing license
- Picnic supplies
- Trekking pole

GREATER BOSTON

© JACQUELINE TOURVILLE

BEST HIKES

Native Americans who once inhabited the Boston

area were known as the Massachusett, which translates as "near the great hill" or "by the blue hills." Rising out of an otherwise flat coastal plane, Great Blue Hill, the highest point in the Boston area, and its accompanying range of smaller hills, most likely served as a guiding beacon for Native Americans as they navigated the coastal waters and surrounding woodlands.

Today, with the skyline of Boston on the rise – literally – these same blue hills still tower high over the urban landscape. Street maps and MBTA routes may have taken over as the dominant forms of navigation in the city, but for those who dream of walking in a wooded forest, with birdsong their only companion, or who long to stand on a wind-whipped summit, the Blue Hills are still a beacon. When the urban grind of traffic jams and crowded T stops becomes too much, lift your eyes to the shimmering summit of Great Blue and know that escape from Boston's hustle and bustle is never far away.

Blue Hills Reservation is one of the most popular hiking retreats in the Boston area, but the landscape of Greater Boston – an area that conforms roughly to the radiating rings formed around the city by Routes 128/I-95 and I-495 provides hikers with a surprisingly varied mix of trails. From the rocky and scenic Blue Hills and the Middlesex Fells, two oases of quiet, wooded hills just minutes from downtown Boston, to such rare and cherished recreation areas as Walden Pond and the coastal dunes of Plum Island, hikes in Greater Boston lead to unusual microenvironments, history-drenched waypoints, and much-needed breathing room.

Trails closest to Boston occupy compact acreage, but elsewhere in the region, lands such as Bradley Palmer State Park and Myles Standish State Forest offer sprawling, four-season recreation centers for thousands of local residents. Likewise, the Trustees of Reservations properties – Noanet Woodlands, Rocky Woods, and World's End – provide valuable local places to walk, exercise, and sightsee. Maudslay State Park, Walden Pond State Park Reservation, and the Minute Man National Historical Park are not only great places to walk, but preserve invaluable pieces of local history. Great Meadows, Plum Island, and Mass Audubon's Drumlin Farm Wildlife Sanctuary are on the must-see destinations list of many bird-watchers.

You may dread your daily commute on the T, but the same MBTA system that shuttles thousands every day within the city, provides bus routes and commuter rail service to many outlying points that are within short walking distance of many of the trailheads listed in this chapter. Don't have a car? You can still hike Walden Woods to learn more about Henry David Thoreau, someone who really wanted to get away from it all. Don't want to get stuck in yet another traffic jam? Hop on the commuter rail for a quick trip to World's End, a quiet walking area on Hingham Harbor. Other hikes that are within easy range of MBTA service include the Minuteman Battle Trail, Middlesex Fells Reservation, Blue Hills Reservation, Audubon's Drumlin Farm and Moose Hill sanctuaries, and the Boston Harbor Islands.

Strung like a jeweled necklace around the city, the many reservations, state parks, and conservation lands stand in stark contrast to the sprawling suburban and urban landscape, but they are also connected to it. If not for the concern of so many citizens here that green space be saved for recreational use – and spared from the hands of developers – Greater Boston would no doubt look very different. So as you breathe a sigh of relief that you've left the crowds behind as you set out on the trail, also breathe a sigh of gratitude that the crowds worked hard to make sure you had a destination.

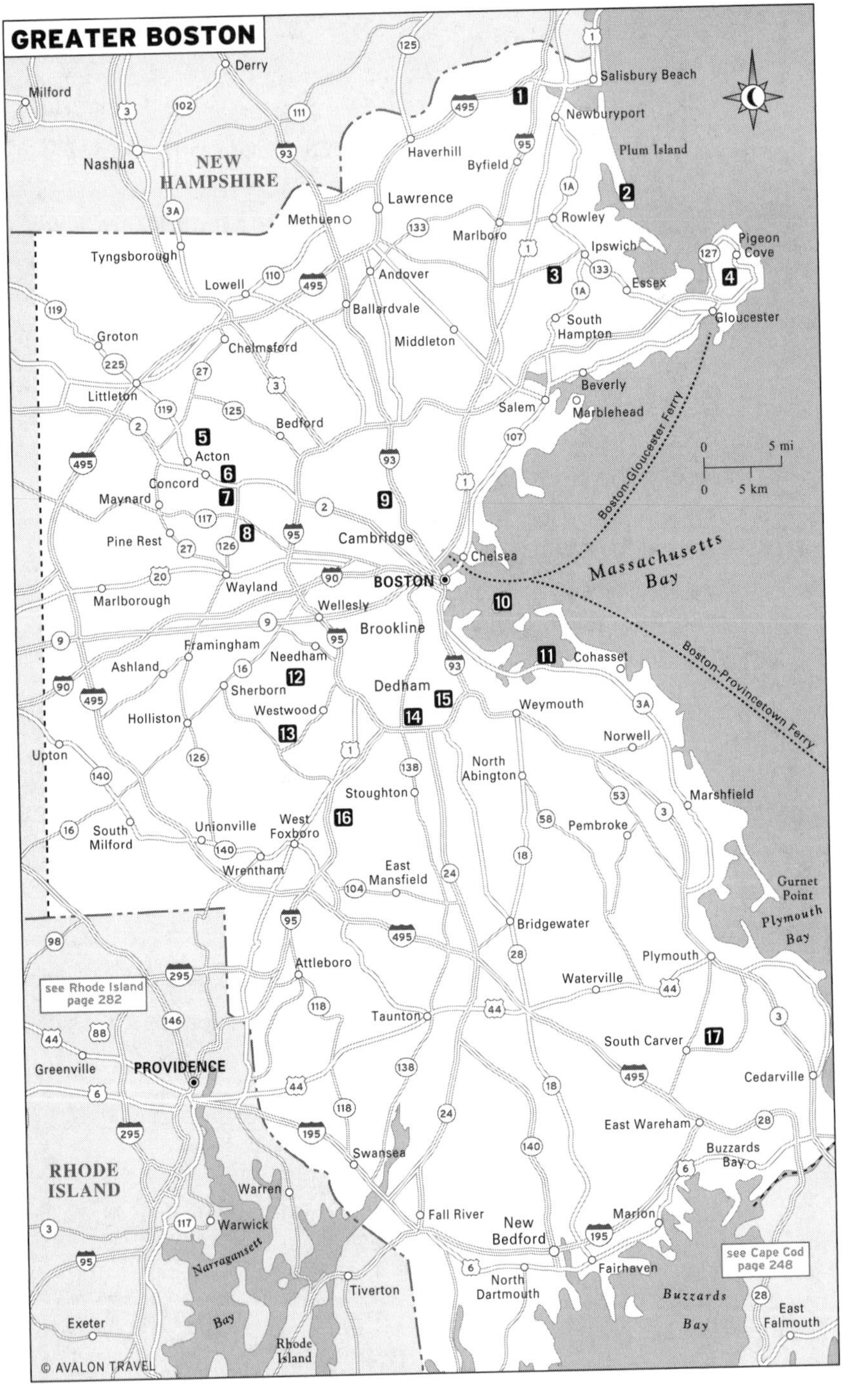

GREATER BOSTON

Map showing the Greater Boston area, including parts of New Hampshire, Rhode Island, and Massachusetts Bay.

Cities and towns shown include: Milford, Derry, Nashua, Tyngsborough, Lowell, Groton, Littleton, Maynard, Pine Rest, Marlborough, Upton, South Milford, Greenville, PROVIDENCE, Exeter, Warwick, Warren, Tiverton, Fall River, New Bedford, North Dartmouth, Swansea, Attleboro, Taunton, Haverhill, Byfield, Lawrence, Marlboro, Methuen, Andover, Ballardvale, Middleton, Chelmsford, Bedford, Concord, Acton, Wayland, Wellesly, Framingham, Needham, Ashland, Holliston, Sherborn, Westwood, Dedham, Brookline, BOSTON, Cambridge, Chelsea, Weymouth, Norwell, Cohasset, Marshfield, Pembroke, North Abington, Stoughton, West Foxboro, Wrentham, East Mansfield, Bridgewater, Waterville, Plymouth, South Carver, Cedarville, East Wareham, Buzzards Bay, Marion, Fairhaven, Salisbury Beach, Newburyport, Plum Island, Rowley, Ipswich, Essex, Pigeon Cove, Gloucester, South Hampton, Beverly, Marblehead, Salem, Unionville.

Water bodies: Massachusetts Bay, Buzzards Bay, Narragansett Bay, Plymouth Bay, Gurnet Point.

Ferries: Boston-Gloucester Ferry, Boston-Provincetown Ferry.

Insets: see Rhode Island page 282, see Cape Cod page 248.

Locations numbered 1–17 are marked on the map.

© AVALON TRAVEL

TRAIL NAME	LEVEL	DISTANCE	TIME	ELEVATION	FEATURES	PAGE
1 Merrimack River Trail and Laurel Walk	Easy/Moderate	3.0 mi	2 hr	200 ft		40
2 Bar Head Drumlin/Plum Island	Easy	2.0 mi	1.5 hr	50 ft		43
3 Blueberry Hill Trail	Easy/Moderate	3.0 mi	2 hr	100 ft		46
4 Dogtown Trail	Moderate	4.6 mi	2.5 hr	Less than 20 ft		49
5 Dike Trail	Easy	2.0 mi	1.5 hr	less than 10 ft		52
6 Battle Road Trail	Easy	11.0 mi	6 hr	0 ft		55
7 Walden Pond Trail	Easy	1.7 mi	1 hr	20 ft		58
8 Drumlin Farm	Easy	2.0 mi	1 hr	200 ft		61
9 Skyline Trail	Strenuous	7.0 mi	4 hr	1,200 ft		64
10 Spectacle Island and Georges Island	Easy	6.0 mi	3 hr	157 ft		67
11 World's End	Easy/Moderate	2.9 mi	1.5 hr	10 ft		70
12 Noanet Peak	Moderate	4.0 mi	2 hr	300 ft		72
13 Rocky Woods	Moderate	2.3 mi	1.5 hr	250 ft		75
14 Blue Hills Skyline Trail	Butt-kicker	4.5 mi	2.5 hr	1,200 ft		78
15 Rattlesnake and Wampatuck Hills	Moderate	2.2 mi	1.5 hr	500 ft		82
16 Moose Hill	Easy	1.4 mi	1 hr	300 ft		84
17 Pine Barrens and Ponds Loop	Moderate	5.5 mi	2.5 hr	50 ft		86

1 MERRIMACK RIVER TRAIL AND LAUREL WALK
Maudslay State Park

Level: Easy/Moderate

Hiking Time: 2 hours

Total Distance: 3.0 miles

Elevation: 200 feet

Summary: This hike through a former 19th-century estate leads to grand gardens and far-reaching views of the Merrimack River.

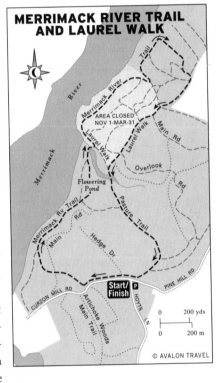

Exploring this garden- and forest-filled chunk of land on the southern bank of the Merrimack River in Newburyport, it's easy to feel like you are tresspassing. In the 19th century, Maudslay State Park was the manorlike estate of the Moseleys, once one of New England's wealthiest families. From the Italian gardens, first planted more than 150 years ago, to the picturesque stone bridge crossings, signs of the estate's former grandeur are everywhere. Taking in the park's best features, this hike leads to lush gardens, breathtaking river views, and one of the largest naturally occurring stands of mountain laurel in eastern Massachusetts.

From the parking lot, cross the street and walk past the headquarters, following Curzon Mill Road west a short distance to a right turn north onto Main Drive, a dirt road marked by large stone entry portals. Follow this dirt road north for 0.25 mile, passing the Italian Gardens on the right and the remaining foundations of the main house on the left. As you come in sight of the Merrimack River through the trees, the trail meets (and ends at) the Merrimack River Trail, marked by blue, white, and green blazes. Turn east (right) with the Merrimack River Trail, following it along high, pine-covered bluffs with constant river views. Tables scattered along the trail here make an inviting spot for a picnic. The Merrimack River Trail eventually heads downhill into shady

view from the Merrimack River Trail

forest cover and crosses two brooks on wooden bridges. At 0.7 mile, the trail turns to the northeast (bearing right) to merge with another trail and cross over a dam at the end of the Flowering Pond. At the hike's mile mark, you reach the Laurel Walk, where the Merrimack River Trail branches right and left. The area to the left is closed November 1–March 31; take the right branch during these months. Otherwise, turn left and follow the Merrimack River Trail/Laurel Walk as it winds between the riverbank and the edge of the grove. Visit in June to see the towering mountain laurel in full bloom; many plants reach well over 20 feet tall.

Where the trail meets the Castle Hill Trail for the first time, bear north (left) to stay with the Merrimack River Trail. Next, reach the unmarked end of a tree-lined road, another outlet of the Castle Hill Trail, about 0.7 mile from the start of the Laurel Walk. Here, turn south (right) to follow the Castle Hill Trail. Most of the hike's elevation gain takes place on this pine-shaded trail on the way to the crest of Castle Hill, with pleasing views of the Merrimack Valley the reward for your efforts. As the trail name implies, there really was once a castle here. Some keen-sighted hikers may even be able to make out the stone steps that once led to the castle's entry.

Once over the hilltop, turn south onto an unmarked woods road and then west (right) onto Line Road. It leads straight onto the Main Road (backtracking over the Merrimack River Trail's right branch). Take the gracefully arched stone bridge over the Flowering Pond, turn south (left) onto the Pasture Trail, and follow it back to the parking lot.

Options

To take in more the estate's former gardens, cross the street from the parking lot and take Hedge Drive, the first trail leaving to the west of the visitor center/ranger station. Heading north, follow the large dirt road until you reach a break in the hedge on your left. Here, like you are stepping into another time, a short path leads you to an English country garden filled with roses, lillies, raspberry bushes, and a colorful assortment of wildflowers. Head west through the garden to an another break in the hedge. Pass through to an ancient orchard and an overgrown terrace garden. Keep following the path west, passing the estate's former well, before reaching a junction with Main Drive. Turn north to reach the Merrimack River Trail.

Directions

From I-95, take Exit 57 in Newburyport for Route 113 west. Drive 0.5 mile then turn right onto Hoyt's Lane/Gypsy Lane. At the road's end, turn right (in front of the park headquarters) onto Pine Hill Road and right again into the parking lot. **GPS Coordinates:** 42.8224 N, 70.9218 W

Contact

A daily parking fee of $2 is collected year-round. The park is open 8 A.M.–sunset year-round. Dogs on leash are allowed. A special-use permit is required for weddings, family reunions, and school groups. A free trail map is available at park headquarters. For more information, contact Maudslay State Park, Curzon's Mill Rd., Newburyport, MA 01950, 978/465-7223. Massachusetts Division of State Parks and Recreation, 251 Causeway St., Suite 600, Boston, MA 02114-2104, 617/626-1250, www.state.ma.us.

2 BAR HEAD DRUMLIN/PLUM ISLAND

Sandy Point State Reservation in Ipswich

Level: Easy

Hiking Time: 1.5 hours

Total Distance: 2.0 miles

Elevation: 50 feet

Summary: This easy hike combines a walk along a sandy beach and a rocky shoreline with a hike onto the glacial drumlin.

Plum Island is an 11-mile long barrier island connected to the Massachusetts mainland by a sole bridge, located at the island's northern end. On the southernmost tip of Plum Island is Sandy Point, a windswept spit of land made up only of ever-shifting dunes and the Bar Head drumlin, an oval, scrub-covered mound of earth deposited by a receding glacier 10,000 years ago. Today several plant and animal species rarely found near a sandy beach thrive on Bar Head drumlin. But even at 50 feet high and covering 15 acres, the drumlin is shrinking under constant erosion by the ocean. Before embarking on this hike, be sure to climb

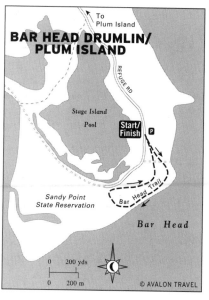

the observation tower directly across from the parking area for views of the adjoining marshlands of the Parker River National Wildlife Refuge.

From the Sandy Point parking lot, pass through a gate onto the beach boardwalk and turn south (right). The trail, a rock-strewn stretch lined with sea roses and beach pea, eventually gives way to sandy beach below the eroded cliffs of the Bar Head drumlin. Continue to follow the waterline to swing around from the south to the west until you reach a fence at the wildlife refuge boundary. Turn north and follow an overgrown road along the refuge boundary to a parking lot for the refuge. Cross the lot to an unmarked, overgrown trail leading up onto Bar Head.

Although the trees and brush atop the drumlin are too dense and high to afford views, a few side trails to the cliffs permit beach and ocean vistas, good perches to watch the sun rise majestically over the open ocean waters. (Visiting in the

© HEIDI J. BROWN

wind-whipped grass on the drumlin

early morning hours also helps you avoid the crowds that typically plague Bar Head in summer.) The trail leads over Bar Head and back to the beach near the boardwalk where you started.

Options

Adjacent to Sandy Point, the sprawling Parker River National Wildlife Refuge is home to numerous bird species in summer, including cormorants, herons, king-fishers, and ducks. You can pay the refuge a visit, but be forewarned, there are many restricted dates. To protect nesting areas for the threatened piping plover, the beach is closed April 1 through at least July 1, portions possibly through late August. Otherwise, the reservation is open daily sunrise–sunset, with limited parking. Visitors are allowed to walk only on trails, boardwalks, roads, parking areas, observation areas, and the beach; all other areas, including the dunes, are closed to the public. And bring bug repellent in summer—there are lots of biting insects, especially on the overgrown road along the refuge boundary.

Directions

From I-95 take Exit 57 and travel east on Route 113, then continue straight onto U.S. 1A south to the intersection with Rolfe's Lane for a total of 3.5 miles. Turn left onto Rolfe's Lane and travel 0.5 mile to its end. Turn right onto the Plum Island Turnpike and travel two miles crossing the Sgt. Donald Wilkinson Bridge

to Plum Island. Take your first right onto Sunset Drive and travel 0.5 mile to the refuge entrance. From the entrance, drive 6.5 miles to a dirt lot at the end of the road and park. Refuge headquarters is located at the north end of Plum Island near the Newburyport Harbor Lighthouse and is open Monday–Friday 8 A.M.– 4:30 P.M., except on federal holidays.
GPS Coordinates: 42.718 N, 70.7812 W

Contact

The fee for entering the Parker River National Wildlife Refuge is $5 per vehicle or $2 for anyone entering on foot or bike, year-round. (All cars pay at the entrance, though you are parking at Sandy Point, which is technically owned by the Massachusetts Department of Conservation and Recreation.) During the warmer months, the refuge often fills to capacity and the entrance closes temporarily, even to visitors on foot. Arrive early to avoid this inconvenience. Dogs are not allowed. For more information, contact Parker River National Wildlife Refuge, 6 Plum Island Turnpike, Newburyport, MA 01950, 978/465-5753 or 800/877-8339 for the hearing impaired, http://parkerriver.fws.gov. U.S. Fish and Wildlife Service, 800/344-9453, www.fws.gov.

3 BLUEBERRY HILL TRAIL

Bradley Palmer State Park in Topsfield

Level: Easy/Moderate

Hiking Time: 2 hours

Total Distance: 3.0 miles

Elevation: 100 feet

Summary: This hike leads you through a sunny hilltop meadow and pine-filled woods on the way to the shores of the Ipswich River.

One of Topsfield's more famous former residents, Bradley Palmer was a noted attorney in the early 1900s who represented Sinclair Oil in the Teapot Dome Scandal and President Wilson at the Versailles Peace Conference after World War I. Palmer's 732-acre estate is now a multi-use recreation area marked by moderately sloping hills, wide carriage roads, and rugged trails offering varied opportunities for easy to moderate treks. This hike, leading to the lush meadow summit of Bluberry Hill and down to the serene shores of the Ipswich River, merely introduces you

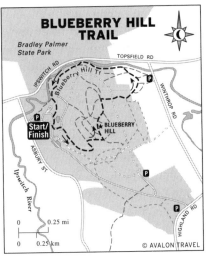

to this park; use it as a jumping off point for further exploration of this North Shore hidden gem.

From the parking area, walk past park headquarters and follow the paved road. Trails and carriage roads in Bradley State Park are unnamed; trail navigation relies on numbered intersections. After only a short walk, you will reach a signpost marked 44. Here, turn southeast with the unpaved carriage road, dipping into the tall pine woods; pass intersection 43. At intersection 42, turn east (left) and within only a few yards, pass through intersection 41. Here, the trail begins to climb Blueberry Hill, with a switchback in the trail turning you to head north.

Reaching intersection 36, head east to continue uphill through the woods. Pass intersection 37. At intersection 38, turn due north, passing several intersections as you crest the open meadow top of Blueberry Hill, about a mile from the point where this hike began. Continue over the hill until you reach the marker for intersection 30. Here, there are two trails—take the one that bears to the northeast, following it only a short distance to marker 28; turn due north and skirt another open meadow. Reaching intersection 27, turn east and begin to descend the rather steep trail, crossing over an unpaved road at intersection 25. At intersection 17, turn onto the trail heading northeast. Pass through intersection 16 and at the next intersection, turn with the trail to head due north. Pass marker 12 and at intersection 11, turn to head northwest. Approximately one mile from leaving Blueberry Hill, the trail now brings you to the quiet shores of the Ipswich River and the land holdings of the Essex County Greenbelt. Turn west (left) with the trail to parallel the river for the mile trip back to the parking area; you'll begin seeing the blue blazes, with a paw print

Ipswich River

on them, of the Discover Hamilton Trail. Where a footbridge leads right over the river, pick up the Healthy Heart Trail at intersection 3. Follow this pleasant tree-lined trail back to the park headquarters and the parking area.

Options

For a long, relatively flat walk or a fun outing for beginning mountain bikers, start from the parking area at the southern end of the park. To reach the trailhead, turn right after entering the main entrance and follow the park access road approximately 0.75 mile to a picnic area and parking lot on the left. Leaving from the parking area, follow the dirt road until you reach a trail branching off to the right at intersection 58. Follow the trail, heading northeast and then northwest to reach intersection 22. Here, turn right to pick up another dirt road, this one heading east. At intersection 21, leave the dirt road to pick up the trail. Walk north, passing by markers 19 and 18. At marker 17, take a right, heading northeast. Use directions from the main hike for reaching the Discover Hamilton Trail.

After turning onto the Healthy Trail at intersection 3 and eventually returning to the park headquarters, continue south from the headquarters to pick up a dirt road. Stay on the road, enjoying the pleasant cover of tall pines, all the way back to the parking area where this hike started.

Directions

From U.S. 1 in Topsfield, turn east onto Ipswich Road (at a traffic light). Drive 1.2 miles and turn right onto Asbury Street. The state park entrance is on the left, a short distance down the road. Park in a dirt area just before the state park headquarters.

GPS Coordinates: 42.6551 N, 70.9123 W

Contact

Trails are open year-round, with a daily parking fee of $5 collected mid-May–mid-October. Dogs on leash are allowed. Maps are available at the park headquarters and on the state park website. For more information, contact Bradley Palmer State Park, Asbury St., Topsfield, MA 01983, 978/887-5931. Massachusetts Division of State Parks and Recreation, 251 Causeway St., Suite 600, Boston, MA 02114-2104, 617/626-1250, www.state.ma.us.

4 DOGTOWN TRAIL

BEST ◖

Gloucester and Rockport

Level: Moderate

Total Distance: 4.6 miles

Hiking Time: 2.5 hours

Elevation: Less than 20 feet

Summary: Explore colonial ruins and discover curiously engraved boulders on this rugged woods walk through the heart of Cape Ann.

Dogtown is a patch of untamed woods found inland—and a world away—from Cape Ann's crowded beaches. The rugged land was once a thriving colonial settlement, dating to the 1660s, but as inhabitants began to increasingly make their living from the sea, the town was abandoned, with the last remaining settlers leaving their dogs behind, according to local lore. Cellar holes, stone walls, and even the town common can still be found here, though forest cover is ever-encroaching. Dogtown's woods are also marked by oversized glacial-erratic boulders, some engraved with inspirational sayings, the legacy of an early 20th century finan-

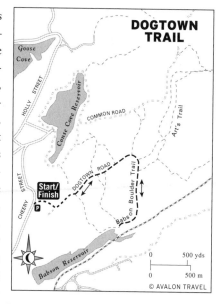

cier named Roger Babson. During the Great Depression, Babson hired stonecutters to carve sayings such as Keep Out of Debt and Never Try Never Win. This hike takes you on a relatively flat, but still demanding tour of this unique New England landscape.

From the parking area, continue to follow the paved Dogtown Road heading northeast, walking around a gate to follow a dirt road (still called Dogtown Road). Passing another gate, Dogtown Road narrows to a gravel path. Note that blazes here are underfoot—every so often, you should see a streak of red paint painted onto the gravel. The woods are thick on both sides of the path, but it is still possible to make out glacial erratics and cellar holes through the cover; numbered spur trails lead to some of the more notable sights. To see your first Babson boulder, take a right at marker 18 and walk a few steps to see Never Try Never Win. On this short spur trail is another rock inscribed as the spot where

one of Babson's Boulders: Prosperity

a former settler was gored by a bull. Return to Dogtown Road and resume your course, reaching Dogtown Square, a junction of trails where a rock is inscribed D.T. SQ., approximately 1.2 miles from the parking area.

From Dogtown Square, turn southeast (right) onto a rock-strewn dirt road and follow it for 0.1 mile, passing the old stone wall boundary of Dogtown. Reaching a junction, take the trail heading south onto the Tent Rock Trail, sometimes called the Boulder Trail. It continues for a mile to the scenic Babson Reservoir, along the way passing deposits of rocky glacial morraine and more large boulders inscribed with such messages as Study, Be On Time, Truth, and Industry.

To return to your car, retrace your steps from the reservoir, heading back to Dogtown Square and, eventually, the parking area. And then check for ticks! Trails in Dogtown, though popular with local hikers, tend to be overgrown, especially by late summer. Though this abandoned feeling lends a certain "lost in time" charm to the place, ticks like to hide in tall grasses, so take time to inspect your legs when you emerge from the woods.

Options

If you're up for a longer trek of Dogtown, from the reservoir, the trail turns west (left), crosses railroad tracks, passes a few more inscribed boulders, and then reaches the rough dirt Old Rockport Road behind Blackburn Industrial Park, 1.4 miles from Dogtown Square. Turn left and follow the road 1.2 miles east to the Babson Museum on Eastern Avenue/Route 127 (the museum is an interesting place to visit to learn more about Roger Babson). Behind the museum, turn north onto the red-blazed Beaver Dam Trail. Crossing the railroad tracks, then skipping back and forth across a brook, the trail passes over a small hill, hooks sharply to the south and then swings northwest, reaching Dogtown Square, 1.4 miles from the museum. Be on the lookout for a few more inscribed boulders on the left just before the trail returns to Dogtown Square.

Directions

From the Grant Circle Rotary on Route 128 in Gloucester, take Route 127/ Washington Street north for 0.9 mile and turn right onto Reynard Street. Follow Reynard Street to a left onto Cherry Street. Then turn right onto the access road to Dogtown, 1.5 miles from Grant Circle Rotary. Drive less than 0.5 mile to a parking area and a gate.

GPS Coordinates: 42.6338 N, 70.6681 W

Contact

Parking and access are free at all times. Dogs on leash are allowed. Trail maps are available in a mailbox located next to the parking area. For more information, contact Cape Ann Chamber of Commerce, 33 Commercial St., Gloucester, MA 01930, 978/283-1601, www.capeannvacations.com.

5 DIKE TRAIL

BEST ◖

Great Meadows National Wildlife Refuge, Concord

Level: Easy

Total Distance: 2.0 miles

Hiking Time: 1.5 hours

Elevation: less than 10 feet

Summary: Passing through a landscape of marshy wetlands, this easy hike offers excellent wildlife viewing and some of the best bird-watching in the state.

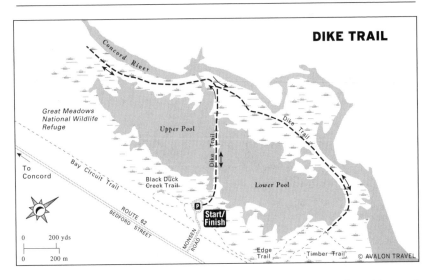

A vast and serene oasis of wetlands, the 3,000-acre Great Meadows National Wildlife Refuge, stretching along 12 miles of the Concord River, may be as much a refuge for the nature-starved city dweller as it is for the many species of wildlife who call this place home. From great blue herons and osprey to songbirds and wood ducks, 221 bird species have been observed here. On this hike, binoculars are a must—the Dike Trail around the broad wetlands is considered one of the best birding sites in the state. Besides birds, animals such as deer, muskrats, foxes, raccoons, cottontail rabbits, and weasels call the refuge home. With all the standing water here, you can bet there are crowds of bugs too, especially in spring. Interestingly, relics of human habitation here date back to 5500 B.C.

Before you begin your hike, check out the view from the observation tower beside the parking lot. Then walk back across the parking lot to pick up the Dike Trail, a level dirt trail (wheelchair accessible) heading northwest. A large information board at the trailhead offers free paper trail maps and also provides a chalkboard

bird-watchers along the Dike Trail, Great Meadows National Wildlife Refuge

for visitors to note spotted bird species. Continue on the trail, traversing the wetland meadows between Upper Pool and Lower Pool. Large stands of reeds frame the trail, with frequent openings for wide views of birds lighting and taking flight from the marshes and ponds. If you have kids along, or are hiking with a group, remember that there is some serious birding going on here. Keeping quiet is necessary for keeping the birds at ease—and in view.

Reaching the other side in just under 0.5 mile, the trail reaches the Concord River banks (where canoeists pull ashore to walk the trail) and splits in two directions. Turn west (left), following the trail along the Upper Pool about 0.25 mile to the refuge boundary, marked by signs. Turn back and follow the trail to explore the area around the Lower Pool. Where this trail ends, retrace your steps back to the trail split and then back across the dike to the parking area.

Options

For added adventure, you can canoe the gentle Sudbury and Concord Rivers through the refuge and put ashore to walk this trail. Depending on how long a day trip you want, put in along either Route 27, Route 117, or Route 62 and take out along Route 225 on the Carlisle/Bedford line.

Directions

From Main Street/Route 62 in Concord Center, drive 0.7 mile east toward Monument Square. Bear left onto Lowell Road at the square and then take a quick right

onto Bedford Street, staying on Route 62. Follow Bedford Street for 1.3 miles, then turn left onto Monsen Road, a dead-end street (you will see a small brown sign for Great Meadows just before the turn). Stay on Monsen Road until it ends in the Great Meadows parking area, next to the observation tower.
GPS Coordinates: 42.4746 N, 71.3277 W

Contact

Parking and access are free. Dogs on leash are allowed. A map of hiking trails and a number of brochures about Great Meadows, including a list of bird species sighted here, are available at the trailhead. For more information, contact Great Meadows National Wildlife Refuge, Refuge Manager, 73 Weir Hill Rd., Sudbury, MA 01776, 978/443-4661, http://greatmeadows.fws.gov.

6 BATTLE ROAD TRAIL

BEST 🌑

Minute Man National Historical Park, Concord

🎒 ⚙️ 🐾 👫 ♿ 🚌

Level: Easy

Hiking Time: 6 hours

Total Distance: 11.0 miles

Elevation: 0 feet

Summary: Stretch your legs – and your knowledge of U.S. history – on this scenic walk retracing the first moments of the American Revolution.

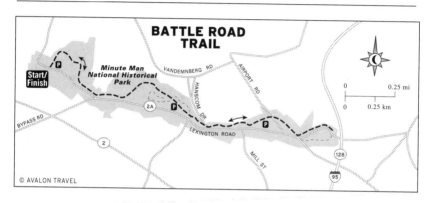

Like an American history textbook come to life, this hike, retracing the route of the American Revolution's opening salvos, is a Bay State gem and can't-miss national treasure. After the fateful "shot heard round the world" was fired on Lexington Green in the early morning hours of April 19, 1775, British soldiers continued their march to Concord on orders to seize a rebel cache of weapons. Turned back at North Bridge in Concord by farmers and villagers turned Minute Men soldiers overnight, British redcoats were unmercifully chased back to Boston by the rapidly growing ranks of rebel fighters. Much of the trail follows original remnants of the Battle Road; other sections leave the historic road to follow the route of the Minute Men, traversing the fields, wetlands, and forests that provided cover and the element of surprise for their guerrilla-style tactics. The flat, easy terrain and opportunity to bring history alive for kids makes this a great hike for families.

From the parking area at Meriam's Corner, the Battle Road begins near the Meriam House, site of the first rebel attacks on the Red Coats. Visit the house if you like, but the flat, wheelchair accessible path heads into the adjacent farmland, notable as remaining in the same configuration as it was in 1775. While some stalwart history buffs may spend their time here visualizing the advancing Minute Men creeping across the freshly tilled earth, it's also easy to forget all about history and simply live in the moment, enjoying the sweet fragrance of the clover-choked fields as you walk along. As the trail continues, it winds into a mixed forest of pine and hardwood and eventually passes historic homes of noted Patriot figures, preserved wayside taverns and inns, sites of intense fighting, and the Paul Revere capture site. Interpretive panels are frequent along the Battle Road path and original buildings still standing are open for visits during the summer tourist season. At mile 4 on this hike is the Minute Man National Historical Park. Staffed spring through fall, the visitors center contains bathrooms, a gift shop, maps, and a ranger station; it also screens a free movie about the events of April 19, 1775. Continuing on from

joggers on the Battle Road Trail

the visitors center, the path ends at Fisk Hill and the Ebenezer Fiske house site. Retrace your steps on the return trip back to your car.

Options

If an 11-mile round-trip is not feasible, a walk to the Hartwell Tavern (at this hike's halfway point) creates a round-trip of about five history-rich miles. For even shorter walks to points along the trail, other parking areas off Lexington Road take you within steps of the Josiah Brooks House and Brooks Tavern (mile 1.5 of this hike), Hartwell Tavern (mile 2.5 of this hike), the Paul Revere capture site (mile 3.2 of this hike), and the Thomas Nelson House site (mile 4 of this hike).

Directions

From Lexington, follow Route 2 west for approximately 6.5 miles to a right turn onto Bypass Road/Route 2A. At the end of the road, take a left onto Lexington Road. Follow brown signs for Minute Man National Historical Park/Meriam's Corner, taking a right about 0.5 mile down the road into the parking area for Meriam House. The Battle Road trail starts here. From Boston, take the MBTA bus 76, leaving from the Alewife T station in Cambridge/Arlington, for stops along Lexington Road.

GPS Coordinates: 42.4593 N, 71.3229 W

Contact

Parking and access are free. Dogs on leash are allowed. Free trail maps are available at Minute Man Visitor Center and online. For more information, contact Minuteman Visitor Center, 250 North Great Rd., Lincoln MA, 01773, 978/369-6993, www.nps.gov.

7 WALDEN POND TRAIL   BEST ◖

Walden Pond State Reservation in Concord

🦌 🛶 🚲 👫 🚌 🚻

Level: Easy   **Total Distance:** 1.7 miles

Hiking Time: 1 hour   **Elevation:** 20 feet

Summary: Get in touch with your transcendentalist side as you explore the woods and pond made famous by Henry David Thoreau's *Walden* or *Life in the Woods*.

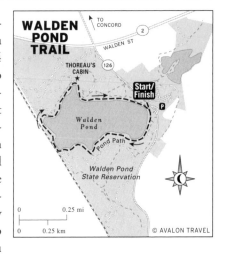

In 1845, a 27-year-old former school-teacher named Henry David Thoreau came to Walden Pond to live on 14 acres owned by his friend, Ralph Waldo Emerson. Thoreau built a small one-room cabin and began his "experiment in simplicity," living a sustenance lifestyle on the pond. At the time, much of Concord was already deforested and the land converted to farms, but the woods around Walden Pond had remained untouched because the sandy soil was not very fertile. Two years, two months, and two days later, Thoreau closed up his house and returned to village life in Concord. Emerson sold the cabin to his gardener. (The cabin no longer stands, but a replica can be seen beside the parking lot.) In 1854, Thoreau published *Walden, or Life in the Woods,* still considered a classic of American literature. Ever since, Walden Pond has stood as a symbol of the American conservation movement.

Today, Walden Pond sits in the middle of a small patch of woods within earshot of busy state routes and a railroad line, yet it remains popular with hikers and cross-country skiers, as well as anglers and canoeists (a boat launch is on the right side of Route 126, just beyond the parking area). This easy loop takes you by the swimming beach and into the woods on a pleasant trek around the pond, with the added excitement of visiting the site of Thoreau's original cabin.

From the parking lot, cross Route 126 at the striped crosswalk and head downhill to the pond swimming beach. The paved walkway curves past the beach and bathhouse before turning into Pond Path, a well-worn footpath that treads just above the shoreline in the shade of the surrounding woods. Erosion in recent years

Walden Pond

led park caretakers to install chicken wire–style fencing on either side of the trail; not the most scenic of conditions, but as you walk, views of the pond are almost constant, with stone steps (and an accompanying break in the fence) at regular intervals offering direct water access. Canada geese and ducks are commonly seen drifting about on placid Walden, with songbirds tweeting their approval from the thick tree canopy overhead.

At approximately 1.2 miles, a short side trail, marked by a sign, leads uphill to Thoreau's house site. There is a plaque commemorating the exact spot. And for no explainable reason, next to it is a huge pile of pond rocks that, over the years, has turned into something of a meditative spot, as visitors stop to balance a few of the waterworn rocks on top of each other before moving on to the rest of the hike. Continuing on the Pond Path from house site returns you to the beach in another 0.5 mile.

Options

Pond Path can often be very crowded, especially on summer weekends when tourists flock here in droves. If you're willing to leave the shores of Walden for part of the hike and explore some alternate trails through Walden Woods, you might actually get to to experience the peace and tranquility Thoreau so magically described finding here.

At the beach bathhouse, follow the asphalt walkway as it turns to head uphill away from the Pond. At the top of the hill, follow the boat launch access road a few steps until you see a sign for the Esker Trail. High on a bank above the water, the Esker Trail still curves with the Pond and will eventually rejoin the Pond Path at the northern edge of Walden, but offers almost a mile of solitude. Esker Trail also intersects with a number of other trails that lead to points of interest, including Emerson's Cliff, the esker's height of land.

Directions

From the junction of Routes 2 and 126 in Concord, drive south on Route 126 for 0.3 mile to the Walden Pond State Reservation entrance and parking lot on the left.

Public Transportation: Take the MBTA commuter rail from North Station in Boston to Concord Depot. Follow Walden Street due south from the train station for 1.4 miles to reach the reservation.

GPS Coordinates: 42.4415 N, 71.3363 W

Contact

A daily parking fee of $5 is collected year-round. Park officials may close the entrance if the park reaches capacity. The park is open to the public 5 A.M.–sunset; check for the closing time posted in the parking lot. Dogs are not allowed. A free map and an informational brochure about Walden Pond are available outside the Shop at Walden Pond, next to the park office at the parking lot's south end, or online. For more information, contact Walden Pond State Reservation, 915 Walden St., Concord, MA 01742, 978/369-3254. Massachusetts Division of State Parks and Recreation, 251 Causeway St., Suite 600, Boston, MA 02114-2104, 617/626-1250, www.mass.gov. The Shop at Walden Pond, 508/287-5477.

8 DRUMLIN FARM

BEST **☾**

Drumlin Farm Wildlife Sanctuary, Lincoln

Level: Easy

Total Distance: 2.0 miles

Hiking Time: 1 hour

Elevation: 200 feet

Summary: Scale a drumlin and visit a working farm on this easy hike kids love.

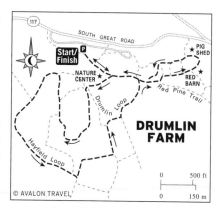

A working farm and 232-acre Audubon sanctuary on the fringes of suburban Boston, Drumlin Farm maintains a variety of habitats for visitors to explore: grasslands, agricultural fields, shrubs and thickets, mature forests, and small ponds and swamps. This easy, ambling loop hike brings you to many of the farm's best features, including the sanctuary's namesake, a whale-shaped drumlin hill created long ago by glaciers and now one the highest points in the greater Boston area. On a clear day, views from the top offer glimpses of Mount Wachusett to the west and New Hampshire's Mount Monadnock almost due north.

From behind the Drumlin Farm Nature Center, pick up the wide, well-worn Drumlin Loop trail, marked with a signpost. The trail passes by a horse corral to the left, crosses a bridge and then splits in two directions. Bear left to head south onto the loop, soon passing though mixed woods as the trail sweeps in a gentle curve to bring you to the top of the drumlin without much effort. Take in nice landscape views and be sure to look skyward: goshawks, red tail hawks, and turkey vultures are a common sight circling overhead. Continuing over the drumlin, pass the first junction with the Hayfield Loop Trail. A little farther, the trail reaches a split. To return almost immediately to the nature center, turn northeast (right) to stay on the Drumlin Loop Trail, a completed loop of about just over 0.5 mile. This hike, however, continues straight ahead on the marked Hayfield Loop Trail. Curving north, west, and then south again, the trail wanders along between fields and thickets. Birds spotted in this area include field sparrows, yellow-bellied eastern meadowlarks, and indigo buntings. Reaching a junction, make a hard turn north (left) to follow

© HEIDI J. BROWN

rabbit on the trail, Drumlin Farm

the Bobolink Trail and skirt the dedicated bird conservation area. This is a good place to whip out the binoculars: More than 100 different species of birds call this area home. At the end of the Bobolink, turn north (left) on the Field Trail and follow as it curves by a sheep pasture and vernal pond. Now reaching the working farm itself, the trail reaches a junction. Take the trail heading east/northeast that crests and then heads over Bird Hill. At the bottom of the hill are the Farm Life Center and a variety of barns, stables, and farm animals awaiting your visit. If you have kids, you will probably end up spending a few hours here. From the Farm Life Center, a paved walkway returns you to the visitors center and parking area.

Options

Though only miles from Boston, the still-rural community of Lincoln takes its agrarian roots seriously. Many farms in the area have, over the years, been converted into conservation lands open to hiking and other recreational use. Varying in size from a few acres to tracts that offer pleasant one-mile hikes through rolling pastureland, continue the theme of the day after your trip to Drumlin Farm by adding a shorter trek from Lincoln's public trails. For more information and maps of the town's open spaces, contact the The Lincoln Conservation Commission and Department, Town Office Building, 16 Lincoln Rd., 2nd Floor, Lincoln, MA 01773, 781/259-2612, www.lincolntown.org.

Directions

From Route 2 in Concord (east or west), turn onto Route 126 south (at the sign for Walden Pond, Framingham) and follow for 2.5 miles to the intersection of Route 126 and Route 117. Take a left onto Route 117 east and the sanctuary is one mile ahead on the right.

Public Transportation: Take the MBTA commuter rail to Lincoln Station. Walk south one block on Lincoln Road. Cross Codman Road and continue south on Lincoln Road to the intersection with Route 117. Cross Route 117, turn left and enter Drumlin Farm through the wall onto the grass path.

GPS Coordinates: 42.4086 N, 71.3284 W

Contact

Admission is free for Massachusetts Audubon Society members. Nonmember adults, $6; nonmember children (ages 2–12) and seniors, $4. Dogs are not allowed. Maps are available at the visitors center and online. For more information, contact Massachusetts Audubon Society Drumlin Farm Wildlife Sanctuary, 208 South Great Rd., Lincoln, MA 01773, 781/259-2200, www.massaudubon.org.

9 SKYLINE TRAIL   BEST ◖

Middlesex Fells Reservation in Medford, Malden,
Winchester, Melrose, and Stoneham

🏛 🦌 ✈ 🐕

Level: Strenuous   **Total Distance:** 7.0 miles

Hiking Time: 4 hours   **Elevation:** 1,200 feet

Summary: This challenging loop through one of Boston's premier hiking grounds scales several small rocky hills and ledges.

Even in the midst of some of Boston's busiest suburbs, you can still find quiet and solitude hiking the Fells, a 2,500-acre chunk of woods and hills located a few miles north of the city off I-93. "Fells" is a Saxon word for rocky hills. The Skyline Trail—the premier hiking circuit in the Fells—loops around three of the Winchester reservoirs, passing through forest and traversing countless rocky ledges, some with good views of the surrounding hills and, occasionally, the Boston skyline. Perhaps the best view is from atop Pine Hill and the stone Wright's Tower lookout, near the start of this loop, which overlooks Boston's skyline and the Blue Hills to the south. The trail dries out fairly quickly after the snow melts—it's a glorious hike on the first warm day of spring.

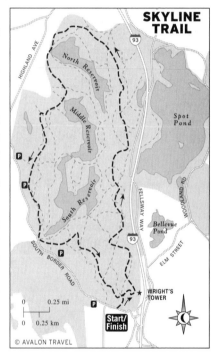

From the parking lot, walk along the east (right) side of Bellevue Pond and onto Quarry Road, a wide dirt road at the opposite end of the pond. Look for the white-blazed Skyline Trail on the northern end of the pond. The leafy trail leads to the east as it scales Pine Hill and reaches Wright's Tower. Footing is generally good on the hill, but in fall and spring, fallen leaves can make conditions very slippery, especially after rain.

Moving on from the summit, the white blazes continue along a rocky ridge before descending west to drop into a valley. Now about a mile into the hike, the trail begins a pattern of moving north and west, ascending and descending the many

© MARGARET COSTELLA

view from Wright's Tower, Middlesex Fells

rocky hills that make up the Fells. Animals spotted in the surrounding forest include fox, deer, and rabbits. The trail stops at the Sheepfold Picnic Area (at mile 3) and then reaches a lovely vista taking in Winchester North Reservoir as the white blazes bring you to Winthrop Hill (at mile 4). All along this route, other trails meet (and sometimes merge with) the Skyline Trail, but careful blazing and good signage makes it easy for even the most of novice of hikers to stay on course.

Continuing on, the trail eventually turns to head south, still dipping and climbing along the way. After passing Panther Cave and crossing Straight Gully Brook (at mile 6), the trail climbs back to the top of Pine Hill to complete the loop. Retrace your steps from Pine Hill on the return to the parking area.

Options

Want to avoid the rocky ridges and hill climbs? The relatively flat Reservoir Trail provides an enjoyable 5.5-mile loop around the three Winchester reservoirs. The circuit can be accessed from many points in the reservation. One of the most convenient spots is the Sheepfold Picnic Area (with parking). To find the trail head, look for the orange blazes heading back into the woods from the picnic tables. As you walk, be mindful that the adjacent reservoir lands are not for public use; heed all no trespassing signs and remain on the trail.

Directions

Take I-93 to Exit 33 in Medford. From the traffic circle, turn onto South Border

Road. Drive 0.2 mile and turn into a parking area on the right, at Bellevue Pond.

Public Transportation: Take the orange line T to Wellington Station, and then take MBTA bus 100 to Roosevelt Circle Rotary. Walk south to the rotary and turn right on South Border Rd. Bellevue Pond entrance to the reservation is 0.2 mile up South Border Road on the right.

GPS Coodinates: 42.4317 N, 71.1074 W

Contact

Parking and access are free. The reservation is open year-round sunrise–sunset. Dogs on leash are allowed. A trail map of the Middlesex Fells Reservation is available for $6 via mail (with SASE) from The Friends of Middlesex Fells Reservation. For more information, contact The Friends of the Middlesex Fells Reservation, 4 Woodland Rd., Stoneham, MA 02180, 781/662-2340, www.fells.org.

10 SPECTACLE ISLAND AND GEORGES ISLAND

Boston Harbor

BEST 🌙

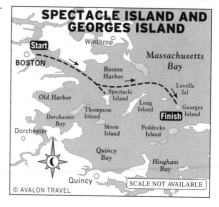

🏛 🌊 ⚙ 🏠 🚌

Level: Easy

Hiking Time: 3 hours

Total Distance: 6.0 miles

Elevation: 157 feet

Summary: For a windswept day of hiking and exploring, take to the seas — and take the ferry — to visit two islands in Boston Harbor.

A bit of the rustic wild in full view of sleek, modern Boston, this fun hike—and quick and easy city escape—takes you on a day trip to Spectacle and Georges Islands, the two most popular destinations in the Boston Harbor island chain; both are maintained by the National Parks Service. Access to the islands is seasonal, with ferries running May–September. When planning for this trip, factor in a little more than an hour total for ferry boarding and the ride through Boston Harbor. How much time you spend exploring the islands is up to you (and the ferry schedule). Try leaving on an early morning ferry to give your trip a more leisurely pace.

Only a 10-minute boat ride from downtown Boston, tiny 105-acre Spectacle Island offers an incredible five miles of walking trails. From the ferry dock, wander out on the island's twisting footpaths. As you follow the windswept shore, turn inland to crest the island's 157 foot-high hill, with panoramic views of the harbor and the city. Tree cover here is sparse and there is really no way to get lost. (Low-lying cover is as much due to wind as it is to the island's once bleak past as a garbage dump for the city of Boston.) Spectacle's visitors center offers exhibits about island history and nature, restrooms, and a café; jazz concerts are held at the visitors center every Sunday afternoon in summer.

Twenty-five minutes from the hustle and bustle of Boston is Georges Island, a 39-acre pinpoint of land that manages to squeeze in a large dock, picnic grounds, open fields, paved walkways, a parade ground, gravel beach, and the remains of Fort Warren, a National Historic Landmark. Built in 1847, Fort Warren served as a training area, patrol point, and prison during the Civil War, gaining a favorable

approaching Spectacle Island

reputation for the humane treatment of its Confederate prisoners. National Park rangers offer guided tours of the fort several times each day during the summer (you can also explore on your own); on weekdays in the spring, the island is a popular destination for school field trips. For a little extra room to roam on what can be a very crowded piece of real estate, visit Georges Island at low tide. The island actually grows to 53 acres, perfect for a meandering stroll along the sandy shore.

Options

From Georges Island, a free water taxi (shuttle) is available to four other harbor islands: Grape, Bumpkin, Lovells, and Peddocks. At 132 acres, Peddocks is the largest of these islands and comes with the most diverse terrain—the long strip of land is actually a string of five drumlin hills. Before you embark, pick up the shuttle schedule for Peddocks at Long Wharf. Camping is also permitted on each of these islands. Contact the Boston Harbor Islands Partnership to make reservations.

Directions

Boston's Long Wharf is next to the Marriott Long Wharf hotel and across the street from Faneuil Hall Marketplace, a short walk from the MBTA's blue line/ Aquarium stop and from both the green and orange lines at Haymarket. Inexpensive parking is available at nearby Fan Pier.

Round-trip ferry tickets from Boston to stops at Spectacle and Georges Islands are $14 for adults and $8 for children ages 3–11. Ferries depart Long Wharf for Georges and Spectacle Islands every hour on the hour 9 A.M.–4 P.M. Monday–Thursday, June 21–September 1. Return trips from Georges Island are every hour on the half-hour. On Fridays and weekends during the summer, ferries depart Long Wharf daily every half-hour 9 A.M.–5 P.M. Return trips from both Spectacle and Georges run hourly.

GPS Coordinates: 42.3601 N, 71.0496 W

Contact

Trail, beach, and Fort Warren access are free. Dogs are allowed. Maps of the islands are available at the Spectacle Island visitors center. For more information, contact Boston Harbor Islands Ferry, 408 Atlantic Ave., Boston, MA 02110, 617/223-8666, www.bostonislands.com. Boston Harbor Islands Partnership, 408 Atlantic Ave., Suite 228, Boston, MA 02110, 617/223-8666, www.nps.gov.

11 WORLD'S END
Hingham

Level: Easy/Moderate

Hiking Time: 1.5 hours

Total Distance: 2.9 miles

Elevation: 10 feet

Summary: This string of four low drumlin hills rising above Hingham Harbor offers good bird-watching and excellent water views.

This 251-acre peninsula in Hingham nearly became a community of 163 homes in the late 1800s, when then-landowner John Brewer hired none other than the famous landscape architect Frederick Law Olmsted to design a landscape of carriage paths lined by English oaks and native hardwoods. That much was accomplished, but the Brewer family continued to farm the land rather than develop it. In 1945, the site was named as a possible location for the United Nations, and in the mid 1960s a proposal was made to build a nuclear power plant here.

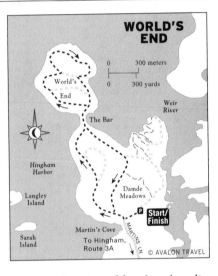

Today, thanks to The Trustees of Reservations, this string of four low drumlin hills rising above Hingham Harbor provides local people with a wonderful recreation area. Bird-watchers flock here, particularly in spring and fall, to observe migratory species. From various spots, you'll enjoy views of the Boston skyline, Hingham Harbor, and across the Weir River to Hull. This hike loops around the property's perimeter, but four miles of carriage paths and three miles of foot trails, all interconnected, offer many other possible routes for exploration. Easy terrain makes World's End a good pick for kids, too.

From the entrance, follow the paved access path west past the public bathrooms to reach a junction with a carriage road. Turn right (northwest) and follow the flat, wide path for 0.25 mile. The landscape here is grassy, but marked occasionally by groves of trees and rocky outcroppings. At the next forked junction, choose the trail leaving to the left (northwest) and follow it to bear around the west flank of Planter's Hill, the tallest of the park's drumlin hills. A quarter mile past Planter's, cross the narrow land bar between the harbor and river. Known simply as The

Bar, the causeway offers spectacular views west to Hingham Harbor and east to the Weir River estuary. Once you've crossed, turn west (left) onto another carriage road. This follows a 0.5-mile curve around another hillside, with pleasant water views; turn west again (left) at the next junction of carriage paths. After another half mile, turn at the junction to head south (a left turn), reaching the land bar 0.25 mile farther. After crossing back over The Bar, take the trail leaving to the east (left) and continue another 0.7 mile back to the parking area, passing by the reserve's Dame Meadows salt marsh area on the way.

Options

To explore the bucolic side of World's End, visit Rocky Neck, along the reserve's less-visited eastern shore. From the parking area, leave on the carriage road heading east, soon entering a coastal woods and marsh environment. You will see glimpses of water as you walk and at 0.25 mile, you will notice the marsh to your right give way to the rocky shore. Continue on and at 0.5 mile, reach a junction. Here, take the carriage road heading due north. Winding through the forest cover, the trail first visits the Ice Pond and then takes you out out to the tip of Rocky Neck for excellent water views. There is much less foot traffic here and chances are you can take in the splendor in solitude. Retrace your steps to return to the parking area.

Directions

From the junction of Routes 228 and 3A, drive north on Route 3A for 0.6 mile. Turn right on Summer Street, drive 0.3 mile, proceed straight through the traffic lights, and then continue another 0.8 mile to the World's End entrance.

Public Transportation: Take MBTA commuter rail service from South Station to Nantasket Junction in Hingham. World's End is a 10- minute walk north along Summer St./Martins Lane.

GPS Coordinates: 42.2480 N, 70.8727 W

Contact

There is an entrance fee of $5 per person ages 12 and older, except for members of The Trustees of Reservations, who enter for free. The reservation is open daily 8 a.m.–sunset year-round. Horse permits are free but must be obtained in advance by contacting the Trustees of Reservations Southeast/Cape Cod Regional Office. Dogs on leash are allowed. Maps are available at the entrance and online. For more information, contact The Trustees of Reservations Southeast/Cape Cod Regional Office, The Bradley Estate, 2468B Washington St., Canton, MA 02021-1124, 781/821-2977, www.thetrustees.org.

12 NOANET PEAK   BEST ☾
Noanet Woodlands, Dover

🏕 🦌 🌳 🐴

Level: Moderate   **Total Distance:** 4.0 miles

Hiking Time: 2 hours   **Elevation:** 300 feet

Summary: Climb to the top of Noanet Peak for a unique view of the Boston skyline and then explore the preserve's woods and ponds.

From 1815 to 1840, Noanet Brook powered the Dover Union Iron Company. A flood breached the huge dam at Noa-
net Falls in 1876 and it wasn't until 1954 that then-owner Amelia Peabody decided to restore the dam. And she didn't stop there. Peabody, on a mission to preserve open space in this once rural area, bought up hundreds of acres in Noanet woods and then promptly invited the public to enjoy its natural beauty.

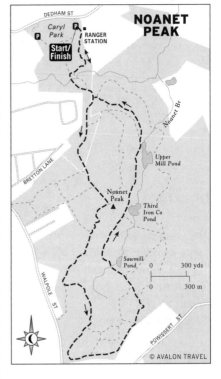

Today, the 695-acre Noanet Woodlands is a surprisingly quiet and seclud-
ed forest patch plunked down in the middle of suburbia. It might come as a shock to many first-time hikers of 387-
foot Noanet Peak to find that virtually the only sign of civilization visible from this rocky knob is the Boston skyline 20 miles away, floating on the horizon like the Emerald City. You have to scan the unbroken forest and rolling hills for a glimpse of another building. And you may hear no other sounds than the breeze and singing of birds. This hike brings you to the summit of Noanet Peak and then winds through the lush preserve to visit ponds, wetlands, and a rebuilt 19th-century mill dam.

From the parking area, walk past the ranger station to pick up the yellow-
blazed Noanet Peak Trail heading south. Follow the shady path to Junction 6 (trail junction signs are on trees) and turn left onto an unmarked trail. The Noanet Peak Trail makes a sharp turn west, but you should keep heading

Just steps into the Noanet Woodlands, suburbia is left far behind.

south, now on an unnamed trail. At the next junction (not numbered), skip the trail leaving to your left (east) and stay on your southern route, as it heads up the hill. Passing three other trail junctions, you soon reach the open ledge atop Noanet Peak. After enjoying the view, take the trail leaving the summit to the southwest, following a wooded ridge crest that slowly descends back to a junction with the Larabee Trail. At the junction, turn left to head south with the Larabee Trail. (You'll almost immediately recross the trail leading to Noanet's summit, but do not turn onto it). Follow the trail as it curves along the edge of the reserve and eventually turns to a northerly direction. Reaching Junction 18, walk straight onto the blue-blazed Peabody Trail. Continue on this flat, shady path to pass ponds and the site of an old mill. Wildflowers, including pink lady's slipper and marsh marigold, flourish here. Continuing on, bear left through Junction 4 to follow a connector trail west back to the Caryl Trail. Reaching the Caryl Trail, turn north (right) for a short walk back to the parking lot.

Options

To skip the uphill climb on this hike, at Junction 4, leave off the Peabody Trail, heading due south. Follow it as it winds between the ponds and the eastern flank of Noanet Peak, continuing on for over a mile to reach Junction 18, Here, turn at the signpost for the Larabee Trail, to turn northward for a pleasant woods walk back to Junction 4 and the start of the hike.

Directions

From I-95/Route 128, take Exit 17 onto Route 135 west. Drive about 0.6 mile and turn left at the traffic lights onto South Street. Drive 0.7 mile and bear left at a fork. After another 0.4 mile, turn left onto Chestnut Street. Cross the Charles River and enter Dover; turn right onto Dedham Street. Two miles past the river, turn left into Caryl Park; the sign is hard to see, but the parking lot is next to tennis courts.

GPS Coordinates: 42.2483 N, 71.2712 W

Contact

Parking and access are free. Noanet Woodlands is open to the public sunrise–sunset year-round. For those who wish to bike, a special biking permit can be obtained at the Noanet Woodlands ranger station at the Caryl Park entrance on weekends and holidays, or from the Southeast Region office of The Trustees of Reservations. Dogs are prohibited at Caryl Park, but visitors who walk to Noanet Woodlands can bring their dogs. For more information, contact The Trustees of Reservations Southeast/Cape Cod Regional Office, The Bradley Estate, 2468B Washington St., Canton, MA 02021-1124, 781/821-2977, www.thetrustees.org.

13 ROCKY WOODS
Medfield

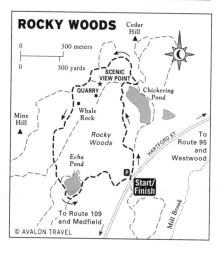

Level: Moderate

Hiking Time: 1.5 hours

Total Distance: 2.3 miles

Elevation: 250 feet

Summary: Ascend a rocky ridge for pleasing views of a seemingly untouched landscape of woods and ponds.

The rugged, rocky terrain of this 491-acre patch of woodlands formed via glacial plucking and scouring during the last Ice Age. Even for New England colonists accustomed to the rockiness of the region's soil, land here was just too rocky to till and so remained a forest, with the land divided into common woodlots for use by the neighboring townspeople. Logging activity continued into the 1800s and today Rocky Woods is crisscrossed by more than 12 miles of cart paths and former logging roads. Granite was also once quarried at the site and a string of artificially constructed ponds built for water storage and fire suppression are seen. This hike crosses through wetlands and pine-filled woods, visits two of the reserve's ponds, and then climbs a granite ridge with scenic views of the surrounding landscape.

From the parking area, pick up the flat, yellow-blazed Loop Trail as it bears north out of the lot and into the woods. Trail navigation within the reserve uses named trails, different color blazes, and numbered trail junctions. Within 0.1 mile, the trail begins sweeping west and soon reaches Junction 2. Here, turn north (right) to follow the Bridle Trail, a flat, wide trail continuing under forest cover for the next 0.25 mile. Reaching Junction 5, turn east (right) with the trail to reach Junction 4, along the upper reaches of Chickering Pond. Visit the clear waters of the pond and then return to the junction, picking up the Ridge Trail as it heads to the northwest. The trail is shaded by tall pines and stands of cedar, and much rockier soil under foot. After a rather sudden uphill ascent to the top of the ridge, the green-blazed trail continues for the next 0.5 mile, treading along ground that alternates between pine needle covered path and rocky outcroppings.

At about the halfway point of the Ridge Trail, look for a marker pointing the way to the scenic vista. It's only steps off the main path and well worth a look.

At Junction 7, the Ridge Trail ends, but the green blazes continue straight ahead as the Harwood Notch Trail begins. Still following the ridge, the Harwood Notch Trail eventually leads to another scenic vista marker and then drops steeply from the ridge to reach Junction 6, about 0.25 mile from where the Ridge Trail ended. Continuing on for only 0.10 mile, the trail reaches an unmarked junction. Bear to the southeast (taking the trail to your left) which eventually becomes yellow-blazed. Crossing on a long, narrow footbridge over the shimmering waters of Echo Pond, the trail winds another 0.25 mile before returning you to the parking area.

The cart paths in Rocky Woods are wider than typical footpaths.

© JACQUELINE TOURVILLE

Options

For more climbing (and an added distance of about 0.3 mile), add a side trip to the summit of 435-foot Cedar Hill, the reserve's height of land. From Junction 4, instead of taking the Ridge Trail to the northwest, bear east (right) onto the Tower Trail for a moderate, but unrelenting uphill climb to the top of this rocky knob. Look for the scenic vista marker for a surprisingly wide view stretching to the north. The trail loops off the summit to return you to Junction 4.

Directions

From I-95/Route 128 in Westwood, take Exit 16B onto Route 109, driving west for 5.7 miles. Take a sharp right onto Hartford Street and continue 0.6 mile to the reservation entrance on the left. Or from the junction of Routes 27 and 109 in Medfield, drive 1.7 miles east on Route 109 and bear left on Hartford Street and park along that street. The reservation is open daily sunrise–sunset year-round.
GPS Coordinates: 42.2011 N, 71.2794 W

Contact

Admission is free for Trustees members. Nonmember adults $4; nonmember children (ages 12 and under) free. Fees collected by ranger on weekends and holidays; honor system applies at all other times. Dogs on leash are allowed. Maps are available from the ranger on duty weekends and holidays or online. For more information, contact The Trustees of Reservations Southeast/Cape Cod Regional Office, The Bradley Estate, 2468B Washington St., Canton, MA 02021-1124, 781/821-2977, www.thetrustees.org.

14 BLUE HILLS SKYLINE TRAIL   BEST ◖
Blue Hills Reservation in Canton

🔭 🦌 ✈ 🏕 🐕 🚌

Level: Butt-kicker   **Total Distance:** 4.5 miles

Hiking Time: 2.5 hours   **Elevation:** 1,200 feet

Summary: Scenic and strenuous, if you're looking for a butt-kicking hike that's close to Boston, this is it!

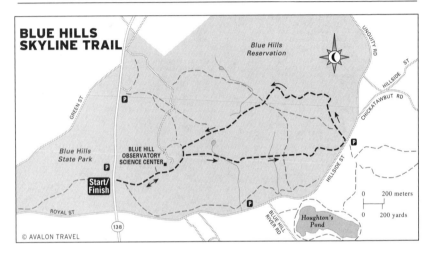

With 5,800 forest acres spread over 20 hilltops, the Blue Hills Reservation in Quincy, Braintree, Randolph, Canton, and Milton comprises the largest tract of open space in greater Boston. It hosts a broad diversity of flora and fauna, including the timber rattlesnake, which you are extremely unlikely to encounter given the snake's fear of people. The reservation harbors an extensive network of trails and carriage roads. But be aware that some are unmarked and confusing, and many are rocky and surprisingly rugged. At 635 feet, Great Blue Hill, near the reservation's western end, is the park's highest point and probably its most popular hike.

This 4.5-mile loop on the north and south branches of the Skyline Trail passes over Great Blue and four other hills, climbing a cumulative total of about 1,200 feet. It incorporates several good views—the best being the panorama from the stone tower on Great Blue, reached near this hike's end. In fact, while the native granite tower is less than 50 years old, it symbolizes this high point's long history. Patriots used Great Blue as a lookout during the Revolutionary War, lighting beacons up here to warn of any British attack. For several hundred years, fires have

white mist flower growing along the Blue Hills Skyline Trail

been lit on Great Blue to celebrate historic occurrences, beginning with the repeal of the Stamp Act and including the signing of the Declaration of Independence.

From the parking lot, walk back on Route 138 in the direction you came, watching for blue blazes that cross the road within 100 feet. Enter the woods at a granite post inscribed with the words Skyline Trail. The trail heads east and then northeast as it ascends steeply for 0.5 mile, reaching open ledges and a carriage road just below the summit. Turn east (right) on the carriage road, where blue blazes are marked on stones. The trail curves north, passing the path leading to the summit (there aren't any views, and the weather observatory here is private property). Within 0.1 mile turn east (right) with the blue blazes onto a footpath marked by a post inscribed South Skyline Trail. It descends ledges with good views of the Boston skyline and Houghton Pond, enters the woods, and, within a mile of Great Blue, reaches wooded Houghton Hill. Descend a short distance to Hillside Street, cross it, turn left (north), and follow the blue blazes about 150 feet to where the blazes direct you back across the street toward the reservation headquarters (passing a post marked North Skyline Trail). Walk up the driveway and past the headquarters to pick up a carriage path. In about 75 feet, turn right (north) at a sign onto the North Skyline Trail. In minutes you reach an open ledge on Hancock Hill with a view of Great Blue Hill. All along the route, you might spot red-tail hawks circling overhead, foxes scurrying about in the thicket, and wild turkey waddling about. Wildflowers make a pretty frame to the trail in places; look for the distinctive bloom of the rare pink lady slipper in mid to late June.

Continuing over Hemenway Hill and Wolcott Hill in the next mile, watch for side paths leading north to views of Boston. The Skyline Trail drops downhill, crosses a carriage path, and then climbs the north side of Great Blue to the stone tower. Climb the stairs to the tower for a sweeping view of woods, city, and ocean. From the tower's observation deck looking west (out over the stone building beside the tower), you may see Mount Wachusett. Standing on the side of the tower facing Boston, look left: On a clear day, you'll spy Mount Monadnock between two tall radio towers in the distance. Descend the stone tower and turn right (south) on the Skyline Trail, circling around Great Blue and descending 0.5 mile to Route 138, where you began this hike.

Options

Still want to make it to the stone tower, but need a route that is a bit easier on the knees? Just south of the parking lot where this hike begins, find Blue Hill River Road and follow it in your car as it turns into Hillside Street and eventually reaches a parking area. Leaving from here, cross back over Hillside Street and walk back toward Route 138 until you see the trailhead for the red-blazed Accord Path leaving to the north (on your right). Follow the Accord Path a few steps to the Wildcat Notch Path and then follow this slowly ascending trail until it reaches the South Skyline Trail. Turn west (left) with the blue blazes for a much shorter and gentle push to the top of Great Blue, bearing north at the summit to reach the stone tower. Retrace your steps on the return, a total trip of a little over one mile.

Directions

From I-93, take Exit 2B onto Route 138 north. Continue for nearly 0.5 mile to a commuter parking lot on the left—park here for this hike. The Blue Hills Reservation Headquarters is located at 695 Hillside Street in Milton, 0.25 mile north of Houghton's Pond, beside the State Police Station.

Public Transportation: The Great Blue Hill and Houghton's Pond sections are accessible from the red line to Ashmont Station. From Ashmont, take the high speed line to Mattapan. The Canton and Blue Hills bus services the Trailside Museum and Great Blue Hill on Route 138. For the Houghton's Pond area, exit the bus at Blue Hill River Road. Cross the road and walk one mile east on Hillside Street.

GPS Coordinates: 42.2141 N, 71.1200W

Contact

Parking and access are free. Dogs on leash are allowed. Maps are available at the reservation headquarters or the Massachusetts Audubon Society Blue Hills Trailside Museum. For more information, contact Blue Hills Reservation Headquarters, 695 Hillside St., Milton, MA 02186, 617/698-1802, www.mass.gov. Friends of the Blue Hills, P.O. Box 416, Milton, MA 02186, 781/828-1805, www.friendsofthebluehills.org. Massachusetts Audubon Society Blue Hills Trailside Museum, 1904 Canton Ave./Route 138, Milton, MA 02186, 781/333-0690, www.massaudubon.org.

15 RATTLESNAKE AND WAMPATUCK HILLS

Blue Hills Reservation in Braintree

Level: Moderate

Total Distance: 2.2 miles

Hiking Time: 1.5 hours

Elevation: 500 feet

Summary: Find solitude in this popular hiking area with a trip up two hills tucked away along the reservation's northeastern boundary.

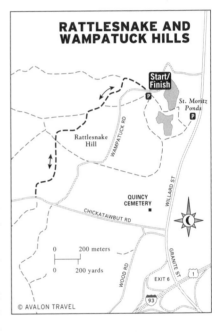

While many hikers flock to the west side of the reservation and to Great Blue Hill, the east side of the reservation remains a fairly well-kept secret—and the views from there are arguably better than those from Great Blue Hill. Standing in a warm summer breeze on Rattlesnake Hill, gazing out over an expanse of woods to the Boston skyline in the distance, many who visit here are amazed to hear only the breeze and the singing of birds, despite having left the interstate behind just a half hour earlier and hiking merely 0.5 mile.

From the roadside parking area, the Skyline Trail begins at a marked trailpost, heading northwest and then west as it quickly ascends a short but steep hillside to a view of the thickly forested, rolling hills of the reservation and the Boston skyline beyond. The trail then bends around an old quarry now filled with water, and turns south. After more uphill gain, the trail reaches the rocky top of Rattlesnake Hill at 0.5 mile from the hike's start, with excellent views of the hills and skyline. The summit is also a bird-watcher's paradise; red-tail hawks, vultures and even bald eagles are often spotted soaring proudly overhead.

Stay with the blue blazes to head west off the summit, dropping in elevation and then gaining it back as you scale Wampatuck Hill in less than 0.5 mile. The trail here offers good footing, but occasional rock outcroppings and tree roots makes it necessary to more carefully watch your step and a short, rocky scramble along the trail here may be intimidating for some inexperienced hikers. But reaching the summit of Wampatuck offers the reward of even more good views. And maybe even better, a real sense of solitude in the middle of this popular hiking retreat. Return the same way.

Options

Still have energy to spare? Continue on the Skyline Trail from Wampatuck Hill for another half mile to take in views of the vast Blue Hills Reservoir (adding one mile round-trip to this hike) or really turn this into a butt-kicker by pushing on for a little over a mile to reach the summit of Chickatawbut Hill, for great views and a chance to visit the Blue Hills Education Center, located near the summit. This adds an additional 2.2 miles to this hike.

Directions

From I-93 in Braintree, take Exit 6 and follow signs to Willard Street. About a mile from I-93, watch for the ice rink on the left (Shea Rink). Drive 0.2 mile beyond the rink, turn left on Hayden Street, and then immediately left again on Wampatuck Road. Drive another 0.2 mile and park at the roadside on the right, where a post marks the Skyline Trail. The reservation headquarters is at 695 Hillside Street in Milton, reached via the reservation entrance on Route 138 or from Randolph Avenue (I-93, Exit 5).

Public Transportation: Take the red line T to Quincy Center and pick up MBTA bus 238 to the Shea Rink stop. The trailhead is found across the street.

GPS Coordinates: 42.2368 N, 71.0321 W

Contact

Parking and access are free. This trail is open dawn–8 P.M. Dogs on leash are allowed. Maps are available at the reservation headquarters or the Massachusetts Audubon Society Blue Hills Trailside Museum. For more information, contact Blue Hills Reservation Headquarters, 695 Hillside St., Milton, MA 02186, 617/698-1802, www.mass.gov. Friends of the Blue Hills, P.O. Box 416, Milton, MA 02186, 781/828-1805, www.friendsofthebluehills.org. Massachusetts Audubon Society Blue Hills Trailside Museum, 1904 Canton Ave./Route 138, Milton, MA 02186, 781/333-0690, www.massaudubon.org.

16 MOOSE HILL

Moose Hill Wildlife Sanctuary, Sharon

🏠 🦌 ✈️ 🌿 👫 🚌

Level: Easy

Total Distance: 1.4 miles

Hiking Time: 1 hour

Elevation: 300 feet

Summary: Start with a walk to the summit of Moose Hill and then explore this 2,200-acre reserve's collection of forest, fields, and wetlands.

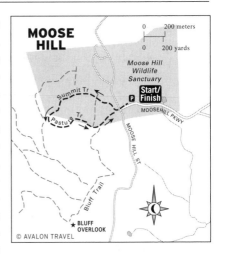

At over 500 feet tall, Moose Hill rises high above the surrounding landscape, making it a striking centerpiece for the Massachusetts Audubon Society's oldest sanctuary. While no one here can ever remember actually seeing any moose, sightings of other wildlife are frequent. Living in this microenvironment of forests, red maple wetlands, and rippling pasture are wrens, kinglets, and woodcock—and furry creatures ranging from rabbits to deer. An excellent time to visit the reserve is in spring, when migrating warblers stop by to sing a few sweet tunes on their journey north. Because it has all the features of a real mountain climb (an uphill trudge followed by splendid views) this hike is a good one for kids just finding their "mountain legs".

From the parking area, cross Moose Hill Street, heading west to reach a wide gravel carriage road that begins just below the corner of Moose Hill Street and the Moose Hill Parkway. Follow this carriage road for 0.1 mile until you reach a junction with the Summit Trail, marked with blue blazes (you will also see white blazes here; these belong to the Warner Trail, as described below). At first cutting through a wet forest of red oak, the Summit Trail veers north and then turns west, passing over a bridge and passing through a gap in a stone wall. In another 0.1 mile, cross a junction with the Moose Hill Loop and begin the scramble up Moose Hill's rocky, pine-covered hillside; just before the summit, the trail splits and then rejoins itself. At 0.3 mile, the trail reaches the fire tower (not open for climbing). Take in pleasant views from the summit and then continue west with the Summit Trail to descend the hill, continuing another 0.4 mile until you reach a junction.

Turning left to head southeast on the Pasture Trail, the next 0.25 mile offers prime bird-watching in summer as swallows, meadowlarks, and butterflies flit about above the wildflower-filled grasses. The Pasture Trail ends at a junction with the Cistern Trail. Bear north here to return through a mix of field and forest on the 0.25-mile return to the starting point of this hike. Cross the street to return to your car.

Options

Moose Hill is a stop on the Warner Trail, a long distance hiking route that stretches more than 30 miles from Sharon, Massachusetts, to the Diamond Hill State Park in Cumberland, Rhode Island. For a short trip on the trail to the summit of Bluff Head, keep track of the white blazes of the Warner Trail as you descend the summit and turn onto the Pasture Trail (the Warner Trail coincides with these trails). Just before the Pasture Trail ends at the Cistern Trail, the white blazes veer off to the right, heading south. Follow the white blazes, continuing through several junctions until reaching Bluff Head, with nice views south, at 1.5 miles from Moose Hill. Retrace your steps to the Pasture Trail and continue on to return via the Cistern Trail. For more information about the rest of the Warner Trail (and future plans for adding more mileage), contact Friends of the Warner Trail, P.O. Box 85, MA 02048 or visit www.warnertrail.org.

Directions

From 1-95 South in Walpole, take exit 10 (Coney St., Sharon, Walpole). Take a left off the exit and take the first right onto Route 27 north (Walpole). Take the first left on Moose Hill Street. Continue past TTOR's Moose Hill Farm. Follow to the top of the hill and turn left onto Moose Hill Parkway. The parking lot is on the left.

Public Transportation: From Boston's South Station, take the Attleboro commuter train to Sharon. From the Sharon station walk to the main road, Route 27. Follow north for two blocks and take a left onto Moose Hill Parkway. Walk 1.5 miles to the top of the hill; the nature center is on the right.

GPS Coordinates: 42.1247N, 71.2090W

Contact

There is a fee of $4 for nonmember adults and $3 for nonmember children (2–12) and seniors; Audubon members enter for free. Trails are open every day, dawn–dusk. Dogs are not allowed. Maps are available at the trailhead and online. For more information, contact Moose Hill Wildlife Sanctuary, 293 Moose Hill Street, Sharon, MA 02067, 781/784-5691, www.massaudubon.org.

17 PINE BARRENS AND PONDS LOOP

BEST **⊂**

Myles Standish State Forest in Carver

🏇 ⛵ 🦌

Level: Moderate

Total Distance: 5.5 miles

Hiking Time: 2.5 hours

Elevation: 50 feet

Summary: Travel deep into a pitch pine forest to visit cranberry bogs and glacial kettle ponds.

Myles Standish State Forest sprawls over more than 14,000 acres, making it one of the largest pitch pine/scrub forest communities north of Long Island, NY—and one of the largest public land tracts in Massachusetts. The forest winds around 16 lakes and ponds, including several ecologically significant glacial kettle ponds. Living in these freshwater refuges is the Plymouth red-bellied turtle, an endangered turtle species only found in this part of the state.

To explore the forest, a grid work of old woods roads cuts through the pine barrens, along with hiking trails and a paved bicycle path. This loop from the forest headquarters connects trails and dirt woods roads on the way to visit a number of the forest's ponds. The grid pattern of roads and the signs at many intersections makes navigating through this vast landscape easier than it might be otherwise, but bring a map. Although the pine-covered terrain is mostly flat, there are slight rises and dips that can make this hike a real workout.

From the parking lot, head north on the healthy heart trail (look for the trail sign marked with a heart symbol) as it skirts East Head Reservoir. Within 0.5 mile, the trail intersects with Lower College Pond Road, a paved road. Follow Lower College Pond Road less than 0.25 mile to the Halfway Pond Road intersection. Here, turn west (left) onto the dirt Halfway Pond Road. Now deep in the barrens, follow the forest-shaded road 0.5 mile to a crossroads and turn north (right) onto the bridle path trail named Jessup Road. Continue about 0.7 mile to reach another intersection. Bear west (left) to stay on the bridle trail, now called Three Cornered Pond Road, and 0.5 mile farther turn north (right) at a crossroads onto West Line Road (still following the bridle path). For the next 0.5 mile, the trail winds north along the edge of a cranberry bog and the shores of Federal Pond.

Reaching the next intersection, turn east to follow Federal Pond Road, continuing straight for a little over one mile to reach the shores of College Pond, the forest's popular swimming beach. From here, head south on the paved Lower College Pond Road for the next 1.5 miles back to the parking area, passing Three Cornered Pond, New Long Pond, and a scattering of smaller, unnamed ponds on the way.

Options

To turn your trip to Myles Standish into an overnight adventure in the barrens, camp at one of state forest campgrounds. Campsites are clustered near Charge Pond and Fearing Pond. For a more remote camping experience, Curlew Pond on the northern end of the forest offers two waterside campsites. Contact the state forest headquarters for more information and to make reservations.

Directions

From 1-95 South in Norwood, take exit 10 (Coney St., Walpole, Sharon). Turn left off the exit onto Route 27 north, turning right in 0.3 mile to stay on this road. At 0.9 mile, turn left onto Moose Hill Street. At 2.2 miles, turn left onto Moose Hill Parkway to reach the sanctuary parking lot.
GPS Coordinates: 41.8389 N, 70.6941 W

Contact

A daily parking fee of $5 is collected mid-May–mid-October. Dogs on leash are allowed. Maps are available at the state forest headquarters or online. For more information, contact Myles Standish State Forest, Cranberry Rd., P.O. Box 66, South Carver, MA 02366, 508/866-2526. Massachusetts Division of State Parks and Recreation, 251 Causeway St., Suite 600, Boston, MA 02114-2104, 617/626-1250, www.state.ma.us.

NEW HAMPSHIRE

© MARGARET COSTARELLA

BEST HIKES

《 Butt-Kickers
Mount Lafayette, **page 105**

《 Fall Foliage
Welch and Dickey, **page 107**
Mount Monadnock, **page 126**

《 Kid-Friendly Hikes
Beaver Brook Trail, **page 129**

《 Summit Views
Mount Lafayette, **page 105**
Mount Monadnock, **page 126**

Poet, naturalist, and avid hiker Henry David

Thoreau once observed, "thousands annually seek the White Mountains to be refreshed by their wild and primitive beauty." Indeed, many hikes in the famous White Mountains of New Hampshire, including Mount Lafayette and Mount Chocorua, are among the most popular in all of New England – and considered some of the best hiking east of the Rockies. You are likely to find trails in Franconia Notch, the state's premier mountain recreation area, crowded with boots on nice weekends in summer and fall – and even in winter. Some of the lower peaks of the Whites, including Welch and Dickey Mountains, offer the best views per ounce of sweat that you'll find anywhere.

The sky-high peaks of the Whites do stand out as the Granite State's star attraction, but for smaller summits in the lower half of New Hampshire – regional favorites such as Monadnock, Kearsarge, and Smarts – the beauty is in the details. Leaving behind the predominant conifer cover found in the northern part of the state, the deciduous forests of maples, beech, oaks, and birch found so abundantly here provide treks with a backdrop of ever-changing color. Lime green in June and lush blue in summer, the landscape gradually heats up to an autumn fire of red, orange, and golden yellow.

Southern New Hampshire is also home to the state's 18 miles of sea-coast (the shortest stretch of seaboard located within the boundaries of one state). Shoehorned between Massachusetts and Maine, New Hampshire's coastal area offers sandy beaches and rocky shoreline, but the heart of this region is found in the tidal estuaries that form a great inland bay. Hikes around aptly named Great Bay take you to a unique marine environment where fertile fields and freshwater rivers meet salt marshes and coastal tides.

Wherever you decide to hike in New Hampshire, access to the outdoors is easy to come by: Almost 85 percent of the state is forest-covered and much of this land is crisscrossed by a constellation of hiking trails and footpaths, including the long distance Appalachian Trail. Wildlife abounds in the thick forests of New Hampshire, including sizable populations of moose, black bear, and deer populations. Bald eagles and peregrine falcons also flock to the Granite State, as do lots of other forest critters, including beaver, fox, fisher cats, wild turkey, and water fowl.

Most state parks and forests allow certain types of hunting in season and hikers will need to take appropriate precautions in the woods at these times. The prime, snow-free hiking season in southern New Hampshire generally runs from April or May through mid-November. In the northern part of the state, weather is less predictable. Trails, especially on Mount Lafayette, may be snow-covered by mid-October. If you do attempt hikes in the White Mountains, especially summit climbs to the higher, exposed peaks, come prepared with emergency and foul-weather gear. White Mountains hikes described in this chapter are each located near a camping shelter, with vary degrees of amenities.

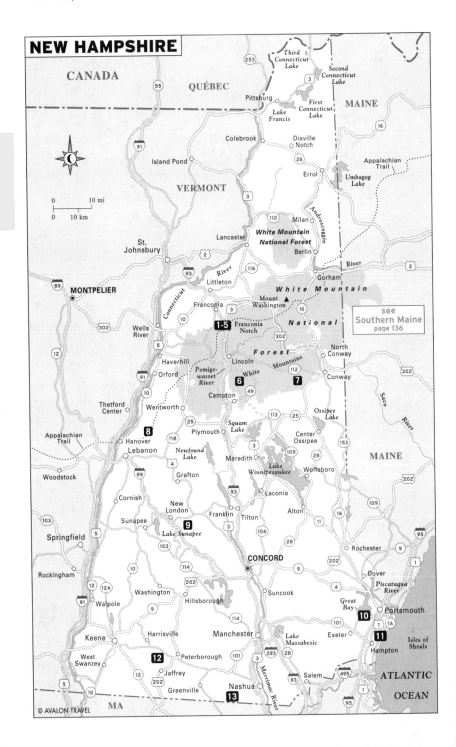

TRAIL NAME	LEVEL	DISTANCE	TIME	ELEVATION	FEATURES	PAGE
1 Cannon Mountain	Butt-kicker	4.4 mi	3 hr	2,100 ft		94
2 Lonesome Lake Trail	Easy/Moderate	3.2 mi	2 hr	1,000 ft		97
3 North and South Kinsman	Butt-Kicker	11.1 mi	8 hr	2,500 ft		100
4 Pemi Trail	Easy	5.6 mi one-way	2.5 hr	50 ft		103
5 Mount Lafayette	Butt-kicker	8.0 mi	6 hr	3,500 ft		105
6 Welch and Dickey	Moderate	4.5 mi	3.5 hr	1,700 ft		107
7 Mount Chocorua	Strenuous	5.4 mi	5 hr	2,600 ft		110
8 Smarts Mountain	Strenuous	8.2 mi	3.5 hr	2,100 ft		113
9 Mount Kearsarge	Moderate	2.9 mi	2 hr	1,100 ft		116
10 Great Bay Estuarine Research Reserve	Easy	1.0 mi	45 min	0 ft		119
11 Odiorne State Park	Easy/Moderate	2.0 mi	1 hr	0 ft		122
12 Mount Monadnock	Strenuous	4.6 mi	3 hr	1,600 ft		126
13 Beaver Brook Trail	Easy/Moderate	2.5 mi	1.5 hr	50 ft		129

1 CANNON MOUNTAIN
Franconia Notch State Park

🏠 🐕 ♿

Level: Butt-kicker

Hiking Time: 3 hours

Total Distance: 4.4 miles

Elevation: 2,100 feet

Summary: Explore scenic views from the mountain that was once home to the state's iconic Old Man of the Mountain profile.

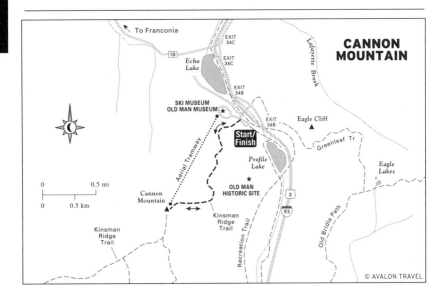

Cannon Mountain (4,077 feet) stands out at the north end of spectacular Franconia Notch because of the 1,000-foot cliff on its east face. A popular place for technical rock climbers to test their skills, the cliff was once the home of the Old Man of the Mountain, the famous stone profile that suddenly gave way to gravity in 2003. The Cannon Mountain Ski area on the northern flank of the mountain operates an 80-passenger tramway gondola that visits the mountain's summit several times a day in summer. As a result, the summit of Cannon is much more developed than other summits in Franconia Notch, offering such amenities as a snack bar and bathrooms. Wheelchair access to the summit is provided by the Cannon Mountain Aerial Tramway, but the hiking trails are not wheelchair accessible.

A number of trails crisscross Cannon Mountain, but only the Kinsman Ridge Trail can be taken uninterrupted from the trailhead to the summit. This trail begins in the aerial tramway parking lot and ascends the north face of the mountain,

view of Franconia Notch from the summit of Cannon Mountain

which is shared by the ski area. It's a steep trip up to the scenic top of Cannon, but it does come with the option of taking the gondola back down the mountain.

From the tramway parking lot, follow the Kinsman Ridge Trail through a picnic area and briefly along a ski area trail before entering the woods, heading south. The trail ascends at a moderate grade, passing a short side path at 1.5 miles that leads to open ledges and a nice view across the notch to Franconia Ridge. At 2.0 miles, the Kinsman Ridge Trail swings west (right), soon climbing more steeply to the summit, where there is an observation platform, summit lodge, and summit tramway station. To the east, the views extend to Mounts Lafayette and Lincoln. To the west, you can see Vermont's Green Mountains and New York's Adirondacks on a clear day. Head back along the same route.

Options

For a real calf burner, the very fit hiker might like the challenge of the steeper Hi-Cannon Trail to the summit. From the Lafayette Campground parking lot off I-93, pick up the Lonesome Lake Trail at the trail marker and follow it west through the campground, ascending steadily toward Lonesome Lake. At 0.4 mile, turn north onto the Hi-Cannon Trail (look for the trail marker at the well-defined trail junction). Hi-Cannon at first climbs steadily through a series of switchbacks, but at 1.2 miles from the campground, the trail suddenly becomes increasingly vertical and rugged on its way up a ridge. Pass a fine overlook with views toward Franconia Notch at 1.6 miles and, a few yards later, climb up a ladder to negotiate a cliff-like rock slab. Tall hikers and those carrying tall frame packs should be mindful of a rock overhang hovering overhead at the top of the ladder. Continuing on, still on rocky, somewhat open terrain, at 2.4 miles from the campground, turn north on the Kinsman Ridge Trail and follow it 0.4 mile to Cannon's summit.

Directions

From Lincoln, follow I-93 north for approximately 10 miles to enter Franconia Notch. Continue driving approximately six miles until reaching exit 34B. At the end of the exit ramp, follow the signs for Aerial Tramway parking; the southern end of the lot is reserved for hikers.

GPS Coordinates: 44.1419 N, 71.6860 W

Contact

Parking and access are free. Dogs on leash are allowed. Two waterproof trail maps showing this hike are available from the Appalachian Mountain Club (*Franconia–Pemigewasset Range* map and *Crawford Notch–Sandwich Range/Moosilauke–Kinsman* map, $10 each). For more information, contact Franconia Notch State Park, Franconia, NH 03580, 603/745-8391, www.franconianotchstatepark.com. White Mountain National Forest Headquarters, 71 White Mountain Drive, Campton, NH 03246, 603/536-6100, TDD for hearing impaired 603/536-3665, www.fs.fed.us.

2 LONESOME LAKE TRAIL

Franconia Notch State Park

🄰 📷 🄲 👫

Level: Easy/Moderate

Hiking Time: 2 hours

Total Distance: 3.2 miles

Elevation: 1,000 feet

Summary: Take in the sights of the Franconia Ridge from this scenic mountain pond.

Lonesome Lake, like so many other natural features in New England, was formed during the last Ice Age, when glacial action carved the 20-acre pond out of a pocket in the rock between Cannon and Kinsman Mountains. Nestled 1,000 feet above Franconia Notch on the southern flank of Cannon Mountain, the lake is technically classified as a tarn, or high elevation, glacially formed mountain pond.

Despite its name—and the somewhat steep climb it takes to get there—Lonesome Lake is far from lonesome; the tarn is actually one of the most popular destinations in Franconia Notch. Campers from nearby Lafayette Campground, especially families with young kids in tow, visit in droves on sunny summer days; Appalachian Trail through-hikers stop by to cool off their feet as the AT skirts the southern shore of the lake; and still other hikers make their way here as a worthy detour on the way to Cannon or other nearby mountains.

Nonetheless, if you accept the likelihood of sharing this beautiful spot with dozens of other visitors (or you make it a point to get here in the early morning or late afternoon to avoid the crowds), the view from the lake's southwest corner across its crystal waters to Mounts Lafayette and Lincoln on Franconia Ridge has no comparison. And though you may bring along your bathing suit to take a dip, don't forget your hiking gear—especially your boots and some extra socks. The trail to Lonesome Lake passes through extensive boggy areas, which, combined with heavy foot traffic, can make for a muddy hike.

From the parking lot, pick up the Lonesome Lake Trail at the trail sign near the entrance to the Lafayette Place Campground. Crossing though the campground on a well-worn path heading almost due west, the trail enters the forest and begins its moderate ascent. Pushing west before gradually turning southwest and growing steeper, the trail reaches the northeast corner of the lake at 1.2 miles. You can stop here to swim, but to continue in a loop around the lake, turn south (left) at the trail junction to take the Cascade Brook Trail, following it nearly 0.3 mile to the south end of the lake, and another junction. Turn west (right) on the Fishin' Jimmy Trail/Appalachian Trail, crossing the lake's outlet and reaching another small beach area where people swim. An Appalachian Mountain Club hut lies a short distance off the lake, in the woods. Bear north (right) off the Fishin' Jimmy Trail onto the Around-Lonesome-Lake Trail, which heads north along the lake's west shore, crossing boggy areas on boardwalks. In 0.3 mile, turn east (right) on the Lonesome Lake Trail and follow it 1.4 miles back to the campground.

a rocky section of the Lonesome Lake Trail

© MARGARET COSTARELLA

Options

Want to turn this pleasant little trek into a overnight backpacking adventure? Explore Lonesome Lake and Cannon Mountain (or North Kinsman) and then backtrack to spend the night at the Appalachian Mountain Club Lonesome Lake hut, located on the Fishin' Jimmy Trail near Lonesome Lake. The hut has a 46-person capacity and is more like a rustic hotel, complete with beds, showers, and home-cooked meals. Contact the AMC for reservation and rate information.

Directions

From Lincoln, follow I-93 north for approximately 10 miles to reach Franconia Notch. At signs for the Lafayette Place Campground, park in one of the large parking lots on the east side of I-93 (for southbound vehicles, another parking lot is on the west side of the highway). From the east side parking lot, hikers can cross under the highway to the Lafayette Place Campground on the west side, where the trail begins.

GPS Coordinates: 44.1419 N, 71.6860 W

Contact

Parking and access are free. Dogs on leash are allowed. Two waterproof area trail maps available from the Appalachian Mountain Club show this hike (*Franconia–Pemigewasset Range* map and *Crawford Notch–Sandwich Range/Moosilauke–Kinsman* map, $10 each). For more information, contact White Mountain National Forest Headquarters, 71 White Mountain Drive, Campton, NH 03246, 603/536-6100, TDD for hearing impaired 603/536-3665, www.fs.fed.us. Franconia Notch State Park, Franconia, NH 03580, 603/745-8391, www.franconianotchstatepark.com. Appalachian Mountain Club Pinkham Notch Visitor Center, P.O. Box 298, Gorham, NH 03581, 603/466-2721, www.outdoors.org.

3 NORTH AND SOUTH KINSMAN
White Mountain National Forest and Franconia Notch State Park

Level: Butt-kicker

Hiking Time: 8 hours

Total Distance: 11.1 miles

Elevation: 2,500 feet

Summary: Take in the tumbling waters of Cascade Falls on the way to these two towering peaks overlooking Franconia Notch.

Two 4,000-footers in a single day? For very fit hikers ready for a butt-kicking good time, it's hard to beat this trek to North Kinsman (4,293 feet) and South Kinsman (4,356 feet), two towering peaks rising high above the western flank of Franconia Notch. Spectacular scenery awaits at both mountain summits, but the more popular attraction on this 11.1-mile hike just may be the 1.5 miles of falls and cascades along Cascade Brook. Many hikers, especially families with young children, explore only as far as the brook—a refreshing place on a hot summer day (and a way for more novice hikers to enjoy the mountains).

If you do decide to go for the bragging rights of hiking all 11.1 difficult miles in one day, make sure to come prepared with plenty of food, water, basic camping gear—and at least two pairs of extra socks. Most of the stream crossings on this hike utilize rocks or downed trees and can be difficult at times of high water (and slippery almost any time). Also, heavily used trails in the area are often wet and muddy, making rocks and exposed roots slick and footing difficult. Portions of the route coincide with the Appalachian Trail.

You can begin this hike on either side of I-93. From the parking lot on the northbound side of I-93, follow the signs to the Basin, passing west beneath I-93 and crossing a footbridge over the Pemigewasset River. Beyond the bridge, the trail bends north (right); within 100 feet, bear west (left) at a sign for the Basin-Cascades Trail. From the parking lot on the southbound side, follow the walkway south to the Basin. Turn west (right) on the bridge over the Pemigewasset and watch for the Basin-Cascades Trail branching west (left). Hikers from either parking lot will converge at this trailhead near the Basin, a natural stone bowl carved out by the Pemigewasset River and a popular spot for tourists. Follow the Basin-Cascades Trail west for 1.0 mile before the Basin-Cascades Trail meets the Cascade Brook Trail at a trail crossing.

Even a novice hiker can take in the wild beauty of Cascade Brook.

From this junction to the summit of South Kinsman, the hike coincides with the white-blazed Appalachian Trail (AT). Turn right (northwest) on the AT/Cascade Brook Trail, immediately crossing the brook on stones or a downed tree. A half mile farther, the Kinsman Pond Trail bears left and crosses Cascade Brook; however, you should bear right and continue roughly north on the AT/Cascade Brook Trail another mile to a junction with the Fishin' Jimmy Trail at the south end of Lonesome Lake. Turn west (left) with the AT onto the Fishin' Jimmy Trail, crossing a log bridge over the lake's outlet to a beachlike area popular for swimming. There's an outstanding view across Lonesome Lake to Franconia Ridge and Mounts Lafayette and Lincoln and Little Haystack (from left to right). Stay on the AT/Fishin' Jimmy Trail, passing the Appalachian Mountain Club's Lonesome Lake hut, which sits back in the woods just above the beach area. The trail rises and falls, passing over the hump separating Lonesome Lake from the upper flanks of Kinsman Mountain. After crossing a feeder stream to Cascade Brook, the trail ascends steeply, often up rock slabs into which wooden steps have been drilled in places. Two miles from Lonesome Lake, the Fishin' Jimmy Trail terminates at Kinsman Junction.

From the junction, follow the AT straight (west) onto the Kinsman Ridge Trail, climbing steep rock. Reach the wooded summit of North Kinsman 0.4 mile from the junction; a side path leads 20 feet from the summit cairn to an open ledge with a sweeping view eastward. Continue south on the AT/Kinsman Ridge Trail, descending past two open areas with good views. The trail drops into the saddle between the two peaks, then ascends steadily to the broad, flat summit of South Kinsman, nearly a mile from North Kinsman's summit. From various spots on South Kinsman's summit, you have views toward Franconia Ridge, North Kinsman, and Moosilauke to the south.

Backtrack to North Kinsman and descend to Kinsman Junction. At the crossing, turn south (right) on the Kinsman Pond Trail, reaching the Appalachian Mountain Club shelter at Kinsman Pond in 0.1 mile. The trail follows the eastern shore of this scenic mountain tarn, below the summit cone of North Kinsman. It then hooks southeast into the forest, leading steadily downhill and making four stream crossings; this stretch of trail may be poorly marked, wet, and difficult to follow. It reaches the AT/Cascade Brook Trail 2.5 miles from Kinsman Junction, right after crossing Cascade Brook. Bear southeast (right) onto the AT/Cascade Brook Trail, following it 0.5 mile. Immediately after crossing Cascade Brook again, turn left onto the Basin-Cascades Trail, which leads a mile back to the Basin.

Options

Too much hiking for one day? Split the hike into a two-day trek with a stay at the Kinsman Pond campsite, an Appalachian Mountain Club–operated shelter (and three tent platforms), located along the Kinsman Pond Trail 0.1 mile from Kinsman Junction and 4.5 miles from the Basin. A caretaker collects the $8 per person nightly fee during the warmer months. The AMC also operates the Lonesome Lake hut, where a crew prepares meals and guests share bunkrooms and bathrooms; contact the AMC for reservation and rate information.

Directions

From Lincoln, follow I-93 north for 10 miles into Franconia Notch; take the exit at the sign for the Basin. Park in one of the large parking lots on the east side of I-93 (for southbound vehicles, another parking lot is on the west side of the highway). From the east side parking lot, hikers can cross under the highway to the west side, where the trail begins. This hike begins in Franconia Notch State Park, but much of it lies within the White Mountain National Forest.
GPS Coordinates: 44.1199 N, 71.6826 W

Contact

Parking and access are free. Dogs are allowed. Two waterproof area trail maps available from the Appalachian Mountain Club show this hike (*Franconia–Pemigewasset Range* map and *Crawford Notch–Sandwich Range/Moosilauke–Kinsman* map, $10 each). For more information, contact White Mountain National Forest Headquarters, 71 White Mountain Drive, Campton, NH 03246, 603/536-6100, TDD for hearing impaired 603/536-3665, www.fs.fed.us. Franconia Notch State Park, Franconia, NH 03580, 603/745-8391, www.franconianotchstatepark.com. Appalachian Mountain Club Pinkham Notch Visitor Center, P.O. Box 298, Gorham, NH 03581, 603/466-2721, www.outdoors.org.

4 PEMI TRAIL

Franconia Notch State Park

🦆 ✈ 🌲 🐴 👫

Level: Easy

Hiking Time: 2.5 hours

Total Distance: 5.6 miles one-way

Elevation: 50 feet

Summary: Not up for a climb? Explore the base of Franconia Notch on this easy and scenic walk.

Winding through the dense woods and along the rushing waters of the Pemigewasset River, the Pemi Trail is excellent proof that Franconia Notch offers as much scenic beauty at ground level as it does from the soaring peaks that flank the notch. Flowing water, cascading brooks, thick forest, wildflowers, occasional views, wildlife sightings, and very little elevation gain makes the Pemi Trail an easy and pleasant amble for hikers of all ages.

This hike can be done as a long, flat out-and-back hike, or a one-way trek if you can shuttle cars at both the beginning and end of the trail. The entire Pemi Trail runs a total distance of 5.6 miles, though for a shorter hike you could park a second car by the hikers' parking lot at the Lafayette Campground, about halfway between the Basin and Profile Lake.

The Pemi Trail runs in a north-south line, roughly running parallel to I-93. You can hike the trail starting from either direction. To make the most of views along the trail, this hike starts at the northern terminus of the trail.

From the parking area, the trail follows the west shore of Profile Lake, with excellent views across the water to Eagle Cliff on Mount Lafayette. When the light is right, you can distinguish a free-standing rock pinnacle in a gully separating two major cliffs on this shoulder of Lafayette. Known as the Eaglet, this pinnacle is a destination for rock climbers and has been a nesting site in spring for peregrine falcons, which you might see flying around in spring. After crossing the paved bike path through the notch just south of Profile Lake and a second time just north of Lafayette Place Campground, the Pemi Trail follows a campground road along the west bank of the Pemigewasset River, then leaves the campground and parallels the river all the way to the water-sculpted rock at the Basin. It crosses the Basin-Cascades Trail, meets the Cascade Brook Trail, crosses east beneath I-93, and finishes at the parking lot immediately north of the Flume. Return the way you came or find the second car you left earlier waiting in the lot.

Thistle is one of the many plants growing in sunny patches along the Pemi Trail.

© JAROSLAW TRAPSZO

Options

Another option for easy hiking is the universally accessible Franconia Notch Bike Path, a paved trail that also runs parallel to I-93. The nine-mile stretch passes Echo Lake, the Basin, the Flume Gorge, and other state park attractions, including the Lafayette Camp Ground. Access the bike path at the same trailhead parking areas used for the Pemi Trail. The bike path is well-marked.

Directions

This one-way trail requires a shuttling of cars. From Lincoln, follow I-93 north for about 10 miles to Franconia Notch. Leave one car at the parking area off I-93, immediately north of the Flume (the end of the Pemi Trail). The hike begins from the tramway parking lot at Exit 34B off I-93, at the northern end of the notch.
GPS Coordinates: 44.1003 N, 71.6827 W

Contact

Parking and access are free. Dogs on leash are allowed. Obtain the free map of Franconia Notch State Park, available at the state park or from the New Hampshire Division of Parks and Recreation. Two waterproof area trail maps available from the Appalachian Mountain Club show this hike (*Franconia–Pemigewasset Range* map and *Crawford Notch–Sandwich Range/Moosilauke–Kinsman* map, $10 each). For more information, contact Franconia Notch State Park, Franconia, NH 03580, 603/745-8391, www.franconianotchstatepark.com.

5 MOUNT LAFAYETTE   BEST ◖
White Mountain National Forest and Franconia Notch State Park

Level: Butt-kicker   **Total Distance:** 8.0 miles

Hiking Time: 6 hours   **Elevation:** 3,500 feet

Summary: Want a workout? This hike's steep elevation gain ranks it as one of most difficult in the White Mountains.

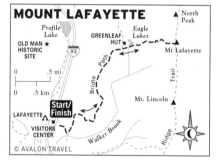

Named for the Marquis de Lafayette, the French military hero who significantly assisted George Washington and the Continental Army during the American Revolution, 5,260-foot Mount Lafayette is the tallest peak in the Franconia Ridge, the spectacular spine of high peaks that soar up to form the eastern flank of Franconia Notch. The mountain also ranks as the sixth highest peak in New Hampshire and the tallest mountain outside the Presidential Range of the northern White Mountains.

Hiking Mount Lafayette is not for the novice, but for hikers up to the challenge of gaining 3,500 feet of elevation in four very steep miles, the reward of this stunning alpine summit may be too good to pass up. From the wind-whipped, treeless top, the views from Mount Lafayette offer a panorama spanning the peaks and valleys of the northern White Mountains to Vermont's Green Mountains, and on a clear day, all the way to the Adirondack Mountains of New York state. Beyond the views, there's just something about climbing to a place where vegetation more closely resembles mosses and flowers found in northern Canada, than flora found only a few hours south in Boston, that really helps you feel like Downtown Crossing and Storrow Drive are a world away.

From the parking lot on the east side of I-93, walk to the east side of the lot and look for the Falling Waters Trail/Old Bridle Path sign marking the trailhead. The two trails coincide as a well-worn path for 0.2 mile before splitting. Where the Falling Waters Trail turns sharply south (right), continue straight ahead (northeast) on the Old Bridle Path. It climbs fairly easily at first through mostly deciduous forest, then grows steeper as it ascends the prominent west ridge of Lafayette. Once on the crest of that ridge, you'll get great views from a few open ledges of the rocky, moss-covered Lafayette summit. At 2.9 miles from the trailhead, the Old

Bridle Path terminates at the Greenleaf Trail and Greenleaf hut. From there, follow the Greenleaf Trail as it dips down into a shallow basin, passes through sub-alpine forest of scrub growth, and soon emerges onto the rocky, open west slope of Lafayette, climbing another 1.1 miles and 1,000 feet in elevation to Lafayette's summit. The views from the summit take in most of the White Mountains and the North Country as well as Vermont's Green Mountains to the west. Stay on the trail to avoid trampling on the delicate alpine growth. But feel free to look all you want at these tundra-loving plant species—especially if you come in late spring to catch alpine-zone wildflowers in bloom. Return the way you came.

a view of Franconia Ridge from the summit of Mount Lafayette

Options

Need to rest your legs? Stay overnight for a little R&R at the the Appalachian Mountain Club–operated Greenleaf hut, located at the junction of the Greenleaf Trail and Old Bridle Path. Bunks, meals, and shower accommodations provided; contact the AMC for reservations and rate information.

Directions

From Lincoln, follow I-93 north for approximately 10 miles to reach Franconia Notch. At the signs for the Lafayette Place Campground, park in the large parking lot on the east side of I-93, where the trail begins. For southbound vehicles, another parking lot is located on the west side of the highway. From the west side parking lot, hikers can walk under the highway to the east lot and trailhead.
GPS Coordinates: 44.1411 N, 71.6818 W

Contact

Parking and access are free. Dogs are allowed. Two waterproof area trail maps available from the Appalachian Mountain Club show this hike (*Franconia–Pemigewasset Range* map and *Crawford Notch–Sandwich Range/Moosilauke–Kinsman* map, $10 each). For more information, contact White Mountain National Forest

Headquarters, 71 White Mountain Drive, Campton, NH 03246, 603/536-6100, TDD for hearing impaired 603/536-3665, www.fs.fed.us. Franconia Notch State Park, Franconia, NH 03580, 603/745-8391, www.franconianotchstatepark.com. Appalachian Mountain Club Pinkham Notch Visitor Center, P.O. Box 298, Gorham, NH 03581, 603/466-2721, www.outdoors.org.

6 WELCH AND DICKEY   BEST 🅒
White Mountain National Forest

Level: Moderate

Hiking Time: 3.5 hours

Total Distance: 4.5 miles

Elevation: 1,700 feet

Summary: Get beautiful White Mountains views for only moderate effort on these two popular southern peaks.

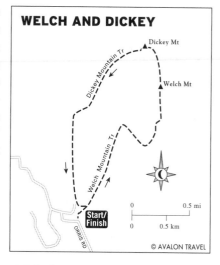

There are only five places in the White Mountains that support communities of jack pine, and Welch Mountain (2,605 feet), the prominent peak that forms the western gateway to Waterville Valley, is one of them. Jack pine is serotinous, meaning the cones of the tree require temperatures of at least 160°F to open and release seeds; the trees took hold in the late 1880s when a fire ravaged the mountain. More than a century later, stands of jack pine are still prominent on Welch, but are in a state of decline as birch and other deciduous trees push their way into the forest—and lack of fire keep the jack pine cones tightly shut.

Welch Mountain is almost always mentioned in the same breath as nearby Dickey Mountain (2,736 feet), not only for the summits' proximity to one another, but because the loop trail that visits both mountains takes you on a delightful hike with pleasing views from open ledges and relatively easy footing. Really, there are few other hikes in the White Mountains where you can visit two summits in just a few hours (and still be able to stand at the end of your hike).

A good pick for a trek in July or August, this 4.5-mile loop may best be saved

Distinctive clustered berries are found in abundance on the forest floor.

for September or October when views from the mountains' many open ledges simply burst with autumn color. The trail is relatively flat, with just a few brief, steep stretches, making it ideal for older children honing their skills on the big hills—and novice hikers ready to add some White Mountains challenge to their outdoor repertoire.

From the parking area, a single trail leaves from the sign marker for the Welch-Dicky loop and quickly enters thick pine cover. To identify jack pine, look for ir-regularly shaped pines (almost scrub-like) with closed cones that sometimes curl around the branches. Within 0.1 mile, you reach a fork. Here, you have a choice between the Dickey Mountain or the Welch Mountain Trail. Bear northeast on the Welch Mountain Trail; the Dickey Mountain trail is used on the loop's return (views are best when hiking this loop in a counterclockwise direction). Within a mile of a gentle, but steady incline, the trail hooks south and emerges onto open ledges just below the summit of Welch Mountain, with a wide view across the Mad River Valley south to the Sandwich Mountains of the Lake Winnipausaukee region. During peak fall foliage season, the vista here will be ablaze with yellow, orange, and red.

From the ledges, the trail turns north again (left) and ascends another, some-what more steep mile to the summit. At the open top of Welch, take in broad views in every direction, including Dickey Mountain to the north, your next des-tination. Continuing north on the trail, you drop steeply into a shallow saddle between the two peaks, then climb up onto Dickey, 0.5 mile from Welch. The footing here is rocky and can be dangerously slippery in wet weather. Watch for a sign pointing to nearby ledges, where there is a good view northwest toward Franconia Notch.

From Dickey's summit, follow an arrow onto an obvious trail north, which soon descends steeply to slab ledges above the cliffs of Dickey Mountain and begins leading southwest, overlooking a beautiful, narrow valley between Welch and Dickey that lights up with color in the fall. The Dickey Mountain Trail continues descending the ridge, reentering the woods, then reaching the parking area, two miles from Dickey's summit.

Options

For a more rigorous trek, the trailhead for the 3,993-foot Sandwich Mountain is just down the road. On this 8.3 mile butt-kicker, expect to ford a brook (difficult in spring and after rains) and ascend steeply to a rocky summit with spectacular views reaching all the way to the Presidential Range. The parking area for the Drake's Brook Trail (the main trail used on the hike) and Sandwich Mountain is in a well-marked turnout off Route 49, about six miles from where you turned onto Mad River Road for the Welch-Dickey hike (10.2 miles from the Route 49 exit off I-93 north).

Directions

From I-93 in Campton, take Exit 28 onto Route 49 north, toward Waterville Valley. After passing through the traffic lights in Campton, drive another 4.4 miles on Route 49, then turn left onto Upper Mad River Road, immediately crossing the Mad River on Six Mile Bridge. Continue 0.7 mile from Route 49, then turn right onto Orris Road at a small sign reading Welch Mountain Trail. Drive another 0.7 mile to a parking area on the right.

GPS Coordinates: 43.9038 N, 71.5886 W

Contact

A $3 day-use permit is required; purchase at the self-serve trailhead kiosk, area stores, or directly from the national forest office. Dogs are allowed. Two waterproof area trail maps from the Appalachian Mountain Club show this hike (*Franconia–Pemigewasset Range* map and *Crawford Notch–Sandwich Range/Moosilauke–Kinsman* map, $10 each). For more information, contact White Mountain National Forest Headquarters, 71 White Mountain Drive, Campton, NH 03246, 603/536-6100, TDD for hearing impaired 603/536-3665, www.fs.fed.us.

7 MOUNT CHOCORUA
White Mountain National Forest

Level: Strenuous

Total Distance: 5.4 miles

Hiking Time: 5 hours

Elevation: 2,600 feet

Summary: One of the most photographed mountains in the world, a climb to the top of this "mini Alp" is worth the exertion.

The eye-catching eastern end of the Sandwich Range, Chocorua's distinctive horn-shaped summit cone makes this 3,500-foot peak a natural draw for visitors. An equal match to the mountain's unusual shape may be the unusual story behind the mountain's namesake. Though no official records exist to substantiate the legend, according to local lore, Chocorua was a Penacook warrior who lept to his death from the mountain after being chased there by white settlers.

Some visitors to Chocorua just to stand in the parking lot and snap photos of this "mini Alp," but during peak hiking season, Chocorua is one of the most traveled mountains in New Hampshire. From its rocky, bare summit, the 360-degree views are nothing short of spectacular. The Brook-Liberty loop gets away from the crowds (as much as possible) for a more solitary experience of Chocorua's splendor.

This hike ascends via the Brook Trail, which is steep, and descends via the Liberty Trail, known as the easiest route on Chocorua. (Hikers looking for a less demanding route could opt to go up and down the Liberty Trail.) From the parking area, walk past the gate and follow the gravel woods road north, which the Brook Trail leaves within 0.5 mile at a marked junction. The trail passes a small waterfall along Claybank Brook less than two miles up, and after some easy to moderately difficult hiking emerges from the woods onto the bare rock of Chocorua's summit cone at three miles. The trail's final 0.6 mile ascends steep slabs and ledges; the Liberty Trail coincides with the

the view from Mount Chocorua

Brook Trail for the last 0.2 mile to the top. Open summit views stretch north to Mount Washington, west across the White Mountains, south to the lakes region, and east over the hills and lakes of western Maine. To descend, follow the two trails down for that 0.2 mile, and then bear south onto the Liberty Trail. It traverses somewhat rocky ground high on the mountain, passing the U.S. Forest Service's Jim Liberty cabin within 0.5 mile. The descent grows more moderate, eventually following an old bridle path back to the parking area, 3.8 miles from the summit.

Options

Want to spend the night on this mythic mountain? The U.S. Forest Service maintains the Jim Liberty cabin (which has a capacity of nine) on the Liberty Trail, 0.5 mile below Chocorua's summit; a fee is charged and the water source is unreliable in dry seasons. Contact the White Mountain National Forest for rate and reservation information.

Directions

From the junction of Routes 113 and 113A in Tamworth, drive west on Route 113A for 3.4 miles and turn right onto the dirt Howler's Mill Road. Continue for 1.2 miles and turn left (at trail signs) onto Paugus Road/Fire Road 68. The parking area and trailhead lie 0.8 mile up the road.

GPS Coordinates: 43.9174 N, 71.2932 W

Contact

A $3 day-use permit is required; purchase at the self-serve trailhead kiosk, area stores, or directly from the national forest office. Dogs are allowed. A waterproof area trail map is available from the Appalachian Mountain Club (*Crawford Notch–Sandwich Range/Moosilauke–Kinsman,* $10). For more information, contact White Mountain National Forest Headquarters, 71 White Mountain Drive, Campton, NH 03246, 603/536-6100, TDD for hearing impaired 603/536-3665, www.fs.fed.us.

8 SMARTS MOUNTAIN

Lyme

Level: Strenuous

Hiking Time: 3.5 hours

Total Distance: 8.2 miles

Elevation: 2,100 feet

Summary: Hike the Appalachian Trail to splendid fire tower views of the Connecticut River Valley.

A popular hike for students from nearby Dartmouth College and one of the first summits encountered along the New Hampshire stretch of the northbound Appalachian Trail, Smarts (3,240 feet) blends a walk in the woods and along the rocky crest of a ridge with a rigorous push to the summit. Though mostly wooded at the top, an abandoned fire tower can still be climbed and is what makes the finish of this hike so spectacular. On a clear day, panoramic views take in the upper Connecticut Valley, the nearby Green Mountains, and north to more rugged peaks (Smarts is actually an isolated southern summit of the White Mountains).

The mountain is also a worthy climb for its unique subalpine environment. Thanks to its location as a gateway to the uplands of New Hampshire, cold wind currents coming down through Canada (and Vermont) tend to strike Smarts Mountain first. Depending on when you visit, you may or may not encounter windy conditions near the summit, but you will see the results of such constant exposure to harsh air currents. Despite its relatively diminutive size, Smarts displays scrub growth—krummolz—near its summit and is home to a lush boreal forest, the same cold-loving spruce and fir forest that covers the mountains of the northern Whites.

Near the entrance to the parking area, pick up the white-blazed Lambert Ridge Trail at the large trail marker (this is also the Appalachian Trail). An unmarked wide path seen at the end of the lot is the Ranger Trail, your route of descent. The hike starts as a slightly steep trek through mixed woods, with several switchbacks

A hiker takes in the view from Smarts Mountain.

helping to reduce the grade. At 0.3 mile, the trail begins the ascent up rocky Lambert Ridge—itself a nice destination for a short hike. For the next 1.3 miles, tree cover thins and views become frequent. The trail then drops slightly, changes direction a few times—watch for white blazes—and ascends the relentlessly steep west slope of Smarts, passing an unmarked junction with the Ranger Trail at 3.5 miles from the parking lot. Here, you will also notice the beech and maple trees giving way to a boreal forest of firs and evergreen (the only boreal forest found this far south in New Hampshire). A half-mile more and you've reached the mountain's flat, wooded summit. Continue on for another 0.1 mile, noting the scrub growth and watching on the left for a spur trail to the fire tower. Another summit spur trail leads to a tent camping site. Return to the parking area by backtracking 0.6 mile to the trail junction and bearing left for the 3.5-mile descent along the more moderately graded Ranger Trail.

Options

For a shorter hike that's a bit easier on the knees, but still leads to amazing views, try the 2.2-mile round-trip climb to nearby Holt's Ledge (a net climb of about 1,000 feet). This section of the AT leaves from a well-marked trailhead at the Dartmouth Skiway. To reach it, at the fork located 1.3 miles from Lyme Center, bear right and continue driving 0.1 mile to the Dartmouth Skiway parking area. Holt's Ledge is also one of the largest nesting grounds in New Hampshire for peregrine falcons; respect closed off areas on the trail that protect these fragile habitats.

Directions

From Route 10 on the Green in Lyme, take Dorchester Road (at the white church), following signs for the Dartmouth Skiway. Two miles from the Green, you'll pass through the village of Lyme Center. Continue for another 1.3 miles and then bear left onto the gravel Lyme-Dorchester Road. Follow for 1.8 miles. Just before an iron bridge over Grant Brook, park in a small lot on the left, at the trailhead.
GPS Coordinates: 43.7971 N, 72.0719 W

Contact

Parking and access are free. Dogs are allowed. Local trail maps are available from the Dartmouth Outing Club (including a three-color, double-sided map covering a 75-mile section of the AT from Route 12 in Woodstock, VT, to Route 112 in Woodstock, NH, $2). For more information, contact Appalachian Trail Conference, 799 Washington St., P.O. Box 807, Harpers Ferry, WV 25425-0807, 304/535-6331, www.appalachiantrail.org. Dartmouth Outdoor Programs Office, 119 Robinson Hall, Dartmouth College, Hanover, NH 03755, 603/646-2834, www.dartmouth.edu.

9 MOUNT KEARSARGE
Winslow State Park

Level: Moderate

Hiking Time: 2 hours

Total Distance: 2.9 miles

Elevation: 1,100 feet

Summary: A good hike for kids just getting their "mountain legs," this not-too-tough hike leads to surprisingly long views.

Some landscapes in northern New England are better than others at hiding their icy past, but on 2,937-foot Mount Kearsarge, evidence of the last Ice Age is everywhere. Large glacial erratic boulders, dumped by retreating glaciers, are scattered throughout the forest, and glacial striations, grooves scraped into the rock by the movement of the heavy ice sheets, are clearly visible on the summit and ledge outcroppings. Even the shape of the mountain summit itself, with its relatively flat top, was molded by the advancing glaciers.

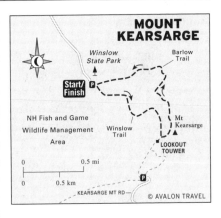

The famous civil war battleship, USS *Kearsarge*, was named for this towering, isolated monadnock in the Sunapee region. And in turn, the mountain's name is derived from the Penacook moniker, Carasarga, meaning "notch-pointed-mountain of pines." Today, the climb to the rocky, bald summit of Mount Kearsarge, with its views of the White Mountains, Green Mountains, and southern New Hampshire, is one of the finest short hikes in New England and, while steep, a great adventure for children.

Two state parks occupy the mountain and offer plenty of options for ascending Kearsage. This loop uses the Winslow Trail to reach the summit and the Barlow Trail, a gentler route that's easy on the knees, for the descent.

From the upper end of the parking lot in Winslow State Park, pick up the red-blazed Winslow Trail heading south. The wide, well-beaten path rises quite steeply and relentlessly and grows even more rugged the higher you go. At 0.8 mile, scramble a large erratic boulder on the left for a good view north. A short distance farther, the trail breaks out of the trees and onto the bald, rocky summit, the result of a forest fire that broke out on the mountain top in the 1780s. (Subsequent wind and soil erosion prevented forest regrowth.)

© JACQUELINE TOURVILLE

Winslow Trail, Mount Kearsarge

From this wide-open and windy spot take in views in every direction, including nearby Sunapee, Ragged, and Cardigan Mountains and more distant Mount Monadnock and Mount Ascutney. On very clear days, views extend to the White Mountains, the Green Mountains of Vermont, the Atlantic Ocean, and Boston. This is a wonderful hike during the height of the fall foliage colors (and because of this, Kearsarge's trails are usually packed during peak fall weekends). A fire tower stands at the summit, and nearby are a pair of picnic tables, along with a very large and very out-of-place-looking communications tower—the one drawback to Kearsarge's otherwise impeccable mountaintop. For the return trip, pick up the yellow-blazed Barlow Trail off the eastern edge of the summit. Follow the blazes and cairns, soon descending into scrubby pine. Follow the trail for 1.8 miles back to the parking area.

Options

Want a shorter climb to the summit? Rollins State Park offers a 0.5-mile trail to the summit, leaving from a parking area (and picnic grounds) located about halfway up the mountain. To reach Rollins State Park, from exit 10, follow signs for Rollins State Park.

Directions

Take I-89 to Exit 10 and follow the signs to Winslow State Park. From the tollbooth at the state park entrance, drive to the dirt parking lot at the end of the road. The last 0.6 mile of the entrance road (beyond the fork at the dead-end sign) is not maintained in winter.

GPS Coordinates: 43.3895 N, 71.8672 W

Contact

Park admission is $4 for adults, $2 for children ages 6–11, and free for children ages five and under and New Hampshire residents age 65 and over. Dogs on leash

10 GREAT BAY ESTUARINE RESEARCH RESERVE
Greenland

🦌 ✈️ 🌸 👫 ♿

Level: Easy

Hiking Time: 45 minutes

Total Distance: 1.0 mile

Elevation: 0 feet

Summary: Explore a unique salt marsh ecosystem on this easy walk along the shore of the Great Bay Estuary.

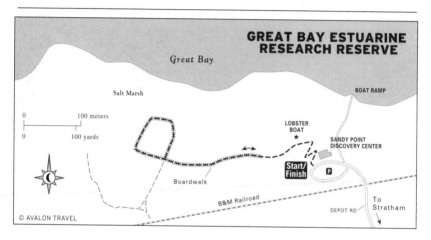

A few miles short of the Atlantic Ocean, the Piscataqua, Cocheco, and Salmon Falls Rivers join together as a tidal estuary, forming a great inland bay. Aptly named Great Bay, this unique marine environment is a place where fertile fields and freshwater rivers meet salt marshes and coastal tides. Probably the state's most ecologically diverse area, the 4,500-acre tidal estuary and 800 acres of coastal land at Great Bay National Estuarine Research Reserve provide refuge for 23 species of endangered or threatened plant and animal species. Bald eagles winter here, osprey nest, and cormorants and great blue heron are readily seen.

Great Bay is accessible for all thanks to the Sandy Point Trail, a wheelchair-accessible interpretive trail and boardwalk that allows visitors to experience the vast diversity of the estuarine ecosystem. Visitors are welcome to climb aboard and explore the lobster boat and gundalow river boat beached near the trail, making this an exciting destination for kids.

From the Great Bay Discovery Center parking lot, a short path zigzags down the slope to the trailhead, marked by the beached lobster boat and gundalow. From here, the graded, gravel trail leaves west, along the southern shore of

© JASON BROWN

a flat-bottomed gundalow river boat on the shore of Great Bay

Great Bay, and enters a mature, upland forest of oak, hickory, elm, and beech. The trail becomes a boardwalk just before reaching the wetter ground of the red maple–sensitive fern swamp ecosystem and continues west. Here, look for jack-in-the-pulpit, spotted touch-me-not-fern, royal fern, and cinnamon fern. Continuing on, the boardwalk reaches a junction. The Woodland Trail enters the forest to the left, heading south away from the bay, but this route takes the boardwalk to the northwest, entering the salt marsh. Almost immediately to your right, take note of the almost pure stand of feather-tufted common reed, a threatened plant species in North America (this is the last known example of the plant in the state). As the boardwalk bends west, Great Bay comes into view. A series of mudflats at low tide, the estuary at high tide becomes a vivid blue lake. This is a good spot for bird-watching: Blue heron, egret, osprey, kingfisher, and waterfowl all frequent this part of Great Bay. Follow the boardwalk as it forms a loop through the marsh and retrace your steps back to the trailhead.

Options

Another reason why this hike is a good one for children? On the return to the trailhead, stop by the Great Bay Discovery Center for lots of fun, hands-on learning about the estuary. Kids (and adults) love the esturine touch tank, filled with a sampling of the maritime creatures who call Great Bay home. Great Bay Discovery Center is open to the public 10 A.M.–4 P.M. Wednesday–Sunday, May 1–September

30 and on weekends in October. Year-round, the Discovery Center hosts frequent nature and learning programs about the estuary for all ages.

Directions

From the Stratham traffic circle at the junction of Routes 108 and 33, drive 1.4 miles north on Route 33 and turn left onto Depot Road at a sign for the Great Bay Discovery Center. At the end of Depot Road, turn left on Tidewater Farm Road. The Discovery Center is at the end of the road and the trail begins behind the center.

GPS Coordinates: 43.0546 N, 70.8964 W

Contact

Parking and access are free. Dogs are not allowed. Trails are open year-round. An interpretive trail pamphlet available at the Great Bay Discovery Center guides visitors along the boardwalk at the estuary's edge and offers information about natural history and the local environment. For more information, contact Great Bay National Estuarine Research Reserve, 89 Depot Rd., Greenland, NH 03840, 603/778-0015, www.greatbay.org.

11 ODIORNE STATE PARK

Rye

🦌 🛶 💧 🎡 🐕 👫 ♿

Level: Easy/Moderate

Total Distance: 2.0 miles

Hiking Time: 1 hour

Elevation Gain: 0 feet

Summary: Visit the site of New Hampshire's first European settlement and the ruins of a World War II bunker as you explore the state's last tract of undeveloped coastline.

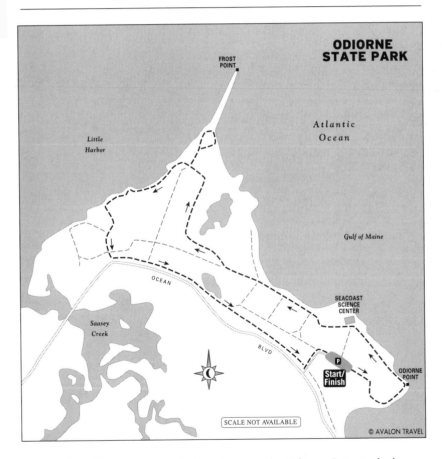

Not far from Hampton's crowded beaches, bucolic Odiorne Point is the largest tract of undeveloped land left along New Hampshire's tiny 18-mile shoreline. Nestled within a 330-acre state park overlooking both the Atlantic Ocean and Portsmouth's Little Harbor, Odiorne is notable as the site of New Hampshire's first English settlement in 1623 and for the remains of Fort Dearborn, a U.S. military defensive installation and lookout built during World War II. With the fort's long-abandoned bunkers looking more like grassy dunes than strategic defense points, Odiorne's crisscrossing paths lead to rocky ocean beaches, sheltered tide pools, salt marshes, and dense upland woods. Odiorne State Park is also home to the Seacoast Science Center, a family-friendly aquarium focused on marine life in the Gulf of Maine.

From the eastern end of the parking lot, a paved walkway curves past a playground and bathroom pavilion to quickly bring you out to the Odiorne Point promontory. Scramble down to the rocky beach to explore the tidal pools or

© JACQUELINE TOURVILLE

on the path to Odiorne Point, Odiorne State Park

simply stop to take in the vast ocean views. On a clear day, you will see the Isles of Shoals, a small chain of low-lying offshore islands. Before the last Ice Age, Odiorne's tree-covered land actually stretched all the way out to these islands. Glacial action scraped the coastal plain away, but at very low tide, petrified tree roots, known as the Sunken Forest, are still visible.

The walkway turns north to follow the shore for approximately 20 yards, leading to a picnic area and views of Whaleback Lighthouse, located off the coast of nearby Kittery, Maine. (Wheelchair users should note that the paved walkway loops back to the parking lot from the picnic area.) Leaving the picnic area, a loose gravel path continues along the shore, taking you a short distance to the Seacoast Science Center—if you have kids in tow, the center's marine touch tank is a must-see. The trail picks up again on the west side of the science center building, next to the staff parking lot.

Now heading northwest, you will find the open ocean traded for the calmer waters of Portsmouth's Little Harbor. Without the direct impact of battering ocean wind, the land along Little Harbor gradually changes to thick upland forest. As the the path treads between the rocky beach to your right and the wild bramble to your left, it's not uncommon to spot rabbits hopping along the trail or a darting fox on the hunt for shorebirds.

Less than 0.25 mile from the science center, a large stone marker lets you know you are on the spot where in 1623 a small band of English settlers founded Pannaway Plantation, the first European settlement in New Hampshire. A large path breaks to the left from the monument, the remnants of one of the settlement's original carriage roads; this hike stays on the smaller path and continues northwest, hugging the shoreline.

Approximately 0.75 mile from the science center, the trail turns inland, soon bringing you within sight of a freshwater marsh (on your right) and one of Fort Dearborn's abandoned bunkers (to your left). It is possible to step inside the long, low concrete casement for a look around, but be forewarned, graffiti and beer cans await—and little outside light penetrates beyond the doorway.

A few steps beyond the bunker, the trail splits. Bear to the right to walk the short distance out to Frost Point, a natural jetty extending into Little Harbor. The trail circles back from the jetty, returning you to the split. Bear right to stay near the shore. For the next 0.2 mile, note how the rocky coast eventually gives way to salt marsh as Little Harbor meets the oncoming waters of Witch Creek. Taking the first trail you reach that breaks to your left, curve around another bunker to reach a trail junction. Here, continue straight on the large carriage road. In less than 0.1 mile, you will reach the bike path, running parallel to Route 1A. Turn left to take the tree-lined path, a pleasant 0.75 mile walk back to the parking lot where this hike began. Interpretive panels along the path provide information about Odiorne's history. Before returning to your car, be sure to visit Fort Dearborn's Battery 264, located adjacent to the parking lot. A climb to the top of this former military lookout offers blissfully peaceful views of water, sky, and shore.

Options

For a longer trek along Odiorne's oceanfront, bear right (south) when you reach the playground to explore even more rugged, rocky beach. The state park extends another 0.25 mile south, adding a total of 0.5 mile to this trip.

Directions

From I-95, take exit 5 to the Portsmouth Traffic Circle. From the Circle take Route 1 bypass south (follow sign for Beaches/Hampton). After one mile, the road connects with Route 1 south. Follow Route 1 south for approximately one mile. At the sixth light from the traffic circle, take a left onto Elwyn Road. Follow for approximately 1.3 miles to the roundabout at Foye's Corner. Go halfway around the roundabout to Route 1A south. Continue for 1.8 miles, past the Odiorne Point State Park boat launch parking area (on left), to the main entrance of Odiorne Point State Park (on left).

Contact

The park is open daily year-round. In early May–mid-October, admission is $4 for adults, $2 for children 6–11, and children 5 and under and New Hampshire residents age 65 and over enter for free. The Seacoast Science Center charges separate admissions fees. Trail maps are available at the park entrance. For more information, contact Odiorne State Park, Rte. 1A, Rye, NH 03870, 603/436-7406. New Hampshire Division of Parks and Recreation, P.O. Box 1856, Concord, NH 03302, 603/271-3556, www.nhstateparks.org. Seacoast Science Center, 570 Ocean Blvd., Rye, NH 03870, 603/436-8043, www.seacoastsciencecenter.org.

12 MOUNT MONADNOCK BEST **C**

Monadnock State Park, Jaffrey

Level: Strenuous

Hiking Time: 3 hours

Total Distance: 4.6 miles

Elevation: 1,600 feet

Summary: Join the ranks climbing this landmark peak, considered a rite of passage among New England hikers.

At 3,165 feet high, majestic Mount Monadnock (also called Grand Monadnock) rises high above the surrounding countryside of southern New Hampshire, making it prominently visible from many other lower peaks in the region. The mountain's name comes from an Abenaki phrase likely meaning "place of an unexcelled mountain." Borrowing from the Abenaki, modern geologists use the term monadnock to mean an isolated peak in an otherwise eroded plain (there are actually several of these monadnocks in both New Hampshire and Vermont). With

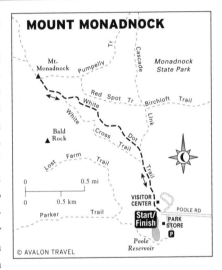

its large, rocky summit and unhindered view encompassing all six New England states, Grand Monadnock is the region's most popular peak. It's often claimed that Monadnock is hiked more than any mountain in the world except Japan's Mount Fuji—although any ranger in the state park would tell you that's impossible to prove.

This hike is one of the most commonly used Monadnock summit routes and through the years has reached the status of a rite of passage of sorts for New England hikers. On your trek, you will no doubt encounter first-timers grimacing their way up the hill in brand new hiking boots, as well as visiting experts who seem to be speed-walking to the summit. It's true that all trails on Monadnock can see quite a bit of boot traffic in the spring, summer, and fall, but if you come here midweek or early in the morning, you have a good chance of having the mountain to yourself.

From the parking lot, walk up the road to find the marked trailhead for the very well-trod White Dot Trail, just past the state park headquarters. The wide path dips

A hiker sits atop the summit of Mount Monadnock.

slightly, crosses a brook, and then begins a gradual ascent north into the woods. At 0.5 mile, the White Cross Trail, another summit route, leaves to the west, but this hike stays to the right, pushing north up the White Dot. Check blazes—dots versus crosses—to make sure you stayed on track. Leaving the junction, the trail begins to climb steeply, with some limited views, until emerging onto open ledges at 1.1 miles. It then follows more level terrain, enters a forest of low evergreens, and ascends again to its upper junction with the White Cross Trail at 1.7 miles. Now combined, the two trails climb the open, rocky terrain of the upper mountain for the final 0.3 mile to the summit. On clear days, Boston skyscrapers and even the Atlantic Ocean can be seen in the distance. Descend along the same route.

Options

Just not up for the push to the summit? Following the White Dot Trail, at 0.7 mile, a marked spur trail turns west (left), leading a short distance to Falcon Spring, a burbling water source that's a big hit with kids. At the state park headquarters, pick up the nature interpretive guide that explains the geology of Falcon Spring and different types of flora spotted along the trail.

Directions

This hike begins from a parking lot on the north side of Route 124, 7.1 miles east of the junction of Routes 101 and 124 in Marlborough and 5.4 miles west of the junction of Route 124, Route 137, and U.S. 202 in Jaffrey.

GPS Coordinates: 42.8348 N, 72.1140 W

Contact

During April–November, an entrance fee of $4 per adult and $2 per child (ages 6–11) is collected at the state park entrance. Children under 5 and New Hampshire residents 65 and older enter state parks for free. Dogs are not allowed. A free map of trails is available from the state park or the New Hampshire Division of Parks and Recreation. A waterproof trail map is available from the Appalachian Mountain Club (*Monadnock/Cardigan,* $8). For more information, Monadnock State Park, P.O. Box 181, Jaffrey, NH 03452, 603/532-8862, www.nhstateparks. org. New Hampshire Division of Parks and Recreation, P.O. Box 1856, Concord, NH 03302, 603/271-3556, www.nhstateparks.org.

🔢 BEAVER BROOK TRAIL

Hollis and Brookline

BEST 🌜

🦌 🏷️ 🦌 👫

Level: Easy/Moderate

Total Distance: 2.5 miles

Hiking Time: 1.5 hours

Elevation: 50 feet

Summary: Just over the state line, this secluded nature preserve offers backwoods adventure and a true sense of solitude.

Tucked away along the edge of sleepy Hollis, a small, rural community known for its centuries-old old apple orchards and quaint village center, Beaver Brook Association is a sprawling 2,000-acre nature conservancy comprised of forest, fields, and wetlands. With over 35 miles of trails, this local jewel attracts hikers in every season, as well as snowshoers and cross-country skiers in winter. The terrain varies from ponds and marshes dotted with beaver dams and duck nests to rolling meadows, thick forest, and gentle hills.

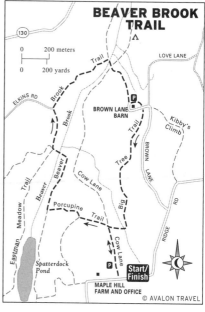

For Bostonians, the lure of Beaver Brook may be its close proximity; Hollis is only an hour away from Boston and just minutes down the road from the popular tax-free shopping strip of Nashua, New Hampshire. Many of the trails are ideal for beginning hikers and children; some are appropriate for people with intermediate skills. Nature learning programs for kids and adults take place year-round, including guided "full moon hikes" for after-dark hiking. This loop through the reserve helps first-time visitors explore the area's natural diversity.

From the office and parking area, walk north to the large trail information sign (a map is posted on the board) and head into the reserve following the wide woods road called Cow Lane. In less than 0.1 mile, turn west (left) on a turnoff for the Porcupine Trail. The forested path is a somewhat steep downhill incline leading to Beaver Brook's extensive wetlands. Chipmunks, garter snakes, and tree frogs are readily spotted here, but the trail's namesake is somewhat elusive (though a sign marker about halfway down the trail helps hikers identify a porcupine habitat).

At the end of the trail, turn north (right) at the sign for the Beaver Brook Trail, a relatively flat stretch running parallel to a broad marsh dotted with bird nesting boxes, proving a breeding habitat for local wood ducks, a protected species of waterfowl. Soon reaching a boardwalk and bridge, cross over the marsh and continue west (straight) until you reach the Eastman Meadow Trail junction. Here, take a right turn north and follow a short distance before bearing east onto the wide forest road called Elkins Road. Follow the road about 0.5 mile until it ends at a trail junction with Cow Lane.

boardwalk and bridge crossing Beaver Brook

Turn south onto Cow Lane, crossing a bridge back over Beaver Brook and reaching a junction. Here, ignore the path marked with a sign for the campground and walk straight ahead onto the wide, uphill connector trail that takes you to Brown Lane Barn, another of the reserve's learning centers. Pass the information sign and cross the parking lot to pick up the Big Tree Trail, marked with a crab apple tree and plank boardwalk at its entrance. Follow the Big Tree Trail south over a rolling, forested landscape inhabited by an impressive assortment of old growth trees, including towering black birch, red oak, and beech; trees are marked with signs to make identification easy.

The Big Tree Trail ends in 0.7 mile at the Wildflower Trail. Turn west (right) and pass by the flower-filled meadow before returning to Cow Lane. Here, turn south (left) for a brief return to the parking area.

Options

If you have time, make a detour to see one of Beaver Brook's signature, human-made attractions: an authentically constructed wigwam. From the Cow Lane trailhead walk approximately 0.3 mile to a junction with the Wigwam Trail. Turn east (right) and head downhill to visit the bark-covered hut tucked away in a clearing in the woods.

Directions

From the junction of Routes 130 and 122 in Hollis, drive south on Route 122 for 0.9 mile and turn right onto Ridge Road. Follow Ridge Road to the Maple Hill Farm and the office of the Beaver Brook Association. The parking lot is just past the office to the right.

GPS Coordinates: 42.7224 N, 71.6067 W

Contact

Parking and access are free. Dogs on leash are allowed. A trail map is available at the Beaver Brook Association office for a small fee. For more information, contact Beaver Brook Association, 117 Ridge Rd., Hollis, NH 03049, 603/465-7787, www.beaverbrook.org. Office hours are 9 A.M.–4 P.M. Monday–Friday.

SOUTHERN MAINE

© JASON BROWN

BEST HIKES

The varied terrain found in the southernmost

part of the Pine Tree State is a microcosm of what makes Maine such a natural magnet for hikers. From easy trail to more moderate outings, hikes here lead to mountains with spectacular summit views, out along craggy ocean cliffs, to secret swimming holes, and deep into the woods where your only company is likely a wandering moose or wild turkey.

The southern portion of the state is also Maine's most populated region. But even the tourist towns that crowd the Atlantic coastline – and Portland, Maine's largest city – offer hikers some treasured gems. Wolfe's Neck Woods in busy Freeport takes you within view of nesting osprey, the Laudholm Reserve in Wells will have you edging along the banks of an estuary on the way to a hidden beach, Portland's Eastern Promenade is an urban recreation path with unparalleled views of Casco Bay, and Ogunquit offers the Marginal Way, a classic cliff walk along the craggy Maine coast.

Inland from the coast, population centers dwindle and Maine's nickname comes to life as low-lyings pine forests and pine tree–carpeted hills dominate the landscape. Hikes here lead through lush woods where creatures of the northern woodlands – moose, white-tailed deer, fox, and even coyote (called coy dogs in these parts) are known to roam. Other trails top the summits of some of the region's taller hills. And while their elevations may be less lofty, views from the summits of such favorite local climbs as Mount Agamenticus in York, Bauneg Beg Mountain in North Berwick, and Douglas Mountain in Sebago give you views that are almost identical to what can be seen from Maine's grand peaks to the north and west – vistas stretching as far to the west as Mount Washington and Pinkham Notch in the White Mountains of New Hampshire.

Hikes in southern Maine are generally not very long, with most stretching for only a few miles. But with so many trailheads clustered so close together, you may be able to fit in at least two, or even three hikes in the same day (and still return to Boston with time to spare). Or combine a hike with other Maine travel plans. The Eastern Prom in Portland takes you within easy walking distance of the city's historic downtown, Wolfe's Neck Woods is a good destination for trying out that new pack you just picked up at L.L. Bean in Freeport, and there may be no better way to end a lazy day at the beach than a quick hop back in the car to reach the trailhead for Mount Agamenticus.

The hiking season in southern Maine generally extends much longer than for the rest of the state, stretching from May through November or December. While you may see news coverage of early fall or late spring snowstorms in Maine, these are generally much farther north of Portland. In summer, temperatures are more moderate closest to the coast, thanks to the cooling effects of the Atlantic Ocean; temperatures inland can be as much as 10 degrees warmer on a sunny day in mid-July. And inland, it's blackfly country, with swarms of the pesky insects arriving by June, joined in early July with an equally thick mosquito population. Assume ticks may be present on any hike in Maine (coastal or inland); wear bug repellent and check skin for ticks upon completing your hike.

One especially notable aspect of the southern Maine landscape is that despite the number of people who live – and vacation – here, the land is remarkably open and free from the crowding that marks so many other resort areas up and down the east coast. This is thanks, in large part, to the tireless efforts of land conservation groups. The majority of hikes in this chapter take place on land that was saved from development, including Mount Agamenticus in the York Land Trust, Laudholm Farm (Laudholm Trust), and Bauneg Beg Mountain and the Savage Wildlife Preserve, two highlights of the Great Works Regional Land Trust. In most of the reserves, trail work is ongoing. Hikers should heed trail detours, posted hiking hours, and other trail rules as a courtesy to land reservation agencies.

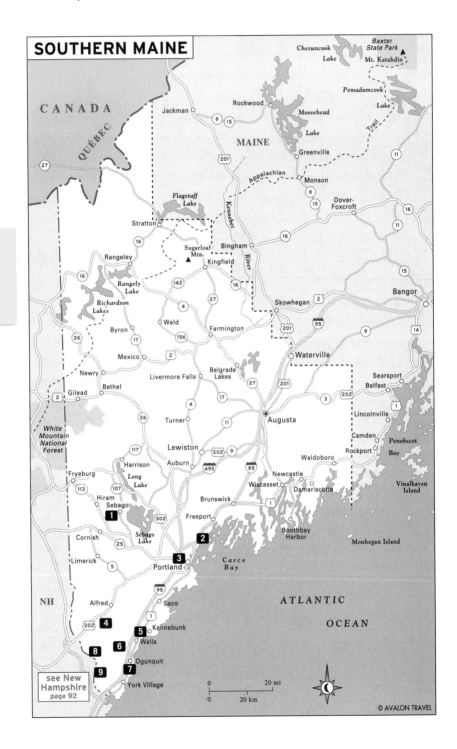

SOUTHERN MAINE

Trail Name	Level	Distance	Time	Elevation	features	Page
1 Douglas Mountain	Moderate	2.5 mi	1.5 hr	400 ft		138
2 Wolfe's Neck Woods	Easy	2.0 mi	1 hr	20 ft		141
3 Back Cove Trail and Eastern Promenade	Easy	5.0 mi	2.5 hr	10 ft		144
4 Bauneg Beg Mountain	Easy/Moderate	1.8 mi	1 hr	300 ft		147
5 Laudholm Beach	Easy	2.0 mi	1 hr	10 ft		150
6 Mount Agamenticus	Easy/Moderate	1.0 mi	45 min	400 ft		153
7 Ogunquit Cliff Walk	Easy	2.5 mi	1 hr	0 ft		156
8 Vaughan Woods	Easy	2.0 mi	1 hr	20 ft		159
9 Raymond & Simone Savage Wildlife Preserve	Easy	2.0 mi	1 hr	10 ft		162

1 DOUGLAS MOUNTAIN
South of Sebago Lake

🏕 🦌 🐕 🚶

Level: Moderate

Total Distance: 2.5 miles

Hiking Time: 1.5 hours

Elevation: 400 feet

Summary: This pleasant trek takes you to a stone observation tower and views of Sebago Lake and the White Mountains.

Southern Maine's other large body of water, Sebago Lake is the deepest and second largest lake in the state. For a different perspective on the lake, this leisurely loop hike to the top of nearby 1,307-foot Douglas Mountain and its stone observation tower yields far-reaching views of Sebago and the surrounding landscape. Popular among locals and visitors alike, this is a good hike for kids (they love the turretlike summit tower). If it's a moose sighting you're after on your trek to Maine, you have a good chance of finding one here, along with a bevy of other northern wildlife, including white-tailed deer, black bear, fox, and wild turkey.

From the parking area, a sign blazed with orange circles points the way to the Eagle Scout Trail. A relatively new trail up the mountain (created as a community service project by some hiking-savvy local scouts), the path enters the pine woods as it begins a gentle one-mile wind up the hill, flowing south as it skirts the hillside. With a swing north in its final few steps, the trail reaches the summit and observation tower. Take in the views—on sunny days, vistas reach as far away as Mount Washington in New Hampshire. (A handy plaque at the summit tower identifies far-off peaks and nearby landforms.) The summit vista is especially pleasant in fall when the red oak and striped maple that intersperse the mountainside pine cover burst like pockets of flame.

Leaving the summit, descend via the yellow-blazed Ledges Trail, a shorter route off the hill that takes you back to Douglas Hill Road in just under 0.5 mile, joining with the Woods Trail just before reaching the road. When you reach Douglas

© JASON BROWN

view of Mount Washington from Douglas Mountain

Hill Road, turn east (right) to walk a few hundred feet to the trailhead parking on the right.

Options

As any local you meet at Douglas Mountain will tell you, the "old way" up the hill is the best—if a short, somewhat steep up-and-down trek is what you seek. To reach the trailhead of the Ledges Trail (once the main route up the hillside), leave the parking area and walk back to Douglas Hill Road. Turn left to continue up the road and in another few hundred feet, reach a clearing on the left that is marked with stone pillars and a registration box. From the registration box, walk through the stone pillars, follow the yellow-blazed Woods Trail a short distance, and then bear south (left) onto the Ledges Trail (also blazed yellow). This trail leads over interesting open ledges with good views, though they are slick when wet. For a descent that is slightly easier on the knees, return to the parking area via the Woods Trail.

Directions

From the junction of Routes 107 and Macks Corner Road in East Sebago, drive 0.5 mile north on Route 107 and turn left onto Douglas Hill Road (which is one mile south of Sebago center). On some maps, the road is not labeled. Drive 0.8 mile to a hilltop and take a sharp left. In another 0.5 mile, turn left into a small parking area.

GPS Coordinates: 43.8741 N, 70.6985 W

Contact:

The preserve is open only during daylight hours. A $3 parking fee is charged for all vehicles (leave payment in the parking area drop box). Dogs allowed. A free guide and map to Douglas Hill is available at the trailhead registration box. For more information, contact Sebago Town Hall, 406 Bridgton Rd., Sebago, ME 04029, 207/787-8884.

2 WOLFE'S NECK WOODS
Freeport

Level: Easy

Hiking Time: 1 hour

Total Distance: 2.0 miles

Elevation: 20 feet

Summary: Observe the northern nesting grounds of the graceful osprey on the way to stunning views of Casco Bay.

A five-minute drive from Freeport's busy shopping district, the marshes, forests, and open fields of Wolfe's Neck State Park are a welcome pocket of calm in the midst of what can be a very crowded tourist city. (Plus, it's a great place to try out some of that hiking gear you just loaded up on at L.L. Bean.) This flat loop of approximately two miles winds through the Wolfe's Neck Woods, taking you to many of the park's best features, including a white pine forest, salt marshes, and

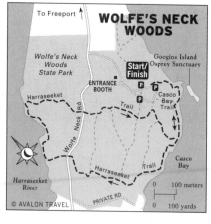

the rocky shorelines of Casco Bay and the Harraseeket River estuary. The White Pine Trail portion of this hike is wheelchair accessible.

From the parking area, pick up the White Pine Trail, a level, universally accessible trail that leads deep into a tall forest of pine and hemlock. Meandering a bit at first, the trail reaches the marshy shore of Casco Bay within 0.2 mile. Kid-friendly interpretive panels explain sites along the trail, including information about the park's signature resident: the osprey. Nearby Googins Island (just offshore and clearly visible from the trail) is a popular northern nesting ground for the graceful bird. Dozens can be seen summering on the island; bring binoculars for the best views of young osprey taking flight for perhaps the very first time. The Casco Bay Trail, a footpath, continues on past the island overlook; those who wish to stay on the universally accessible path can turn right to return to the parking area (the White Pine Trail loop is approximately 0.4 mile long). Following the shores of the bay for another 0.3 mile, the trail turns inland and becomes the Harraseeket River Trail. In less than 0.5 mile, the trail brings you to the shores of the Harraseeket River. Hugging the shoreline for approximately 0.2 mile, the trail offers nice views west toward Freeport. Turning inland again, follow the trail another 0.3 mile back to the parking area.

Casco Bay

Options

For more woods exploration on this hike, just before the number 7 interpretive panel on the Casco Bay Trail, bear south on the Ledge Tail. Taking you up on a ridge covered with dense white pine and hemlock, it's hard to believe you are not on a mountainside in the Maine North Woods, though occasional breaks in the tree cover do show glimpses of Casco Bay. Within 0.4 mile, the trail curves east, passes a number 9 interpretive panel and reaches an unmarked trail junction to the south (right). Take this unmarked trail only a short distance before reaching another junction. Here, turn east (right) on the Old Woods Trail and enjoy a pleasant amble through the woods before rejoining the Haraskeet Trail. Turn (south) right on the Haraskeet Trail to continue the hike to the shore of the Haraskeet River and then back to the parking area.

Directions

From downtown Freeport, drive 4.5 miles east on Route 1 to a right turn at Bow Street. Follow a short distance to Wolfe Neck Road and the park entrance.
GPS Coordinates: 43.8217 N, 70.0840 W

Contact

Visitors to Wolfe's Neck Woods pay $3 per adult for Maine residents, $4.50 per adult nonresident, and $1.50 per child May–October. Trails are still open in the off-season. Dogs on leash are allowed. A trail map and informational brochure is available at the trailhead. For more information, contact Wolfe's Neck Woods State Park, 426 Wolfe's Neck Rd., Freeport, ME 04032, 207/865-4465. Maine Department of Conservation, Bureau of Parks and Lands, 286 Water St., Key Bank Plaza, 3rd and 5th floors, Augusta, ME 04333-0022, 207/287-3821, www.state.me.us.

3 BACK COVE TRAIL AND EASTERN PROMENADE

BEST ◖

Portland

🏊 🏕 👫 ♿ 🚌

Level: Easy	**Total Distance:** 5.0 miles
Hiking Time: 2.5 hours	**Elevation:** 10 feet

Summary: Explore Portland and Casco Bay on the city's premier recreation paths.

Portland is consistently rated as one of the healthiest places to live in the United States, and you'll see why as you join dozens of Portlanders for a walk or jog along the Back Cove Trail and the Eastern Promenade, the two crown jewels of the city's extensive urban recreation system. Follow the entire route for a fun few hours exploring this northern New England hub (Portland is Maine's largest city), or take to the path in segments; numerous access points exist along the mostly flat, wheelchair-accessible trail.

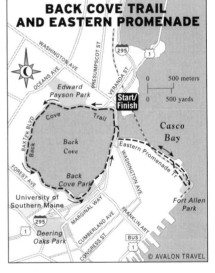

This hike starts on the Back Cove Trail. Just off I-295, and not far from Portland's bustling city center, the trail circles the beautiful shores of Back Cove and serves Portlanders as an urban oasis for jogging, biking, and just strolling along taking in great views of the city skyline. Wheelchair users will find a universally accessible combination of stone dust and paved surfaces—mostly flat with a slight rise along the stretch that parallels I-295. And with its numerous benches along the trail and portable toilets available near both parking areas, it's a great place to bring kids.

Leaving from the Payson Park parking area, bear west (right) on the trail to circle the cove in a counterclockwise direction. On your left, for the first mile or so, is the Portland city skyline to the east, a mix of old brick buildings and gleaming modern structures. Continuing to skirt the southern and eastern shores of the cove, take in views looking back over the water, before reaching a bridge over the watery entrance to Back Cove. Here, on the southern end of the bridge, another

Eastern Promenade

wheelchair-accessible trail leads to the east (right). This is Eastern Promenade Trail, a two-mile loop along Casco Bay. The waterfront trail, part of an old rail line, offers spectacular harbor and ocean views.

Approximately one mile from leaving Back Cove, the Eastern Prom, as it's known locally, reaches East End Beach and the waterside Fort Allen Park. (The blocklike island remains of Fort Allen can be seen just offshore in the middle of the bay.) If you have a dog, try to come here in the off-season when East End Beach is open to off-leash dog running. During the summer months, East End Beach becomes a favorite spot for locals to take a quick dip at the end of the workday. The trail loops back from Fort Allen Park for the return to Back Cove. Reaching the bridge to Back Cove, bear northwest on the Back Cove Trail for the return to the parking area.

Options

Both Back Cove and the Eastern Prom can be reached from various access points to create a custom-length hike. Alternate parking for Back Cove can be found at Preble Street Extension. From this parking area to the bridge that connects Back Cove with the Eastern Prom can be reached in approximately 0.5 mile. The Eastern Prom trailhead can also be accessed at the corner of Commercial and India Streets in downtown Portland. To reach the East End Beach parking area, descend from Fort Allen Park down Cutter Street to the parking area.

Directions

To reach Payson Park and the parking area off Preble Street, from the intersection of Marginal Way and Forest Avenue/U.S. 302 in Portland, turn onto U.S. 302, heading west under I-293. After passing the highway exit ramps, take the first right onto Baxter Boulevard/Route 1 North. Follow 1.7 miles to a right turn at Preble Street. (The Preble Street parking area is at the end of the street to the right.) To reach Payson Park, continue on Preble Street.

Public Transportation: Amtrak service from Boston to Portland is provided by the Downeaster line. In Portland, the #8 Peninsula Loop Bus (part of the Greater Portland METRO system) makes stops at Back Cove.

GPS Coordinates: 43.6790 N, 70.2681 W

Contact

Access and parking are free. Dogs on leash are allowed. Trail maps of both Back Cove and the Eastern Promenade are available from Portland Trails. For more information, contact Portland Trails, 305 Commercial St., Portland, ME, 04101, 207/775.2411, www.trails.org.

4 BAUNEG BEG MOUNTAIN
North Berwick

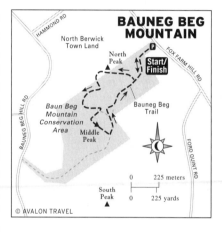

Level: Easy/Moderate

Hiking Time: 1 hour

Total Distance: 1.8 miles

Elevation: 300 feet

Summary: This hidden gem offers impressive views and the chance to spot one of the rarest orchids in eastern North America.

Home to the one of the rarest orchids in North America and a natural habitat for the endangered Blanding's turtle, 866-foot Bauneg Beg Mountain is as worthy a hike for what you may find on the forest floor as it is for the pleasant views from its summit. (Bauneg Beg is Gaelic for pleasant and small, though why the mountain has an Irish-derived moniker appears to have been lost to time.) A former ski area, Bauneg Beg is covered by a surprisingly thick new-growth forest. This summit loop hike, an easy climb for beginners and children, explores interesting rock formations known as the Devil's Den as it winds through the woods on a gentle ascent to the top.

From the parking area on Fox Farm Hill Road, a wooden sign marks the start of the Bauneg Beg Trail, a rocky path leaving west from the lot. As the trail crosses on planks over wet areas at the base of the hill, this is a good place to be on the lookout for small whorled pogonia, one of the eastern United States' rarest orchids. Typically found near fern cover and among humid, peat-type soil, the flower grows to about 10 inches in height and has two lime green flowers that grow from a pale green whorl of leaves. The orchids typically bloom the second week of June, with flowers lasting only 7–10 days before wilting. Because of its endangered status, it is strictly prohibited to pick the orchid.

Moving away from the wetlands, the trail quickly shoots uphill in a somewhat steep stretch before reaching a junction at 0.25 mile. Here, bear north (right) to take the trail marked as the way to North Peak. As the trail begins its upward climb in a north and then westerly direction, the forest changes to a mixed woods of white pine, beech, red oak, and maple.

Continuing uphill, the trail reaches North Peak, a lower subsidiary peak of Bauneg Beg, with limited views. From North Peak, the trail dips south into a saddle before the climb to the summit, again crossing areas that tend to collect water in spring and after summer rains, making it a good place to look for orchids—and the endangered Blanding's turtle, another wetland inhabitant. To identify a Blanding's turtle, look for the distinctive yellow neck and yellow spotted shell.

taking in the view from Bauneg Beg Mountain

As the trail rises up to reach the summit, you push east and then south to the rocky overhang known as the Devil's Den. Scrambling over some boulders before reaching the Middle Peak (the mountain's true summit), views take in the low, rolling hills of southern Maine and, on a clear day, can reach as far as Mount Washington in New Hampshire. Bauneg Beg's summit is notable as the only summit in southern Maine not to have a radio tower built on it. But somewhat disappointingly, the view from Bauneg Beg includes lots of cell towers sticking up from just about every upland.

On the return trip, descend the way you came or continue south over the summit and then bear north (left) to take Ginny's Way, a gently sloping trail that returns you to the Bauneg Beg Trail in another 0.5 mile.

Options

If you are on a mission to catch a sighting of the small whorled pogonia, try the Tom's Way trail on the west side of the mountain. To reach the trailhead, stay in your car to continue north on Fox Farm Hill Road past the parking area for the Bauneg Beg Trail. In 0.5 mile, you will reach Hammond Road. Take a left and drive to the end of the road. Take another left on Bauneg Beg Mountain Road and proceed south on the road almost a mile until you see the trailhead marker for Tom's Way on your left (east side of the road). Pull over on the side of the road to park.

Tom's Way winds through a red oak and beech wetlands that provides the rich peat soil the small whorled pogonia prefer. If you decide to go off-trail in search of the orchids, be careful of your footing to avoid trampling any plants. Other endangered plants, including swamp saxifrage, are also found here. Tom's Way will also take you to the summit in a gentle 0.75 mile climb to the top of Bauneg Beg.

Directions

Heading north on Route 4 from the center of North Berwick, proceed 2.1 miles to a left turn on Boyle Road. Continue straight on Boyle Road for 5.5 miles. The road turns into Ford Quint Road and then reaches a left turn on Fox Farm Hill Road. Follow Fox Farm Hill for 0.3 mile to a sign on the left for Bauneg Beg Conservation Area.

GPS Coordinates: N 43.3921, W 70.7793

Contact

Parking and access are free. Dogs on leash are allowed. Trail maps are available at the trailhead bulletin board. For more information, contact Great Works Regional Land Trust, P.O. Box 151, South Berwick, ME 03908, 207/646-3604, www.gwrlt.org.

⑤ LAUDHOLM BEACH
Wells Reserve

Level: Easy   **Total Distance:** 2.0 miles

Hiking Time: 1 hour   **Elevation:** 10 feet

Summary: Explore the salt marshes and dramatic views of this estuary reserve on the way to Laudholm Beach and the Atlantic Ocean.

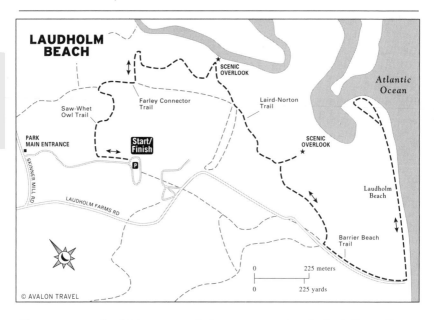

This scenic stretch of Atlantic coastal plain, encompassing the Little River, Ogunquit River, and Webhannet River estuaries, was once the largest saltwater farm in southern Maine, shipping milk, butter, and eggs as far away as markets in Boston. As agricultural production dropped off by the 1970s, local conservation efforts stepped up and today the former Laudholm Farm is one of 27 centers in the United States designated as a National Estuarine Research Reserve. Open to the public and with many of the original buildings of the old Laudholm Farm still intact (serving as an education and visitor center), Wells Reserve protects 2,250 acres of salt marsh, freshwater wetland, beach, dune, forest, and field—the dynamic components of an estuarine microenvironment. This rambling hike takes you on a tour of the reserve's diverse landscape, culminating with a visit to Laudholm Beach and the crashing surf of the Atlantic Ocean.

From the parking area, find the footpath leading west out of the lot. Within a

Laudholm Beach

few feet, the footpath ends at a junction with the Saw-whet Owl Trail. Named for the Saw-whet, or Acadia, owls who live in the area (almost unseen during the day, diminutive saw-whets hunt at dawn and dusk), the trail pushes north through a mixed forest of beech, ash, and oak, the trail ends in 0.25 mile when it reaches the Laird Norton Trail. Jog east (right) for only 0.1 mile before reaching the Farley Connector Trail, departing the Laird Norton Trail to the north (left). Follow this trail a short distance to reach the Farley Trail. Bear to the northeast on the Farley Trail to reach a scenic viewing point overlooking the salt marshes of the Little River estuary. As the flat expanse of the river winds toward the sea, salt marsh grasses are busy with bird activity; heron, cormorants, and gulls are commonly seen here, fishing for dinner or simply taking a stroll at low tide on the tidal flats.

Turning away from the viewing area, head east with the trail, ducking back into the upland forest. The trail ends at a junction with the Laird Norton Trail. Ignore the other two trails heading south from the junction and instead bear east (left) to follow the Laird Norton Trail to an even more dramatic estuary overlook. What you see here is truly the point where the river meets the sea. The mouth of the Little River is a dramatic break in the coastline that swells or empties with the tide; be here as the tide goes out to see just how powerful the force of tidal action is on the meandering river.

From this overlook, the trail retreats back into the woods one more time before bringing you to a junction with the Barrier Beach Trail. Turn east (left) with the trail to reach Laudholm Beach on the Atlantic Ocean. A sandy beach with the classic Maine outcroppings of jagged rock, head north on the beach (hanging left once you reach the end of the Barrier Beach Trail). With only a wall of trees behind you and nothing but white capped waves in front of you, the ability to feel such solitude on Maine's busiest stretch of shoreline may be the crowning achievement of Wells Reserve. Once you've had your fill of surf and sand, retrace your steps to the Barrier Beach Trail, following it all the way back to the parking area.

Options

A longer loop trail creates a pleasant 2.5-mile stroll that takes in the southern section of the reserve. From the parking area, walk toward the education center and look for the Muskle Trail (blazed red), leaving to the south of the education center. Follow the gently curving trail for a little over a mile as it skirts the woods and sweeps past old farmland. Reaching a junction with the Pilger Trail, follow a spur of the Pilger south a short distance to a viewing point overlooking the river and salt marsh. Retrace your steps from the viewpoint and then continue to follow the Pilger Trail east, back through the woods, until it reaches the Barrier Beach Trail. Turn east again (right) with the Barrier Beach Trail to reach the sea. Use this trail for the return to the parking area.

Directions

Driving north on 1-95 from Boston, cross into Maine and continue to Exit 19 (Wells) and follows signs to Route 1 north. Follow Route 1 north 1.5 miles to Laudholm Farm Road (just north of the Lighthouse Depot and south of the Maine Diner, at the second flashing traffic signal). Turn right and follow signs to the Reserve.

GPS Coordinates: 43.3375 N, 70.5509 W

Contact

Trails are open year-round, but admission is charged for trail use between Memorial Day and Columbus Day. Rates are $3 per adult, $1 for children 7–16, children under six are free (maximum $10 per carload). Dogs and pets are prohibited. Trail maps are available at the visitors center. For more information, contact Wells National Estuarine Research Reserve, 342 Laudholm Farm Road, Wells, ME 04090, 207/646-1555, www.wellsreserve.org.

6 MOUNT AGAMENTICUS   BEST [

West of Ogunquit

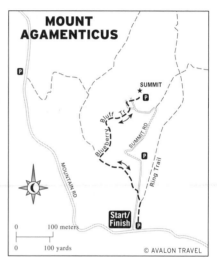

Level: Easy/Moderate   **Total Distance:** 1.0 mile

Hiking Time: 45 minutes   **Elevation:** 400 feet

Summary: A short, easy trek up leads to panoramic views and one of the best hawk-watching spots in Maine.

A landmark hump on the otherwise flat coastal plain of southern Maine, 689-foot Mount Agamenticus is still used as a navigational tool by local fishing boats and other seafarers. But "Mount A" is perhaps best known as one of Maine's premier sites for hawk-watching. Birds, too, use the mountain as a guide during their annual migrations and each fall, thousands of migrating raptors, including peregrine falcons, bald eagles, osprey, and northern goshawks, can be viewed from the summit. On an early October day with strong northwest winds, hundreds of raptors may soar over the mountain in just a few hours. This one-mile up-and-down hike is an easy walk to a summit with a fire tower and two viewing platforms that offer 360-degree views of the Seacoast region of southern Maine and New Hampshire. Even very young children can have fun scampering up this oversized hill.

From the parking area at the base of Summit Road, look for a brown box that holds maps and other trail information. Nearby is the beginning of the Ring Trail, an old woods road that quickly disappears into the tree cover. Reaching a fork within 0.1 mile of the trailhead, bear west (left), crossing over Summit Road and soon reaching another junction. Here, turn north (right) on the Blueberry Bluff Trail and continue uphill to the broad summit area. Mount A's summit is grassy and broad with two viewing platforms, a town recreation lodge, and a fire tower; despite all this development, there's still plenty of room to picnic and just roam about. The only mar to this beautiful place is the very large (and very out of place) cell tower. Return the way you came or descend via the Summit Road, a 0.5-mile walk to the bottom of the hill.

hawks circling the summit of Mount Agamenticus

Special Note: Mount Agamenticus sits in the middle of over 9,000 acres of conservation land, with much of it open to hunting in season. Dog owners should be aware that hunters on the mountain are allowed to bait traps with meat while looking to attract bobcat, coyote, fisher, fox, and marten. If you take your dog to the mountain during hunting season (bait season generally starts in late fall), be sure to keep your pet leashed and on-trail at all times.

Options

To learn more about the history and ecology of the mountain, try the self-guided Interpretive Trail. At the trailhead for the Ring Trail, look in the trail map box for copies of the Interpretive Trail guide. Numbered sites and directions in the guide lead you to significant locations on Mount A. The trail follows the Ring Trail around to the western side of and finally to the summit for a round-trip of approximately two miles.

Directions

From the corner of U.S. 1 and York Street in York, drive north on U.S. 1 for 4.1 miles to a left turn on Mountain Road. Follow 2.6 miles to a right turn on Summit Road (listed as the Mount A Road on some maps). Park in the turnouts at the base of the road.

GPS Coordinates: 43.2169 N, 70.6922 W

Contact

Parking and access are free. Dogs allowed. No wheelchair facilities on the trail, but Summit Road leads to a level parking area with wheelchair access. A trail map and informational brochure is available at the trailhead. For more information, contact York Parks and Recreation Department, 186 York St., York, ME 03909, 207/363-1040, www.parksandrec.yorkmaine.org.

7 OGUNQUIT CLIFF WALK   BEST ☾
Ogunquit

Level: Easy   **Total Distance:** 2.5 miles

Hiking Time: 1 hour   **Elevation:** 0 feet

Summary: Tread above the crashing surf of the Atlantic on this popular cliff walk to Ogunquit's Main Beach.

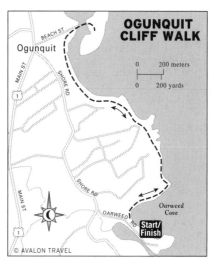

Along the Ogunquit coast winds the famous Marginal Way, a cliff walk that edges between the manicured lawns of Ogunquit's magnificent beachfront homes and rocky ledges hovering just above the crashing surf of the Atlantic. Connecting Perkin's Cove and Main Beach, the 1.25-mile-long cliff walk is a universally accessible path that makes for a pleasant oceanfront stroll. If you come here in summer, be prepared for crowds; during the peak tourist season Marginal Way can feel more like a traffic jam than a walk. Come here in the off-season for a bit more solitude on the trail, but you will likely never be alone. Year-round, in good weather and bad, painters, photographers, bird-watchers, and ocean lovers can be found on Marginal Way, taking in the rugged beauty of the Maine coast.

From the parking area on Oarweed Road, follow the signs for Marginal Way as they lead north to the beginning of the Cliff Walk. Continuing north and east to skirt Perkins Cove, the flat tarred trail soon emerges on top of the rocky cliffs with full ocean views. Lined with dense thickets of beach rose, breaks in this natural hedge reveal side paths that lead directly down to the rocks. A good example of Maine's distinctively jagged coast of black, basaltic rock, the many tide pools that collect at low-tide here are well worth checking out. From hermit crabs and sea urchins to sea stars and periwinkles, these temporary pools are fun to explore—especially for kids. Low tide also brings with it frequent sightings of harbor seals sunning themselves on the outermost stretches of rock.

Continuing along, you pass no shortage of grand homes and grand hotels to your left, but it's the powerful action of the sea that will likely hold your attention.

© JASON BROWN

the Cliff Walk

Benches scattered frequently along the path make it easy to sit for a while to contemplate the crashing waves and bird-watchers will want to bring the binoculars for excellent shorebird viewing opportunities, especially during the migration seasons. From mid-May to early June, and then again from mid-July through September, an impressive number of osprey, green heron, plover, and sandpipers follow the coastline, stopping to rest and feed in the shallow coastal waters and protected marshes of Ogunquit. Local birders claim as many as 17 different species of migratory birds use Oguinquit as a staging area during their twice yearly journey.

As the Marginal Way nears its end, the large barrier beach (Ogunquit's main public beach) appears offshore, trading open ocean views for the pleasant scenery of a salt marsh and a river of sea water on the western (land-facing) side of the beach. The trail takes you to Beach Street, where an access road leads across the shallow bay to the white sands of Ogunquit Beach. To return, retrace your steps.

Options

If you are don't want to make the return 1.25-mile trip on foot, Ogunquit runs a number of trolleys during the summer season that make stops in and around the village, including the beginning and end of the Marginal Way. Look for the trolley stop at Main Beach.

Directions

From I-95 north, take Exit 7. At the end of the exit, turn left (north) onto

Route 1 north. Continue about seven miles; you will pass the Ogunquit Theater on your right. Take the next right after the theater onto Bourne Lane. At the stop sign, take a right onto Shore Road. Perkins Cove is about 0.25 mile down Shore Road. You will see a Perkins Cove sign directing you to bear left into the Cove on Oarweed Road. Look for the signs for public parking and Marginal Way access to your left.

GPS Coordinates: N 43.2371, W 70.5903

Contact

Parking at Perkins Cove costs $3 per hour during the peak summer season ($2 per hour in the off-season). Access to the Cliff Walk is free. Dogs and pets are not allowed. No map is necessary for this hike, but for a free map of Ogunquit village and beach, contact the Ogunquit Chamber of Commerce, 36 Main Street, P.O. Box 2289, Ogunquit, ME 03907, 207/646-2939, www.ogunquit.org.

8 VAUGHAN WOODS
South Berwick

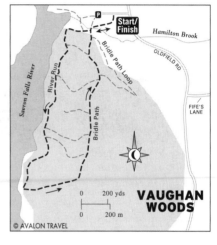

Level: Easy

Hiking Time: 1 hour

Distance: 2.0 miles

Elevation: 20 feet

Summary: Feel lost in time on this serene hike through the primeval forest of southern Maine.

Who knew the Maine North Woods could be found so close to Boston? Though technically not part of the forest system that dominates the northern part of the Pine Tree State—Vaughan Woods is just a few miles west of the bustling outlet centers of Kittery—the forest has every bit the same remote feel. A lush woods of white pine and hemlock running for nearly one mile along the banks of the placid Salmon River, this hike in the Vaughan Woods takes you through stands of giant pines more than a hundred years old and to views of the historic Hamilton House, an 18th-century mansion that was once the centerpiece of bustling farmlands.

From the parking area, walk between the information board and public bathroom to leave on the unmarked River Run Trail; since quite a few of Vaughan's trails are unmarked, it's wise to take a paper trail map from the box on the information booth before departing. Heading downhill a short distance, the trail is immediately surrounded by soaring pines. Following a rocky stream dropping off to the left, the trail reaches the river within 0.1 mile. A small spur path explores a marshy area before taking you within view of the Hamilton House.

Retrace your steps from the spur path and then bear southeast (right) to stay on the River Run Trail, stepping carefully over exposed tree roots. Benches at scenic overlooks along the trail invite you to stop and gaze for a few moments at the bucolic beauty of the Salmon River, a tidal tributary of the Piscataqua River estuary. Across the water is the rural town of Rollinsford, New Hampshire, and in keeping with Vaughan's lost-in-time feel, all that's visible on the other shore is ancient farmland that's still in active use; on quiet days, you may even hear the

Hamilton House, Vaughan Woods

lowing of a grazing dairy herd. If you have a canoe, bring it along to put in along the River Run Trail.

After a mile, the trail ends at the Bridle Path. Turn left and head steeply uphill through the woods, passing the old Warren homesite, marked with a plaque for one of the area's first inhabitants (there are no structures here). Continue on the Bridle Path for the next mile back to the park area and enjoy the quiet solitude of the woods.

Options

For a loop through the forest that penetrates deep into the woods, try the one-mile Old Indian Trail. The trail, winding under some of the oldest pines in this corner of southern Maine is an almost silent trek, thanks to the thick coating of pine needle duff underfoot.

Directions

From the intersection of Routes 4 and 236 in South Berwick, drive south on Route 236 for approximately 0.5 mile. Turn right opposite the junior high school at Vine Street. Go about one mile to the intersection of Vine Street and Old Fields Road. Turn right and watch for the park entrance on the right.

GPS Coordinates: 43.2116 N, 70.8088 W

Contact

Visitors pay a self-service fee of $2 per adult for Maine residents, $3 per adult non-resident, and $1 per child; leave admission fee in the locked payment box at the entrance to the park. Dogs allowed. A trail map and informational brochure is available at the trailhead. For more information, contact Vaughan Woods State Park, 28 Oldsfields Rd., South Berwick, ME 03908, 207/490-4079. Maine Department of Conservation, Bureau of Parks and Lands, 286 Water St., Key Bank Plaza, 3rd and 5th floors, Augusta, ME 04333-0022, 207/287-3821, www.state.me.us.

9 RAYMOND & SIMONE SAVAGE WILDLIFE PRESERVE

Eliot and South Berwick

Level: Easy

Hiking Time: 1 hour

Total Distance: 2.0 miles

Elevation: 10 feet

Summary: Enjoy the company of northern wildlife on this winding walk to a secret swimming hole on the shore of the Salmon Falls River.

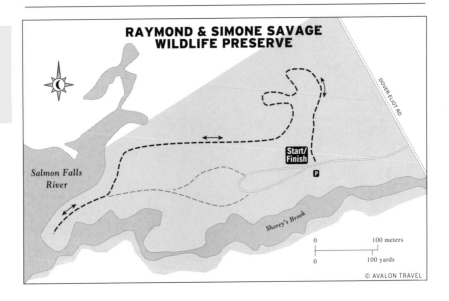

Thanks to the hard work of several local land conservation groups, Southern Maine is filled with a patchwork quilt of land preserves that offer hikes to some really interesting and unique places. With a secret swimming hole (that kids will love) at the end and a gentle walk through a wildlife-filled forest and salt marsh, Savage Wildlife Preserve is one of the best examples of these protected local gems. This easy hike, to a bank above the Salmon Falls River and back, is best in summer when the fields and marsh fill with wildflowers, forest creatures dart about in the shady splendor, and a refreshing dip in river sounds like the perfect way to beat the summer heat.

From the parking area, cross the dirt access road to pick up a dirt footpath that begins between a gap in a split rail fence. Winding along the edge of a field filled with alder, sumac, and birch, the trail gradually pushes deeper under tree cover

Salmon Falls River

until you find yourself in a pine-filled forest wonderland. Squirrels and chipmunks scatter before you, woodpeckers peck away in trees, a wild turkey may strut by, and deer, fox, rabbit, and even a rare sighting of the endangered Blanding's turtle may await lucky hikers. (Deer ticks may also be waiting for you, so be sure to inspect your skin and clothing after the hike.)

Continuing on past the wetlands, the trail curves west and then east before emerging from the woods and following the boundary of a salt marsh along the Salmon Falls River estuary. Reeds and rippling marsh grasses hint at the land's connection with the Atlantic; as you walk, you may notice marsh giving off a briny sea smell. Bird-watchers may want to linger here along the trail. According to local birders, the salt marsh is a great place for loon, grebe, cormorant, and heron sightings.

Flowing east again, the trail ducks back under forest cover as it brings you out onto a bluff above the river. The views are constant through the trees and at the end of the trail, a bluff-point picnic table offers a nice place to take in the sights. You can turn around from here and retrace your steps for an equally lovely stroll back to the trailhead. For those who wish to take a dip before heading back, a faint path just across from the picnic table leads down the bluff about 10 feet or so to the river. There is no lifeguard or really any beach there, but the river stays shallow for several feet with a somewhat rocky bottom; swim at your own risk.

Options

For a shorter return trip, as you return from the bluff, you reach a split in the trail. Here, bear north (right) to head toward a building in the distance. Just as it looks like you are on the way to walking up to their front door, the trail suddenly swings west (left) to return you to the dirt access road and the parking area.

Directions

Traveling north on I-95 from Boston, enter Maine and take Exit 3, bearing east at the end of the exit and following signs for South Berwick/Route 236 North.

Follow Route 236 toward Eliot/South Berwick for 4.3 miles, until reaching an intersection with Route 101/Depot Road. Here, take a left (turning south) and follow Depot Road 0.5 mile to a left turn at a sign for the preserve.
GPS Coordinates: 43.1452 N, 70.7980 W

Contact

Parking and access are free. Dogs and pets are not allowed. Trail maps are available at the trailhead bulletin board. For more information, contact Great Works Regional Land Trust, P.O. Box 151, South Berwick, ME 03908, 207/646-3604, www.gwrlt.org.

THE
BERKSHIRES

© JAROSLAW TRAPSZO

BEST HIKES

A straight drive west from Boston along the Mass

Turnpike brings you to the rural hills and pastoral landscape of western Massachusetts. Offering little evidence that such a large urban center could be so close by, this is a place where summit views miraculously still yield rolling farmland, quaint village skylines, and unbroken acres of forest; and where traffic jams often come in the form of wild turkeys slowly strutting across a backwoods trail.

The Berkshires region harbors the Bay State's highest peak, 3,491-foot Mount Greylock (technically a part of the Taconic Range running up the spine of westernmost Massachusetts), as well as other rugged mountains, including Monument Mountain and Mount Toby. Also found cutting through the region is the Bay State portion of the long-distance Appalachian Trail; the AT runs for 89 miles through the Berkshires, including parts of Mount Greylock and Beartown State Forest.

Though the higher summits of the Berkshires tend to draw the heaviest hiker traffic, there's plenty of other fine hiking in western Massachusetts, from hidden gems like the dramatic Hubbard River Gorge to fire tower views from the DAR State Forest to a walk along the centuries-old Mohawk Trail in the Mohawk Trail State Forest. Lining the Connecticut River valley is the much-loved Mount Tom (part of the steprock Metacomet Ridge) and the multiuse Norwottuck rail trail, a bike path located near many of the area's colleges. Other trails in this rural region simply ramble through the woods and make for great wildlife viewing: hawks, owls, frogs, fish, beaver, otter, fox, gray squirrel, muskrats, white-tailed deer, snowshoe hares, and even the reclusive black bear all call this region home.

The best time of year to hike the Berkshires? You might want to plan a hike in autumn when fall color in the heavily deciduous forests of the Berkshires is simply spectacular. Foliage usually peaks around Columbus Day weekend, the perfect opportunity for a long weekend in the mountains. (Leaf peepers often use Stockbridge or Lenox as a homebase for outings – each is close to many of the area's most scenic trailheads.) Winters are typically cold and see plenty of snow in the hills, but some trailheads are maintained year-round for cross-country skiing and snowshoeing.

Many of the hikes in this chapter are found in Department of Conservation state forests that offer convenient access to trailheads, good maps at state forest headquarters, and, for those who wish to turn their day hike into an overnight getaway, a number of well-maintained campgrounds.

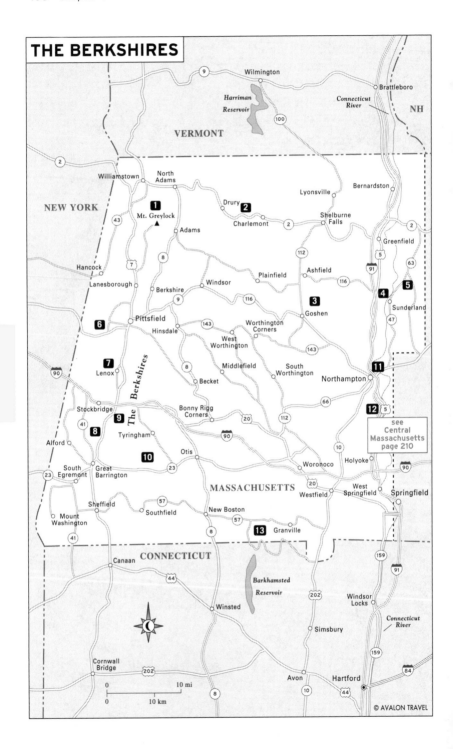

TRAIL NAME	LEVEL	DISTANCE	TIME	ELEVATION	FEATURES	PAGE
1 Mount Greylock	Butt-kicker	12 mi	8 hr	2,500 ft		170
2 Mohawk Trail	Moderate	5.0 mi	3.5 hr	700 ft		173
3 Fire Tower Trail	Easy/Moderate	3.0 mi	1.5 hr	250 ft		176
4 South Sugarloaf Mountain	Moderate	1.5 mi	1 hr	300 ft		178
5 Mount Toby	Butt-kicker	5 mi	3.5 hr	800 ft		181
6 Tranquility Trail	Easy	1.5 mi	1 hr	0 ft		184
7 Beaver Loop	Easy	1.6 mi	1 hr	10 ft		187
8 Monument Mountain	Moderate	1.6 mi	1 hr	720 ft		190
9 Ice Glen and Laura's Tower Trails	Moderate	3.3 mi	2 hr	650 ft		193
10 Benedict Pond and The Ledges	Easy/Moderate	2.5 mi	1.5 hr	200 ft		196
11 Norwottuck Trail	Easy	10.1 mi one-way	5 hr	10 ft		199
12 Mount Tom	Moderate	5.4 mi	2.5 hr	450 ft		201
13 Hubbard River Trail	Moderate	6.0 mi	2.5 hr	450 ft		204

1 MOUNT GREYLOCK

BEST [

Mount Greylock State Reservation

Level: Butt-kicker

Total Distance: 12 miles

Hiking Time: 8 hours

Elevation: 2,500 feet

Summary: A long loop leads to the tallest summit in Massachusetts and beyond to explore the mountain's best features.

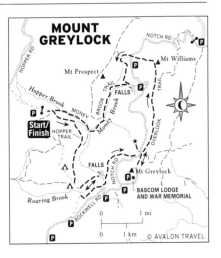

Boston hikers looking to put some serious wear on your hiking boots, this is it! A long, scenic loop around the highest peak in Massachusetts, 3,491-foot Mount Greylock, this 12-mile circuit takes in as many of the mountain's best features as possible on a day hike. Climb through and around the spectacular glacial cirque known as the Hopper, pass two waterfalls, travel over the summit, follow a stretch of the Appalachian Trail, and then descend through the rugged ravine of beautiful Money Brook.

Because you are almost guaranteed to be out on the trail all day on this hike, a trek like this one is no time to skimp on supplies. Make sure to pack sunscreen, bug spray, water, food, extra socks, and other necessities before heading out. While you are never truly "away from it all" on Mount Greylock (park access roads crisscross the mountain, including an auto road to the summit), you do not want a bad sunburn—or hungry tummy—to ruin this superstar trek.

From the parking area, walk past the gate onto the Hopper Trail and follow a flat, grassy lane 0.2 mile to a junction with the Money Brook Trail. Bear south (right) with the Hopper Trail, ascending an old, and sometimes steep logging road, another two miles until you reach Sperry Road. Turn south (left) and walk the road 0.1 mile until you reach a sign for the March Cataract Falls Trail. Here, turn left to head west with the trail one mile, descending through switchbacks, to March Cataract Falls, a 30-foot falls that usually maintains a flow even during dry seasons.

From the falls, backtrack to Sperry Road and take a left to walk south on the road about 100 yards to a sign for the Hopper Trail on your left. Turn north with

a dog's eye view from the Mount Greylock summit

the Hopper Trail; the wide path climbs at a moderate grade past a short falls. Within a mile of Sperry Road, where the Hopper Trail makes a sharp turn south (right), turn left to bear north onto the Overlook Trail. You reach the first view of the Hopper within minutes, though trees partially obstruct it. A half mile down the Overlook Trail lies the second view, which is better; Stony Ledge is visible across the Hopper to the west.

Continue on the Overlook Trail to the paved Notch Road, 1.2 miles from the Hopper Trail junction. Turn north (left) to walk downhill on the road 0.1 mile, past a day-use parking turnout, then take the first trail you come to on the west side of the road, a footpath marked by blue blazes. It descends steeply 0.2 mile to Robinson Point and a view of the Hopper superior to anything on the Overlook Trail. Double back from Robinson Point to the Notch Road and head back uphill to where you left the Overlook Trail. Here, cross Notch Road and look for where the Overlook Trail picks up again on the east side of the road. Follow the Overlook Trail uphill for 0.4 mile to the white-blazed Appalachian Trail. Turn north (left) on the AT, following it across the parking lot to the Greylock summit, where you find the mountaintop's signature War Memorial Tower. The best views are to the east from the meadow beyond the tower; there are also good views to the west.

From the tower, follow the AT north. About a mile from the summit is a good eastern view. About 2.4 miles from the summit, a side trail leads west (left) to Notch Road, but continue 0.2 mile straight ahead on the AT over Mount Williams, one of Greylock's secondary summits. The AT swings west (left) here, descending easily 0.9 mile to Notch Road. Cross the road and, after 0.1 mile in the woods, turn south (left) onto the Money Brook Trail; in another 0.9 mile, a short distance to rugged Money Brook Falls (figured in the distance of this hike). Backtrack from the falls on the side path and continue on the Money Brook Trail, following the brook through a wild, narrow valley, with a few crossings that could be tricky in high water. Nearly a mile past the falls, the Mount Prospect Trail branches west (right); stay on the Money Brook Trail another 1.5 miles to the Hopper Trail; continue straight ahead on the Hopper Trail 0.2 mile back to the parking area.

Options

Too much hiking for one day? You can shave the distance by two miles by skipping the side trail to March Cataract Falls, and another mile by skipping Robinson Point.

Directions

From Route 43 in Williamstown, 2.5 miles south of the junction of Routes 43 and 2 in Williamstown and 2.3 miles north of the junction of Route 43 and U.S. 7, turn east onto Hopper Road at a sign for Mount Hope Park. Drive 1.4 miles and bear left onto a dirt road. Continue 0.7 mile to the parking area on the right.
GPS Coordinates: 42.6546 N, 73.1986 W

Contact

A daily fee of $2 is collected mid-May–mid-October at some parking areas. Dogs on leash are allowed. Find free, basic trail maps of Mount Greylock State Reservation at the park visitors center or online at the Massachusetts Division of State Parks and Recreation website. A map of area trails is available from the Appalachian Mountain Club (*Northern Berkshires/Southwestern Massachusetts/Wachusett Mountain,* $6). For more information, contact Mount Greylock State Reservation, P.O. Box 138, Rockwell Rd., Lanesborough, MA 01237, 413/499-4262 or 413/499-4263. Massachusetts Division of State Parks and Recreation, 251 Causeway St., Suite 600, Boston, MA 02114-2104, 617/626-1250, www.mass.gov.

2 MOHAWK TRAIL
Mohawk Trail State Forest in Charlemont

BEST 🌙

🏕 🌐 🐾 👫

Level: Moderate

Total Distance: 5.0 miles

Hiking Time: 3.5 hours

Elevation: 700 feet

Summary: Walk the famous path used for centuries by Mohawk and Mahican tribes as a shortcut through the Berkshires.

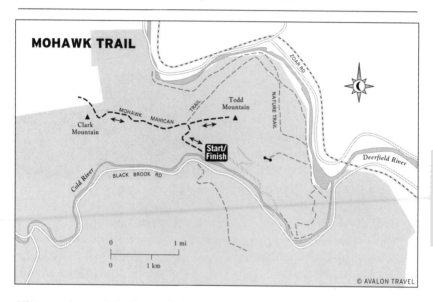

This mostly wooded ridge walk follows a historical route: the original Mohawk Trail, used for hundreds of years by the area's Native Americans as a connector path between the Connecticut and Hudson River Valleys. It was along this route that Mahican and Mohawk tribes traveled for trade and warfare; as you walk the high crest of the Todd-Clark Ridge, rising prominently above the Deerfield River and Cold River valleys, it is easy to see that this trail is, indeed, a very speedy shortcut through this section of the Berkshire highlands.

With such a storied past and still-rustic feel (parts of the route pass through a towering old-growth hardwood forest), the Mohawk Trail is a great way to bring history alive for kids. This moderate hike first visits the summit of Todd Mountain before traveling the ridgetop Mohawk-Mahican Trail to just below the summit of Clark Mountain.

From the visitors center parking area, continue walking west up the paved road, bearing west again (left) where the road forks at the camping area. Approximately

0.7 mile past the parking area, you will see a sign for the Indian Trail, a well-worn path that heads northwest into a pleasant forest of birch and oak. The trail remains flat for only about 200 feet before making a hard turn north (right) to begin the steep and relentless 0.5-mile ascent to the ridge. Unfortunately, the Indian Trail is not well marked and can be easy to lose in a few places, especially in early spring and fall when green leaf cover is not present to frame to the path. (Other hikers have bushwhacked their own faint trails, too, adding to the confusion.) Once atop the ridge, the walking almost immediately levels out. As you quickly come to a well-marked trail junction, turn east (right) onto the Todd Mountain Trail, following it 0.5 mile to the the top of Todd Mountain and an

on the Mohawk Trail

open ledge with good views overlooking the Cold River Valley.

Doubling back to the trail junction, continue straight through the junction to head west on the Mohawk-Mahican Trail as it rides the saddle between Todd and Clark Mountains. The towering forest along this part of the trail is largely old-growth oak and hemlock. Tree ages are 170–300 years, with a small population of hemlocks around 400 years old; you will see disks on trees indicating that this is the old Mohawk Trail. About 0.8 mile past the trail junction, the trail heads back uphill to narrowly bypass the true summit of 1,923-foot Clark Mountain (no views) before reaching the end of the ridge. Double back from here to the junction and descend the Indian Trail back to the start. Can't tell if you've made it to the top of Clark Mountain? If you continue on the Mohawk-Mahican Trail and notice the trail swinging to the north (right) and starting to descend, you've gone too far.

Options

There are plenty of other trails to explore in this gorgeous patch of woods, rivers and hills. On the south side of Route 2, approximately 0.5 mile west past the state forest entrance, find a dirt parking pull off and the trailhead for the Totem Trail, which, despite its name, was blazed in recent times by state forest rangers. This pleasant 1.8 mile out-and-back hike winds through hardwood forest as it takes you to the top of an unnamed ridge overlooking Trout Brook Cove and Hawks Mountain, the large ridge directly to the east.

Directions

From the junction of Routes 2 and 8A in Charlemont, follow Route 2 west for 3.7 miles to the state forest entrance road on the right. Drive the state forest road for 0.2 mile, through a gate, and park just beyond the gate on the left, behind the headquarters building.

GPS Coordinates: 42.6430 N, 72.9464 W

Contact

A daily parking fee of $5 is collected mid-May–mid-October. Dogs on leash are allowed. A free, basic trail and contour map of Mohawk Trail State Forest is available at the state forest headquarters or at the Massachusetts Division of State Parks and Recreation website. For more information, contact Mohawk Trail State Forest, P.O. Box 7, Rte. 2, Charlemont, MA 01339, 413/339-5504. Massachusetts Division of State Parks and Recreation, 251 Causeway St., Suite 600, Boston, MA 02114-2104, 617/626-1250, www.mass.gov.

3 FIRE TOWER TRAIL

BEST **C**

DAR State Forest in Goshen

Level: Easy/Moderate

Total Distance: 3.0 miles

Hiking Time: 1.5 hours

Elevation: 250 feet

Summary: For not too much effort, take in glorious views of the Connecticut River valley from the state forest fire tower.

A tract of former farmland in the eastern foothills of the Berkshires, this sprawling 1,800-acre forest was given as a gift to the state by the Daughters of the American Revolution (DAR) in 1929. Popular among locals for the swimming beaches located on Upper and Lower Highland Lakes, the forest also contains 18 miles of mixed-use trails. This winding walk along Upper Highland Lake and then through the lush hardwood-conifer forest leads to panoramic views from the state forest's fire tower. If you want long views of the Connecticut River valley and into five states—without the effort it takes to

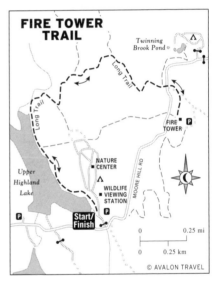

make it to one of the higher summits in the Berkshire region—this hike is a good choice. Out and back, the total elevation gain on this trek is a modest 250 feet.

From the parking area at Moore Hill Road, head west between the boat launch and the night registration office to a sign marking the beginning of the Long Trail (not to be confused with the trail running the length of neighboring Vermont). The dirt path leads to the eastern shore of Upper Highland Lake and then turns north, treading just above the beach areaa popular summer swimming hole during the summer. Reaching the northern tip of this somewhat boot-shaped body of water, the path suddenly veers east into the forest. Over the next mile passing through several well-marked trial junctions, the trail twists and turns its way to reach the fire tower atop Moore's Hill (1,697 feet). Climb the tower's steps for views of the surrounding countryside stretching all the way northeast to New Hampshire's Mount Monadnock, southeast to the Holyoke Range and Mount Tom, and northwest to Mount Greylock. Descend the same way you hiked up.

Options

What else is there to see in the DAR forest? This easy mile-long out-and-back hike leads to the Balancing Rock, a gravity-defying glacial erratic set in the middle of a beautiful deciduous woods (a fiery sight in fall). Other erratics are tucked away along the trail, all dumped here thousands of years ago by melting Ice Age glaciers.

From the parking lot along Moore Hill Road, cross the road and continue walking north a hundred feet or so to the marked Turkey Trail Head south along the blue-blazed woods road and at the intersection of several trails, turn south onto the trail with orange blazes and follow it all the way to Balancing Rock. Return the way you came.

© JAROSLAW TRAPSZO

Balancing Rock is a glacial erratic.

Directions

From North Main Street in Northampton, follow Route 9 west for 12 miles to Goshen. Turn right onto Cape Street/Route 112 north and continue for 0.7 mile. The park entrance is on the right at Moore Hill Road. In summer, park in the second lot along Moore Hill Road, located just past the left turn for the boat launch and nature center. In winter, park in the first lot, near the restrooms and warming hut (Moore Hill Road is not maintained beyond that point).

GPS Coordinates: 42.4569 N, 72.7917 W

Contact

A daily parking fee of $5 is collected mid-May–mid-October. Dogs on leash are allowed. A free trail map is available at the state forest or at the Massachusetts Division of State Parks and Recreation website. For more information, contact DAR State Forest, Rte. 112, Goshen, MA, 413/268-7098 (mail to 555 East St., RFD 1, Williamsburg, MA 01096). Massachusetts Division of State Parks and Recreation, 251 Causeway St., Suite 600, Boston, MA 02114-2104, 617/626-1250, www.mass.gov.

◢ SOUTH SUGARLOAF MOUNTAIN   BEST ◖

Mount Sugarloaf State Reservation in South Deerfield

🏠 🐴

Level: Moderate

Total Distance: 1.5 miles

Hiking Time: 1 hour

Elevation: 300 feet

Summary: A short, steep hike brings you to some of the region's best views of the Connecticut River valley.

Until the 19th century, sugar was sold packed in a tall cone with a flat top, called a sugarloaf. Perhaps with a sweet snack in mind, early Colonial settlers gave the name sugarloaf to a number of conical and relatively flat-topped mountains in New England. Look at a map of the region and you will find a Sugarloaf Mountain in Maine, Vermont, New Hampshire, and this peak in South Deerfield, Massachusetts. (In Connecticut, you can find the twin Sugarloaf Hills.)

At just 652 feet above sea level, South Sugarloaf is barely a hill. But as it rises abruptly from the flat valley, its cliffs loom surprisingly high over the wide Connecticut River and surrounding landscape of town, farmland, and forest. Reached via a short but steep hike, the South Sugarloaf summit offers some

of the Bay State's best views of the Connecticut Valley's quaint tableau. Save this hike for early autumn when the rolling countryside becomes a riot of fall color.

From the parking lot, the wide (though unmarked) West Side Trail leads north into the woods; the trail doubles as a bridle trail through the reservation. Follow the West Side Trail only a very short distance before leaving on the side trail branching to the east (right). This trail leads across the summit auto road to reach the start of the Pocumtuck Ridge Trail, marked by a wooden post without a sign. (The Pocumtuck Ridge Trail can also be reached by walking up the Summit Road about 100 feet inside the gate.)

view from South Sugarloaf

Follow the Pocumtuck's blue blazes as they head east and then northeast up the steep hillside under power lines; the trail finally makes several switchbacks just below the summit ledges to make for an easier climb. Ignore faint footpaths that other hikers have cut to avoid the switchbacks and watch out for rocky footing in spots, especially near the summit. As the sweeping vista comes in to view from atop the summit cliffs, continue on to the mountaintop observation tower for even longer views of the surrounding countryside. Return the same way.

Options

If you want Sugarloaf's magnificent views, but not the steep climb, drive up the Summit Road approximately 0.5 mile to the first summit parking area you reach (on your left). From here, a trail leads north a short distance to an open ledge and splendid views of the Connecticut River, almost directly below where you are standing. Backtrack to the parking area and then take the other trail heading south along the summit to the observation tower. Retrace your steps on the return.

Directions

From the junction of Routes 47 and 116 in Sunderland, drive 0.7 mile west on Route 116 and turn right onto Sugarloaf Road. The Mount Sugarloaf State Reservation Summit Road begins immediately on the right; park in the dirt lot along Sugarloaf Road just beyond the turn for the Summit Road.

GPS Coordinates: 42.4675 N, 72.5945 W

Contact

A daily parking fee of $2 is collected mid-May–mid-October. Dogs on leash are allowed. For a free, basic map of hiking trails, contact the Mount Sugarloaf State Reservation or see the Massachusetts Division of State Parks and Recreation website. For more information contact, Mount Sugarloaf State Reservation, Sugarloaf St./Rte. 116, South Deerfield, MA 01373, 413/545-5993. Massachusetts Division of State Parks and Recreation, 251 Causeway St., Suite 600, Boston, MA 02114-2104, 617/626-1250, www.mass.gov.

5 MOUNT TOBY   BEST 【

Mount Toby Reservation, Sunderland

Level: Butt-kicker   **Total Distance:** 5 miles

Hiking Time: 3.5 hours   **Elevation:** 800 feet

Summary: Explore the biodiversity of an old growth forest before making a steep climb to splendid views from the mountain's fire tower.

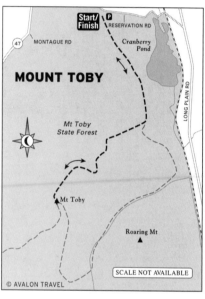

Scenic Mount Toby (1,269 feet) is part of the famed Metacomet Ridge, the narrow line of volcanically formed mountains stretching from Connecticut north into Massachusetts along the Connecticut River valley. Named for Captain Elnathan Toby, the first English colonist to scale the mountain, Mount Toby is considered one of the most biodiverse areas in New England, thanks to remaining relatively untouched by those overly exuberant early American timber harvesters. According to local botanists at the nearby University of Massachusetts (trails at Mount Toby are maintained by the college), the mountain is home to at least 42 native fern species as well as a number of rare orchids, including the showy lady slipper and ram's head lady slipper.

Mount Toby's summit is wooded, but a fire tower open to the public offers panoramic views stretching up to 50 miles across five states when the weather is clear. The well-maintained Summit Road (a restricted road closed to vehicles) provides a route to the top that can be hiked easily—or biked or skied by anyone seeking a fairly challenging climb and a fast descent.

The Summit Road begins behind the Mount Toby Forest sign, with frequent white blazes on the route beginning a short distance down the road. Heading south through a mixed forest of oak, birch, and hemlock, the trail soon takes you past the diminutive Cranberry Pond kettle pond, actually an outlet of the larger Cranberry Pond kettle pond found a few hundred feet to the east; you can visit the larger pond via a short spur path. Less than a mile past the pond, the trail

view from Mount Toby

turns west (right) as it surges upward in a partial ascent of Ox Hill, one of Toby's secondary summits. Continuing west, the trail drops into a col before beginning a very steep trudge to Toby's true summit. Approaching the summit at almost two miles from the trailhead, the road coincides with the orange-blazed Robert Frost Trail to reach the top.

After the strenuous climb you just endured, you might want to rest your legs a few minutes before ascending the 50 or so ladderlike steps to the fire tower observation deck. But when you do reach the top, the views you find from this central location are simply spectacular, stretching from views of Amherst and the Holyoke Range in the south; the Connecticut River and Mount Sugarloaf to the west; Mount Snow, Mount Ascutney, and Mount Monadnock in the north; and the nearby Peace Pagoda in Leverett to the east. This vista is especially lovely in fall when autumn color blazes across the landscape.

Descend the way you came, looking for the white blazes to make sure you picked the correct route. Other trails leave the summit and eventually rejoin the summit road, but these trails are even steeper and can be very hard on the knees.

Options

Roaring Brook Falls, on the eastern flank of Mount Toby, are considered some of the loveliest cascades in the state and are reached in an easy half-mile walk through the woods. To reach trailhead parking for the falls, continue east on Reservation Road from the summit road parking area a short distance to reach

Route 63 and then turn south. Shortly after passing Montague Road on the left, the two entrances to the Roaring Brook Falls Trail dirt parking lot will be on the right. The unmarked Roaring Brook Falls Trail is the dirt path leaving from the lot heading west into the woods. This option is best in late spring when the falls really do roar; by midsummer, the falls tend to run dry.

Directions
From the junction of Routes 47 and 63 in Sunderland, follow Route 47 south for 0.9 mile to a left turn onto Reservation Road. Follow the road for 0.5 mile and park in a dirt lot on the right, just past the sign for the Mount Toby Forest.
GPS Coordinates: 42.5037 N, 72.5311 W

Contact
Mount Toby Reservation is owned by the University of Massachusetts, but is open for public use. Parking and access are free. Dogs on leash are allowed. The *Mount Toby Reservation Trail* map is $4 from New England Cartographics, 413/549-4124 or toll-free 888/995-6277, www.necartographics.com. For more information, contact University of Massachusetts, Natural Resources Conservation, 160 Holdsworth Way, Amherst, MA 01003-9285, 413/545-2665.

6 TRANQUILITY TRAIL

BEST [

Pittsfield State Forest

Level: Easy

Total Distance: 1.5 miles

Hiking Time: 1 hour

Elevation: 0 feet

Summary: This quiet woodland ramble right in the middle of one of the Berkshire's most popular recreation areas is paved for universal access.

Though the hills of western Massachusetts are often lumped together as the Berkshires, the hilly terrain and peaks of the far western portion of the state are actually part of the Taconic Range, a distinct chain of hills that crest along the western border of the New England states, from Connecticut into Massachusetts and north all the way to Burlington, Vermont.

Sitting almost directly on the Taconic Range ridgeline is Pittsfield State Forest, a sprawling 10,000-acre tract of woods, hills, ponds, and streams— and over 65 acres of azaleas, a big tourist draw in June when the flowering shrubs burst into bloom. The paved 0.75-mile long Tranquility Trail is popular with wheelchair hikers and other visitors who favor a smooth walking surface. A quiet woodland ramble right in the middle of one of the Berkshires most popular recreation areas, this satisfying hike really lives up to its name. Other universal access amenities in the state forest include a wheelchair-accessible picnic and restroom, both located very close to the trailhead.

The well-marked Tranquility Trail begins next to the ski area parking lot. Crossing a wheelchair-accessible bridge just steps from the trailhead, the paved path then winds along under a canopy of mixed forest cover to reach its end at a picturesque pond. Along the route, you will probably spot some of the region's more common animal inhabitants—salamanders, turtles, and garter snakes are often fellow travelers along the path and wild turkey, fox, deer, porcupines, and weasel can sometimes be seen lurking among the trees. Red-tail hawks are often spotted overheard, circling for their dinner. To learn more about the flora and fauna of the Tranquility Trail, interpretive audio

Mountain laurel blooms along the trail in June.

© JAROSLAW TRAPSZO

tapes are available from the forest headquarters (near the entrance gate). Return the way you came.

Options

For amazing views that reach far west into New York State, opt for the longer, more strenuous Taconic Crest Trail (not wheelchair accessible). To reach, walk north on the park access road from the parking area approximately 0.5 mile to reach the marked trailhead for the Parker Brook Trail, leaving to the west (left); it is across from a state forest campground. Follow the trail for approximately two miles to its end at the Pine Mountain Trail. Turn south on the Pine Mountain Trail and soon reach the multiuse Taconic Skyline Trail. Jog north and then bear west again on another spur of the Pine Mountain Trail. This takes you west to the top of Turner Mountain and a junction with the Taconic Crest Trail.

With wide-open views sweeping as far as the Catskills to the southwest and north almost to the Adirondacks, follow the trail north for 1.5 miles to the Berry Pond camping area and an intersection with the park access road. Return the way you came or turn south (right) on the park road for a three-mile walk back to the parking area.

Directions

From downtown Pittsfield, head south on North Street to a right turn on U.S. 20 west. Follow U.S. 20 for 2.2 miles and then take a right turn onto Hungerford

Avenue; continue for 0.2 mile, then bear left onto Fort Hill Avenue and continue for one mile. Turn left onto West Street. Continue for 0.2 mile, and turn right onto Churchill Street and continue for 1.7 miles to Cascade Street. Turn left and follow the brown lead-in signs to the park. From the park entrance, follow the access road a short distance to the ski area. The Tranquility Trail begins at the wheelchair-accessible parking lot on the left.

GPS Coordinates: 42.4895 N, 73.2995 W

Contact

The forest is open sunrise–8 P.M. year-round. A $5 day-use fee per vehicle is charged early-May–mid-October. Parking is free for ParksPass holders, vehicles with handicapped, POW, and disabled veteran plates/placards, and seniors 62 and older with the Massachusetts Senior Pass. Dogs on leash are allowed. A basic trail map for Pittsfield State Forest is available at the park entrance. For more information, contact Pittsfield State Forest, 1041 Cascade St., Pittsfield, MA 01201, 413/442-8992, www.mass.gov. Universal Access Program, Massachusetts Department of Conservation and Recreation, P.O. Box 484, Amherst, MA 01004, 413/545-5353 (voice), 413/577-2200 (TTY), www.mass.gov.

7 BEAVER LOOP

Pleasant Valley Wildlife Sanctuary, Lenox

Level: Easy

Hiking Time: 1 hour

Total Distance: 1.6 miles

Elevation: 10 feet

Summary: Explore ponds, marshes, and upland forest as you make an easy loop around this wildlife sanctuary nestled at the foot of Lenox Mountain.

The Berkshires' outpost of the Massachusetts Audubon Society, Pleasant Valley Wildlife Sanctuary is a network of ponds, meadows, marshes, and upland forest at the foot of Lenox Mountain. Known for its enormous beaver population, the sanctuary is also home to a variety or waterfowl and wood warblers and is a nesting ground for the common yellowthroat. This easy, kid-friendly loop takes you through the variety of ecosystems found within the sanctuary and offers the best chance for spotting wildlife. Trails within the sanctuary are clearly signed and marked with two sets of blazes: blue blazes on the trail indicate you are moving away from the office and nature center; yellow blazes mean you are returning to the office.

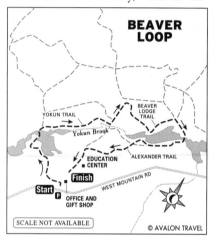

From the parking area near the sanctuary office, follow the gravel path to the nature center, passing a bee balm and wildflower garden filled with fluttering hummingbirds and butterflies. At the center, pick up the Blue Bird Trail and follow briefly to a trail junction. Here, turn east (right) on the Alexander Trail and enter a hardwood forest of linden, black birch, and ash. At 0.3 mile from the office, reach another trail junction. Turn east (right) on the Yokun Trail and then turn north (left) on a short loop path that edges along a marshy beaver pond. Turn east (left) again once you return to the Yokun Trail and follow 0.5 mile to bear northwest (left) onto the Old Woods Road. Crossing over two brooks, the wide, forest-covered path ambles along to a junction with the Beaver Lodge Trail. Bear southwest (left) on the Beaver Lodge Trail and wander along the edge of Beaver Pond, taking in what can only be described as a beaver's version of urban sprawl:

ascending Lenox Mountain

Dams are everywhere. Also living here are muskrats, similar in appearance to beavers, except for their ratlike tails.

At 1.0 mile, the trail leaves the pond and reaches a junction with the Bluebird Trail. Take the Bluebird Trail as it heads southwest on a downhill jaunt through hemlock woods. At 1.3 miles, turn west (right) on the Yokun Trail, skirting two shallow ponds, a favorite haunt of local waterfowl, including heron, mallards, and Canada geese. At 1.6 miles, the trail circles back to the office, crossing a broad swamp before returning to the parking area.

Options

Want to add some mountain views to your outing? Pleasant Valley provides a trailhead for a short, moderately strenuous trek to the top of 2,126-foot Lenox Mountain and a fire tower lookout with views extending to the surrounding Berkshire hills and west into New York State. From the parking area near the sanctuary office, follow the gravel path to the nature center. At the center, pick up the Blue Bird Trail and follow briefly, crossing through a field and over a brook before reaching a well-marked trail junction. Here, bear northwest (left) on the Overlook Trail and follow the blue blazes up the rapidly steepening trail. In about one mile, the mountain's open summit is reached. Enhance your views by climbing the fire tower and then return the way you came, following the yellow blazes back to the parking area.

Directions

From the center of Lenox, follow U.S. 7A north to an intersection with U.S. 7/U.S. 20; turn left and continue approximately one mile to a left turn onto West Dugway Road. The sanctuary and parking area are 1.6 miles ahead on the right.
GPS Coordinates: 42.3852 N, 73.2969 W

Contact

Trails open dawn–dusk on the days the Pleasant Valley nature center is open. Nature center hours are 9 A.M.–5 P.M. Tuesday–Friday, 10 A.M.–4 P.M. Saturday, Sunday, and Monday holidays. Access costs are $4 for nonmember adults and $3 for nonmember children (ages 2–12) and seniors. No dogs or pets allowed. A sanctuary trail map is available at the Pleasant Valley nature center. Pleasant Valley Audubon Wildlife Sanctuary, 472 West Mountain Rd., Lenox, MA 01240, 413/637-0320, www.massaudubon.org.

8 MONUMENT MOUNTAIN   BEST ◖

Great Barrington

Level: Moderate

Hiking Time: 1 hour

Total Distance: 1.6 miles

Elevation: 720 feet

Summary: This storied mountain also comes with some serious views and is considered one of the best hikes in the region.

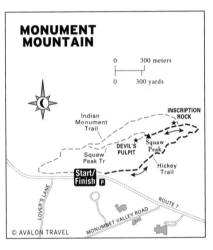

This unique hill has been popular since at least the 19th century: In 1850, so legend goes, Nathaniel Hawthorne, Oliver Wendell Holmes, and Herman Melville picnicked together on Monument's summit. And William Cullen Bryant wrote a poem titled "Monument Mountain" relating the tale of a Mahican maiden who, spurned in love, leapt to her death from the cliffs.

Your hike may be less historic and less traumatic than either of those, but Monument Mountain is one not to miss. A fine trek that rivals even the Mount Greylock region for the best hiking in southern New England, Monument Mountain is an unmistakable gray-white quartzite ridge thrust high above the surrounding landscape. Its summit, Squaw Peak, rises to 1,640 feet and offers three-state views in all directions. Arguably even more dramatic, though, are the cliffs south of Squaw Peak and the detached rock pinnacle known as Devil's Pulpit. A good time to come here is mid-June, when the mountain laurel blooms, or late September when the surrounding hills turn crimson and gold.

Leaving northwest from the parking area, the Hickey Trail is a strenuous and direct route to the top of Monument. Following the Hickey's white blazes into the woods; you first parallel a brook with a small waterfall, a nice way to start this uphill trudge. Continuing to climb and suddenly swinging west as it nears the summit ridge, the trail then takes you to Inscription Rock, on which is carved a brief history of the mountain. Inscription Rock also marks the end of the Hickey Trail and beginning of the Squaw Peak Trail. Continue west on the Squaw Peak Trail. In the next 0.2 mile, footing becomes rocky and a bit tricky as you climb

A cloudy day near the summit of Monument Mountain.

a natural staircase made up of quartzite rock before reaching the summit (at just under one mile from the trailhead).

From the summit, enjoy the views and then continue following the white blazes south about 0.25 mile, passing a pile of rocks, until you reach the cliffs. Devil's Pulpit is the obvious pinnacle at the far end of the cliffs. Return the way you came.

Options

For a gentle, somewhat meandering journey to Inscription Rock, try the Indian Monument Trail, a 1.5-mile former carriage road that makes its ascent up the west side of the mountain. Departing from the same trailhead parking area as the Hickey Trail, the Indian Monument Trail (marked) leaves south from the trail information sign. The Indian Monument Trail reaches the Hickey Trail just below Inscription Rock; to reach the summit, you will still use the Squaw Trail. Return the way you came.

To turn this hike into a somewhat rugged two-mile loop, ascend via the Hickey Trail and continue on the Squaw Peak Trail, past Devil's Pulpit, to eventually head downhill to connect with the Indian Monument Trail, and the return to the trailhead.

Directions

From intersection of U.S 7 and Route 102 at the Red Lion Inn in Stockbridge center, take U.S. 7 south and follow for three miles; entrance and parking are on the right. From Great Barrington, take U.S. 7 north for four miles to the entrance and parking (room for 56 cars) on the left.

GPS Coordinates: 42.2468 N, 73.3325 W

Contact

Monument Mountain is open to the public sunrise–sunset year-round. Parking and access are free. On-site donations welcome. Dogs on leash are allowed. A map of trails is posted on an information board at the picnic area and a paper map is available at the trailhead. A map is also available from The Trustees of Reservations. For more information, contact The Trustees of Reservations Western Management Region, Mission House, P.O. Box 792, Sergeant St., Stockbridge, MA 01262-0792, 413/298-3239, www.thetrustees.org.

9 ICE GLEN AND LAURA'S TOWER TRAILS
Stockbridge

Level: Moderate

Hiking Time: 2 hours

Total Distance: 3.3 miles

Elevation: 650 feet

Summary: Take in nice views of the Stockbridge region before exploring a boulder-strewn ravine that is known to harbor ice well into spring.

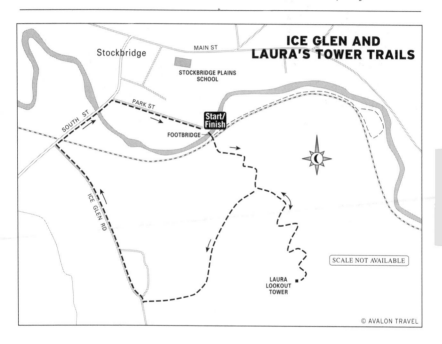

Not far from Stockbridge's quaint village center is the Ice Glen, a boulder-strewn ravine popular with hikers in spring when meltwaters refreeze on the rocks to form a sparkling fairyland of temporary ice sculptures. For summer visitors to Stockbridge, the moss-covered glen provides a cool escape from the heat and from the area's tourist crowds. And don't forget to look up! The Ice Glen contains what is reportedly the tallest pine in Massachusetts. This easy loop hike takes you on a gentle climb to Laura's Tower (1,165 feet), a picturesque overlook with excellent long views from its open observation deck.

From the parking circle, pick up the white-blazed Ice Glen Trail at a large marker and trail map. Only a few steps into this hike, a suspension bridge takes you over the Housatonic River; heading south, the trail then crosses railroad tracks, passes

view from Laura's Tower

under power lines, and enters the woods within the first 0.25 mile. Next, when you reach a trail junction, bear east (left) on the orange-blazed Laura's Tower Trail.

Ascending the hillside as the trail winds its way to the southwest, numerous switchbacks make the uphill trek a breeze. And though you are not far from your start in bustling Stockbridge, towering stands of old growth pine and hemlock found here lend the woods a sense of hushed quiet and true remoteness. In 0.7 mile, the trail reaches the summit of Laura's tower. Climbing up on the open platform reveals postcard-perfect views of Stockbridge's historic village center; on a clear day, views can reach north to Mount Greylock and beyond to the Green Mountains and west to the Catskills of New York State.

Retracing your steps back to the trail junction, turn southwest (left) on the Ice Glen Trail and in another 0.3 mile through the woods, enter the ravine's rocky maze. Pay attention to footing as the trail picks its way along often slippery moss-covered boulders dumped in this configuration sometime during the last Ice Age; some sections of the trail are more of a rock scramble and may be difficult for very young children. After 0.4 mile, the trail leaves the ravine and reenters the woods, heading west (look here for what is the tallest pine tree in the Bay State, according to locals). In 0.1 mile, the trail passes a private driveway and continues west to reach Ice Glen Road. Turn north (right) and follow the road 0.5 mile back to U.S. 7. Turn northeast (right) and follow U.S. 7 for 0.3 mile to turn east (right) onto Park Street. From here, it's only a short distance to the parking circle.

Options

Looking for a wheelchair accessible hike? Once you cross the Housatonic River bridge (universally accessible), look for the yellow-blazed Mary Flyn Trail, a wide, mainly packed-gravel trail that turns east (left) from the Ice Glen Trail to explore the wooded southern bank of the Housatonic River. Built on a former railroad bed, the trail starts with a 100-foot wooden boardwalk and eventually crosses two other bridges as it treads between the river and woods. At 0.6 mile, the trail loops around a former trolley car turnaround and then returns, making a pleasant 1.2-mile round-trip trek.

Directions

From the center of Stockbridge, drive south 0.2 mile on U.S. 7 to a left turn onto Park Street. Drive 0.3 mile to the road's end and parking circle.
GPS Coordinates: 42.2782 N, 73.3076 W

Contact

Parking and access are free. Dogs on leash are allowed. A free trail map is available from the Laurel Hill Association, the village improvement society in charge of maintaining the trails. For more information, contact Laurel Hill Association—Trails, P.O. Box 24, Stockbridge, MA 01262.

10 BENEDICT POND AND THE LEDGES

Beartown State Forest in Monterey

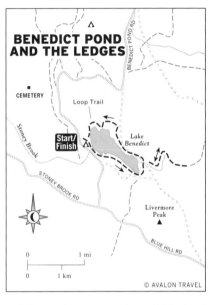

Level: Easy/Moderate

Hiking Time: 1.5 hours

Total Distance: 2.5 miles

Elevation: 200 feet

Summary: Take a short hike on the long-distance Appalachian Trail as it passes near a pretty pond and travels to a scenic overlook.

An easy loop around pristine Benedict Pond, a lake nestled on the more remote southeastern end of Beartown State Forest, this hike takes you to a place simply teaming with critters: hear the tap, tap, tapping of woodpeckers; see beavers hard at work; watch mallards and Canada geese take flight across the water and catch sight of frogs and toads patiently awaiting their next meal. The loop also leads to the Ledges, with excellent views west toward East Mountain and Mount Everett. Kids love this nature trek, a net climb of only a few hundred feet—and for those who have always wanted to journey along the long-distance Appalachian Trail (AT) as it winds its ways from Georgia to Maine, this is your chance! Much of this hike coincides with a section of the Bay State portion of the AT.

From the parking area, follow the blue-blazed Pond Loop Trail as it edges along the southern shores of the pond, taking you to the pond's eastern end. Here, as the trail merges with the white-blazed Appalachian Trail, turn north (left). The coinciding trails soon reach a woods road and split again. Bear northeast (right) to stay on the AT and ascend a low hillside. Where the AT hooks east and crosses a brook, continue straight ahead on a short spur path to an impressive beaver dam that has flooded a swamp. Backtrack to the AT and resume heading east. Within several minutes of a steadily increasing elevation, you reach the upland of the Ledges, with a view west toward East Mountain and Mount Everett.

Return on the AT to the woods road junction and turn west (right) onto the

white blaze marking the Appalachian Trail

Pond Loop Trail. Watch for where the trail bears south (left) off the woods road (at a sign and blue blazes) to continue its loop around the pond. The trail passes through the state forest campground on the way back to the parking area.

Options

For a longer trip on the Appalachian Trail, and the possibility of camping overnight in one of the AT's rustic camping shelters, continue on this hike past the Ledges, following the white blazes for another mile over hilly, forested terrain to reach the Wilcox South shelter. Or, keep on hiking another two miles out from the Ledges to reach the Wilcox North shelter. AT camping shelters are free to use and available on a first-come, first-serve basis.

Directions

From the Monterey General Store in Monterey, follow Route 23 for 2.4 miles west to a left turn on Blue Hill (signs are posted for Beartown State Forest). Follow Blue Hill Road 0.7 mile to the forest headquarters on the left. Continuing north on Blue Hill Road, you pass the Appalachian Trail crossing 1.3 miles from the headquarters; at 1.5 miles, turn right onto Benedict Pond Road (shown as Beartown Road on the park map). Follow signs to the Pond Loop Trail; the trailhead leaves from a dirt parking area. A short distance farther up the road are public restrooms and a state forest campground.

GPS Coordinates: 42.2023 N, 73.2889 W

11 NORWOTTUCK TRAIL

BEST ◖

Elwell Conservation Area, Northhampton

🐾 🦅 🐾 👪 ♿

Level: Easy

Total Distance: 10.1 miles one-way

Hiking Time: 5 hours

Elevation: 10 feet

Summary: Walk, bike, or even stop to shop along this popular rail trail passing through the heart of the Pioneer Valley.

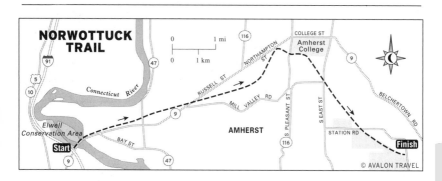

The 10.1-mile-long Norwottuck Trail is a paved, multiuse recreation path that follows a former railroad bed from Northampton, crossing over the Connecticut River and passing through Hadley and Amherst, on its way into Belchertown. Historians believe that the Native Americans who lived here before the European settlers were called the Norwottucks. Translated, Norwottuck means "in the midst of the river," the Native American term for the entire Connecticut River valley.

The trail's flat course provides a linear, universally accessible recreation area for walkers, runners, bicyclists, inline skaters, and wheelchair users. As with any bike or pedestrian path, the Norwottuck is popular with families because it provides a refuge from traffic. The place from which many users access the trail is the large parking lot at its western end; this lot is often full, so it's wise to try one of the other access points listed in the directions.

Options

From grazing dairy cows to shopping mall parking lots, the landscape passed through by the Norwottuck is diverse. In deciding which section of the Norwottuck trail to access, consider the kind of landscape you would find interesting to gaze at as you amble along. From the western end, the trail parallels Route 9 as it cuts across pastoral farm land and winds through Hadley's quaint town commons area.

In miles three and four, the trail passes such enticing stops as a bike and inline skate rental shop, a smoothie stand, and a hamburger drive-in joint, before skirting a large shopping mall. Continuing to cross through a mix of commercial areas and patches of rural beauty on the remainder of its course, the rail trail's final mile might be its most lovely (and undervisited): a marshy wetlands and pond alive with beaver activity and an assortment of ducks, turtles, and even a visiting blue heron or two.

Norwottuck Trail

Directions

To reach the trail's western end from the south, take I-91 to Exit 19 in Northampton. Down the off-ramp, drive straight through the intersection and turn right into the Connecticut River Greenway State Park/Elwell Recreation Area. From the north, take I-91 to Exit 20 in Northampton. Turn left at the traffic lights and drive 1.5 miles to the Elwell Recreation Area on the left. The trail can also be accessed from four other parking areas: behind the Whole Foods store in the Mountain Farms Mall on Route 9 in Hadley, 3.7 miles from the Elwell Recreation Area parking lot; near the junction of Mill Lane and Southeast Street, off Route 9 in Amherst; on Station Road in Amherst (reached via Southeast Street off Route 9), 1.6 miles from the trail's eastern terminus; and on Warren Wright Road in Belchertown, the trail's eastern terminus. Public restrooms are available at the parking area at Elwell Recreation Area.

GPS Coordinates: 42.3350 N, 72.6220 W

Contact

Parking and access are free. Dogs on leash are allowed. A brochure/map is available at both trailheads. The Western Massachusetts Bicycle Map, a detailed bicycling map covering the state from the New York border to the Quabbin Reservoir, including the Norwottuck Trail, is available for $4 from Rubel BikeMaps (P.O. Box 401035, Cambridge, MA 02140, 617/776-6567, www.bikemaps.com) and from area stores listed at the website. For more information, contact Connecticut River Greenway State Park/Elwell Recreation Area, 136 Damon Rd., Northampton, MA 01060, 413/586-8706. Massachusetts Division of State Parks and Recreation, 251 Causeway St., Suite 600, Boston, MA 02114-2104, 617/626-1250, www.mass.gov.

12 MOUNT TOM   BEST [C

Mount Tom State Reservation in Holyoke

Level: Moderate   **Total Distance:** 5.4 miles

Hiking Time: 2.5 hours   **Elevation:** 450 feet

Summary: A popular spot for hawk-watching, this walk along the Metacomet Ridge offers some of the region's most spectacular views.

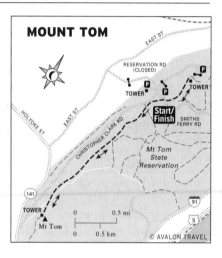

Its dramatic views and relatively easy climb have made the Mount Tom Ridge one of the most popular stretches of the rugged traprock Metacomet Ridge. A steep mountainside capped by tall basalt cliffs defines Mount Tom's west face and the trail follows the brink of that precipice for nearly two miles, treating hikers to commanding views west as far as the Berkshires on a clear day. Mount Tom is also one of New England's premier sites for spotting migrating hawks. Each fall, thousands of hawks and other birds fly past the mountain on their way south. For all the incredible scenery, this hike climbs less than 500 feet and is a perfect outing for young kids to experience the magic of New England hiking.

From the parking area, walk up the paved Smiths Ferry Road for about 75 yards to reach the reservation's interpretive center (located in a stone house). Turn west (right) at the house and enter the woods; the trail is marked by white rectangular blazes and a triangular marker for the Metacomet-Monadnock Trail. Within minutes, the trail turns north and then veers east (right) and climbs steeply toward Goat Peak. Pass a good view westward and then reach the open clearing of Goat Peak, where the lookout tower offers pleasing panoramic views. Double back to Smiths Ferry Road, turn northwest (right), walk about 75 yards, and then enter the woods on the left to head south, following the white blazes of the Metacomet-Monadnock Trail. It crosses the Quarry Trail and then ascends the ridge. Numerous side paths lead to the west (right) to great views from the cliffs, with each view better than the last, until you reach the Mount Tom summit, where there are, unfortunately, a number of radio and television transmission stations (the

© JAROSLAW TRAPSZO

stone observation tower at the summit of Mount Tom

only mar to an otherwise perfect tableau). Take in the sights again as you retrace your steps on the Metacomet-Monadnock Trail to your car.

Options

Continuing north on the Metacomet-Monadnock Trail from Goat Peak brings you in another mile to the castlelike stone foundation remains of Eyrie House, a hotel that was built near the peak in 1861, but subsequently burnt down in 1901. The ruins are what draw most of the attention at this spot, but make sure to take in the long views west—the splendid vista was why a hotel was built here in the first place. The ruins are also accessible via a parking lot on the very northern end of Christopher Clark Road, one of the park's main access roads.

Directions

From I-91, take Exit 18 (Easthampton/Holyoke) to U.S. 5 south. Follow U.S. 5 south for roughly 3.3 miles to a right turn onto Smiths Ferry Road, at the entrance to Mount Tom State Reservation. Follow the road for nearly a mile, passing under I-91 to a horseshoe-shaped parking area on the right. The parking area is about 0.2 mile before the reservation's interpretive center.

GPS Coordinates: 42.2680 N, 72.6320 W

Contact

A daily parking fee of $2 is collected mid-May–mid-October. Dogs on leash are allowed. A free map of hiking trails is available at the reservation headquarters and the stone house, or at the Massachusetts Division of State Parks and Recreation website. Mount Tom State Reservation, 125 Reservation Rd., U.S. 5, Holyoke, MA 01040, 413/534-1186. Massachusetts Division of State Parks and Recreation, 251 Causeway St., Suite 600, Boston, MA 02114-2104, 617/626-1250, www.mass.gov.

13 HUBBARD RIVER TRAIL BEST ◖
Granville State Forest in Granville

🦌 ✈ 🕸 🏠 👪

Level: Moderate   **Total Distance:** 6.0 miles

Hiking Time: 2.5 hours   **Elevation:** 450 feet

Summary: Follow the Hubbard River as it cascades through glacial rock formations to form deep pools and crashing waterfalls.

Located along the southern border of Massachusetts in the towns of Granville and Tolland, Granville State Forest borders with Connecticut's Tunxis State Forest to create a true sense of backcountry solitude. Formerly the hunting and fishing grounds of the Tunxis tribe, the first English pioneer to this area, Samuel Hubbard, settled along the banks of the river now bearing his name in 1749. The woods of the Tunxis soon became open farmland and pastures, but today the landscape is rapidly returning to the hardwood-conifer forest it once was.

This out-and-back hike features the highlight of this out-of-the-way state forest: Hubbard River Gorge, a stunning series of cascades and waterfalls dropping 450 feet over 2.5 miles. Inviting pools of water form at the base of many of the waterfalls, some very deep and perfect for swimming. But don't be tempted to take a dip. Because of the rockiness of the pools (and lack of lifeguards), swimming in the river is strictly prohibited and considered a finable offense by state forest rangers.

From the dirt parking lot, backtrack over the bridge and turn south (right) onto a paved road leading a half mile to the now-closed Hubbard River Campground. The Hubbard River Trail begins at the road's end. Follow the trail, an old woods road marked by blue triangles bearing a hiker symbol, southeast along the northern bank of the Hubbard River. After turning briefly away from the river, the road hugs the rim of the spectacular gorge for the next two miles as you walk downriver, passing many spots that afford views of the cascades. Factor in

© HEIDI J. BROWN

Hubbard River Gorge

extra time on this hike for many "stand still in awe" moments, especially if your visit is in late spring or after a rainfall when the water roars white and foamy over the rocks.

It's also fun as you walk along the river bank to check out what other forest creatures are drawn to this spectacular sight. Judging by the numbers spotted on the trail one lovely summer evening, orange spottted salmanders and frogs seem to love the place, as do ruby-crowned kinglets and other warblers, fluttering about in the nearby treetops.

At 2.5 miles, as the rapids give way to calmer waters, the trail drifts west away from the river and back into the woods. At almost three miles, the trail suddenly hooks to the south (right) before swinging north again to bring you to an old woods road marked on the map as Hartland Hollow Road. Turn back here and retrace your steps back to the gorge and parking area.

Options

If you'd like to see another area similar to the Hubbard River Gorge, turn north on Hartland Hollow Road and watch for a stream through the trees to the east (your right); continue north to discover a small gorge and pools within 0.5 mile of leaving the Hubbard River Trail. This option adds one mile round-trip to the main hike.

CENTRAL MASSACHUSETTS

© JASON BROWN

BEST HIKES

Massachusetts at its midsection is a rumpled

blanket of rolling hills, thick forest, and a string of low but craggy summits that rise above the trees to give long views of the surrounding landscape. Far enough away from Boston, but without the same tourist crowds as the Berkshires region, trails to the top of such notable peaks as Mount Holyoke, Wachusett Mountain, and Mount Wataic tend to be quiet, uncrowded, and easy to reach. These are hikes that are great for beginners and kids as well as serious hikers and backpackers trying to get their legs in shape for more strenuous trips elsewhere. Beyond these hills, you will mostly find pleasant woods walks that are easy to moderately difficult and a number of shorter treks leading to gorges, caves, and summer swimming holes.

Central Massachusetts is also home to two long-distance trails, both of which are largely used by day hikers. The white-blazed Metacomet-Monadnock Trail (Crag Mountain, Mount Holyoke) bounces along the Holyoke Range and through the hills of north-central Massachusetts on its 117-mile course from the Massachusetts/Connecticut line near Agawam and Southwick to the summit of Mount Monadnock in Jaffrey, New Hampshire. In 2009, the federal government designated the Metacomet-Monadnock Trail as part of the new New England National Scenic Trail, a 200-mile trail route comprised of the Metacomet-Monadnock Trail and the Mattabesett Trail in Connecticut. The blue-blazed Midstate Trail extends 92 miles from Douglas (on the Rhode Island border) to Mount Wataic on the New Hampshire line at Ashburham, crossing through woods and over small hills.

This area is snow country in Massachusetts, with the hilly terrain near Worcester and Leominster usually racking up the highest annual snowfall totals in the state. Trails in central Massachusetts usually become free of snow sometime between mid-March and mid-April, though they often will be muddy for a few weeks after the snow melts (New England's infamous mud season).

Many of the hikes in this chapter are in state parks and forests, where dogs must be leashed; horses are allowed in most state forests and parks, as is hunting in season. Trails leading to the Quabbin Reservoir, one of the largest artificially-made public water supplies in the United States, have special access rules: Dogs are prohibited and hikers and mountain bikers should be aware that trails may be closed or rerouted and public access suspended at any time in order to maintain water supply safety.

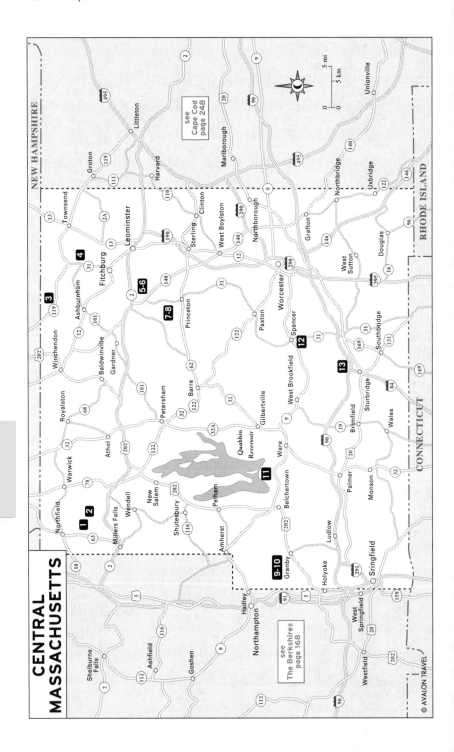

CENTRAL
MASSACHUSETTS

NEW HAMPSHIRE

RHODE ISLAND

CONNECTICUT

see Cape Cod page 248

See The Berkshires page 168

5 mi
5 km

© AVALON TRAVEL

Quabbin Reservoir

TRAIL NAME	LEVEL	DISTANCE	TIME	ELEVATION	FEATURES	PAGE
1 Rose Ledge Trail	Moderate	4.2 mi	2.5 hr	600 ft		212
2 Crag Mountain	Easy/Moderate	3.4 mi	2 hr	350 ft		214
3 Mount Watatic and Nutting Hill	Moderate	2.8 mi	1.5 hr	400 ft		216
4 Willard Brook	Easy	2.0 mi	1 hr	10 ft		219
5 Crow Hills	Moderate	0.7 mi	0.5 hr	200 ft		221
6 Leominster Forest Roads Loop	Moderate	5.5 mi	2.5 hr	50 ft		223
7 Pine Hill Trail	Strenuous	2.0 mi	1.5 hr	500 ft		225
8 Wachusett Summit Loop	Strenuous	5.0 mi	3. hr	700 ft		228
9 Mount Holyoke	Moderate	3.2 mi	2 hr	400 ft		231
10 Rattlesnake Knob and the Horse Caves	Easy/Moderate	4.5 mi	2.5 hr	200 ft		234
11 Quabbin Reservoir	Easy	4.0 mi	2 hr	100 ft		237
12 Howe Pond	Easy	1.0 mi	30 min	10 ft		240
13 Carpenter Rocks	Easy	2.5 mi	1.5 hr	50 ft		242

■1 ROSE LEDGE TRAIL
Northfield Mountain

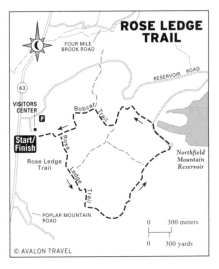

Level: Moderate

Hiking Time: 2.5 hours

Total Distance: 4.2 miles

Elevation: 600 feet

Summary: Known as one of the state's best destinations for technical rock climbing, Northfield Mountain offers a rugged climb with rewarding views.

Traveling west on Route 2 from Boston, Northfield Mountain rises up suddenly from the landscape, a helpful landmark that lets you know you are leaving behind the gently rolling hills of eastern Massachusetts and approaching the more rugged terrain found in the western part of the state. With a feel somewhat more like a peak in the White Mountains of New Hampshire, Northfield's trails are pine shaded and somewhat rocky, with breaks in the forest cover offering stunning views of the surrounding landscape. Especially notable on the mountain is the Rose Ledge, 50-foot tall cliffs made up of stratified bands of rose-hued gneiss.

Northfield Mountain is privately owned by a hydroelectric utility company (which operates the Northfield Mountain reservoir), but the power company–run Northfield Mountain Recreation and Environmental Center provides the public with 25 miles of hiking and multiuse trails—considered by many to comprise one of the best trail systems open year-round in Massachusetts. This hike takes in some of the mountain's best features—including the Rose Ledge cliffs and a view of the reservoir at the 1,100-foot summit—but many other loop options are possible here. The route described here climbs about 600–700 feet in elevation.

From the parking lot and visitors center, enter Northfield's lush evergreen forest by following the wide carriage road of the 10th Mountain Trail, marked by a sign at the north end of the lot. Follow the trail for 0.1 mile as it turns east and reaches a trail junction. Here, turn north (left) onto the Rose Ledge Trail footpath, marked by blue diamonds. Follow the trail 0.2 mile across a carriage road and then turn east (right) with the trail, noting that the trail becomes orange blazed. In the next 0.8 mile, the trail crosses two carriage roads, Hemlock Hill and Jug End, and then bears north (left) at the fork to traverse above the 50-foot tall Rose Ledge, with lovely views of nearby wooded hills.

As the cliffs taper somewhat, and just before reaching the wide carriage road called Rock Oak Ramble, turn east (right) at an easily overlooked connector trail dropping down a short distance to the Lower Ledge Trail. Turn north (left) on the Lower Ledge and you're soon walking below the cliffs. This is one of the most popular places in the Bay State for rock climbing and you should be careful of loose rock falling from above if you venture near the cliff base. At 1.4 miles, the Lower Ledge Trail rejoins the Rose Ledge Trail.

Continuing on as a steady uphill climb through the woods, in another 0.6 mile, the Summit Trail enters on the left and coincides with the Rose Ledge Trail for the final 0.2 mile uphill push to the summit. It's still somewhat wooded, but climb up on the viewing platform and the vista opens northeast to Northfield Reservoir and southwest to the Connecticut River valley. On the return trip, follow the Reservoir Road west off the summit, staying on the road for about 0.1 mile until reaching a junction with the Bobcat Trail. Turn south (left) on the trail and follow downhill a little less than two miles back to the parking area, passing the Chocolate Pot camping shelter a little more than halfway down.

Options

Planning a long-distance trek along the Metacomet-Monadnock Trail? The white-blazed M&M Trail, stretching along the peaks of the Pioneer Valley and north to Mount Monadnock, can be accessed from Northfield Mountain via a marked trail off the 10th Mountain Trail. From where this hike begins, follow the 10th Mountain Trail for approximately three miles to Bugaboo Pass and a trail sign and white triangles pointing the way to the Metacomet-Monadnock Trail.

Directions

From the junction of the Routes 63 and 10 in Northfield, drive south on Route 63 to a left turn for the Northfield Mountain visitors center and recreation parking area. **GPS Coordinates:** 42.6110 N, 72.4720 W

Contact

The visitors center is open 9 A.M.–5 P.M. Wednesday–Sunday, spring–fall. The cross-country center is open 9 A.M.–5 P.M. daily during the ski season. Parking and access are free. Dogs on leash are allowed. Trail maps are available from Northfield Mountain Recreation and Environmental Center. For more information, contact Northfield Mountain Recreation and Environmental Center, 99 Millers Falls Rd./Rte. 63, Northfield, MA 01360, 413/659-3714, www.firstlightpower.com/northfield.

☑ CRAG MOUNTAIN BEST ◖

Northfield

Level: Easy/Moderate **Total Distance:** 3.4 miles

Hiking Time: 2 hours **Elevation:** 350 feet

Summary: Take a short hike on the long-distance Metacomet-Monadnock Trail and take in some of the best views central Massachusetts has to offer.

Taking you to one of the rocky out-croppings of Northfield's Bald Hills region, this not-too-difficult hike leads to Crag Mountain (1,503 feet) and expansive views from its open, knife-edge summit. From the mountain's center-of-New England locale, take in the Berkshires and the southern Green Mountains of Vermont to the west and northwest, New Hampshire's Mount Monadnock to the northeast, the central hills of Massachusetts to the east, and the nearby Northfield Mountain.

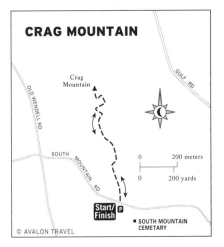

This relatively short up-and-down hike uses the Metacomet-Monadnock Trail, a long distance trail that bounces along the Holyoke Range and through the hills of north-central Massachusetts on its 117-mile course from the Massachusetts/Connecticut line near Agawam and Southwick to the summit of Mount Monadnock in Jaffrey, New Hampshire. In 2009, the federal government designated the Metacomet-Monadnock Trail as part of the new New England National Scenic Trail, a 200-mile trail route comprised of the Metacomet-Monadnock Trail and the Mattabesett Trail in Connecticut. The open top of Crag Mountain is considered one of the most scenic parts of the trail in this north-central part of Massachusetts.

From the parking turnout, follow the white triangular blazes of the Metacomet-Monadnock Trail (labeled as the M&M Trail on some trail signs) as it heads south into the woods. Not far from the trailhead, the path crosses a black gum tree swamp (with some species of black gum here estimated to be more than 150 years old), before beginning a gentle rise through the deep quiet of a hemlock forest. The trail is rocky and root strewn in spots, so watch your step. Breaking out of the woods and crossing on even rockier terrain just yards from the top, the trail reaches Crag's open summit ridge 1.7 miles from the road.

The views from here are gorgeous, thanks to the summit's composition of quartzite, a weather-resistant metamorphic rock that remains jagged, and unfriendly to vegetation, even thousands of years after the mountain formed. Enjoy the scenery, explore Crag's cragginess, and hike back down along the same route.

a steep climb to the top of Crag Mountain

© HEIDI J. BROWN

Options

Want to take a longer trek along the Metacomet-Monadnock Trail? Head southwest off the summit of Crag Mountain, following the blazes back down into the forest. The next five miles of trail take you to an old cemetery before rising again to reach the ledges of Hermit Mountain high above the Millers River. If you keep going, in just over another seven miles, the trail reaches Northfield Mountain at a junction with the 10th Mountain Trail.

Directions

From Route 10/63 in Northfield, about 0.2 mile south of the town center and 0.3 mile north of the southern junction of Routes 10 and 63, turn west onto Maple Street, which becomes Gulf Road. Drive 3.1 miles to a turnout on the right, where the white blazes of the Metacomet-Monadnock Trail enter the woods.

GPS Coordinates: 42.6603 N, 72.4182 W

Contact

Parking and access are free. Dogs are allowed. A map of this trail is included with *The Metacomet-Monadnock Trail Guide,* available for $15 from the AMC Berkshire Chapter. For more information, contact AMC Berkshire Chapter, P.O. Box 9369, North Amherst, MA 01059. (The Appalachian Mountain Club's Berkshire's chapter is charged with maintaining portions of the Metacomet-Monadnock Trail crossing private land.)

3 MOUNT WATATIC AND NUTTING HILL

Ashburnham

Level: Moderate

Hiking Time: 1.5 hours

Total Distance: 2.8 miles

Elevation: 400 feet

Summary: Take in views stretching from Boston to the White Mountains as you walk on one of the oldest interstate footpaths in the northeast.

Once home to a ski area, local conservation efforts prevented a cell phone tower from being erected at the top of 1,832-foot Mount Watatic, forever protecting the mountain's excellent views, stretching from the Berkshires to the nearby peaks of Kidder and Temples Mountains in New Hampshire. The scenery is breathtaking, but for city dwellers who have made the surprisingly easy drive to the trailhead, the real thrill of this hike may be the sudden surge in wildlife populations. If hikes nearer to Boston have yielded only sightings of the occasional squirrel or sparrow, be prepared for trailside spotting of beavers hard at work on their dams, circling turkey vultures and hawks, and even the occasional moose.

This moderate hike, leading first to the scenic outcropping of Nutting Hill, before reaching the Wataic summit, is also a good introduction to the Wapack Trail. First blazed in 1923, the long-distance Wapack Trail stretches from its southern terminus here at the trailhead for Mount Watatic (the "Wa" in Wapack) for 21 miles to its northern terminus at North Pack Monadnock in Greenfield, New Hampshire. From the parking area, find the large brown wooden sign for the Wapack Trail at the north end of the lot. Map information for the Wapack Trail can be found in a weatherproof box next to the trail sign. (However, be aware that parts of this hike use trails other than the Wapack.)

If you are lucky, you might also find a number of walking sticks leaning up against this box. Some kind soul appears to keep a constant supply here, available to any hiker who might need the support of a walking pole (they are fashioned from fallen branches). If you are not sure about your hiking skills, you may want to

Midstate Trail junction, Mount Wataic

grab one of the sticks because, from the start, the old woods road climbs gradually, but relentlessly, uphill.

Leaving from the trailhead, the climb north first passes a wetlands that shows signs of beaver activity and then comes to a trail junction (at 0.3 mile). Here, the yellow triangle blazes of the Wapack Trail turn east (right), but this hike continues north on the blue-blazed State Line Trail to reach Nutting Hill. In another uphill 0.5 mile, reach a junction where the State Line Trail forks west; continue north on the yellow-blazed Midstate Trail, which is rejoined by the Wapack Trail within another 0.2 mile. It is nearly a mile to Watatic's summit from this point. Soon passing over Nutting Hill's open top, stop to take in the views before veering east (right) to stay on the trail; watch for the cairns to help you stay on track.

Reentering the woods, you climb Watatic's northwest slope, passing by the somewhat overgrown trails of the former Mount Watatic ski area. (Make note of the old fire tower foundations that are found just below the summit.) From the summit, the views north and west are tremendous; an unmarked path leads to the lower, southeast summit for excellent views that sometimes reach all the way to Boston. On the return, double back to the fire tower foundations, turn west (left), and descend via the Wapack, passing an open ledge with views and, farther down, an enormous split boulder. At the Midstate Trail junction, turn south (left) for the return leg to the parking area.

Options

For a shorter trip up Watatic, but without the scenic detour to Nutting Hill, turn east with the yellow triangles at the first trail junction reached on this hike. It is approximately 0.7 mile from here to the summit, a complete round-trip of approximately two miles.

Directions

The trailhead parking area is on the north side of Route 119 in Ashburnham, 1.4 miles west of its junction with Route 101.

GPS Coordinates: 42.6870 N, 71.8901 W

Contact

Parking and access are free. Dogs are allowed. A map and guide to the Wapack Trail, including this hike, is available for $11 from the Friends of the Wapack. For more information, contact Friends of the Wapack, P.O. Box 115, West Peterborough, NH 03468, www.wapack.org.

Directions

Following State Route 12 west into Ashburham, reach the intersection with State Route 101. Turn north of Route 101 (Ashby Road) and proceed 3.9 miles to a junction with State Route 119. Turn left (west) to follow Route 119 west 1.4 miles to a marked parking lot for the trailhead on the right.

4 WILLARD BROOK

BEST

Willard Brook State Forest in Ashby

Level: Easy

Total Distance: 2.0 miles

Hiking Time: 1 hour

Elevation: 10 feet

Summary: Follow a babbling brook to a nice little waterfall on this easy walk that is a good pick for kids and families.

There is certainly no shortage of history museums in Massachusetts, but it just may be places like the lush Willard Brook State Forest that offer the truest sense of stepping back into New England's past. You won't find interpretive signs or historical markers here. But what you will discover are trails that lead deep into woods that seem untouched by human activity, and where the quiet is broken only by the sounds of birdsong and the rushing waters of Willard Brook.

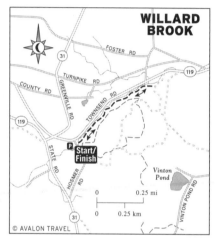

This easy hike, a good one for introducing children to the wonders of the woods, winds through hemlock groves and among huge boulders as it passes through the tight valley of Willard Brook on the way to Traprock Falls. In spring and early summer, the brook runs ferociously, spitting white water as it crashes about the rocky stream bed. But come here in summer and early fall to find a gently babbling brook. It may actually be worth two trips here just to witness this contrast.

From the parking area, walk south (straight) toward the stone bridge over Willard Brook. Just before crossing, bear east (left) and head downhill across a grassy area next the brook. There are a few picnic tables scattered about here (a good stopping place for a picnic on the return trip). You will see a covered footbridge over the stream. Cross the bridge and pick up the footpath as it continues heading northeast (to the left). Following the stream for the next mile, the path weaves in and out of hemlock stands and around large boulders. Uphill on the bank that flanks you to the south, the forest contains enough deciduous cover to make this trek burn brightly in fall. It's a pleasant trek, but exposed tree roots on the trail can make for some tripping hazards, so still watch your footing.

As you reach the other (northeast) end of the trail, the path ascends the hillside above the burbling Traprock Falls and then reaches a forest road; turning north (left) brings you shortly to the state forest headquarters. Most people just double back to the start for a nice two-mile stroll. If it is summer or fall and the water is low enough, you might be able to play a game of hopscotch by carefully stepping on exposed rocks in the streambed.

bridge over Willard Brook

Options

For a longer trek through the Willard Forest, try the Friendship Trail. It leaves from the same trailhead, but instead of heading downhill to the footbridge, continue to cross the stone bridge to look for the orange- and yellow-blazed Friendship Trail. This challenging loop covers approximately five miles as it passes through wetlands and thick forest, and even passes by the state forest's campground area (accessible from another parking area).

Directions

From the junction of Routes 119 and 31 in Ashby, drive 0.2 mile east on Route 119 to the Damon Pond entrance and parking area.
GPS Coordinates: 42.6870 N, 71.8901 W

Contact

A daily parking fee of $5 is collected mid-May–mid-October. Dogs on leash are allowed. A free, basic trail map of the state forest is available at the headquarters on Route 119 in West Townsend, just before the Ashby town line, or at the Massachusetts Division of State Parks and Recreation website. For more information, contact Willard Brook State Forest, Rte. 119, West Townsend, MA 01474, 978/597-8802. Massachusetts Division of State Parks and Recreation, 251 Causeway St., Suite 600, Boston, MA 02114-2104, 617/626-1250, www.state.ma.us.

5 CROW HILLS

BEST C

Leominster State Forest in Westminster

Level: Moderate

Total Distance: 0 .7 mile

Hiking Time: 0.5 hours

Elevation: 200 feet

Summary: One of the most dramatic walks in central Massachusetts, this hike will have you treading along cliff tops for unforgettable views of the surrounding landscape.

From the sheer cliffs of the Crow Hills, archaeologists believe the Penacook Native Americans once built fires to send smoke signals to tribal members in the surrounding countryside. It is easy to understand why the Penacook chose this vantage point as a communication tower. Like that famous peak in New Hampshire, the twin-summit Crow Hills is a monadnock, which in geographical terms means an isolated summit rising up over an otherwise flat plain. Despite its brevity and the climb of just a few hundred feet, and because of the contrast in elevation with the

surrounding landscape, this hike is one of the most dramatic walks in central Massachusetts, traversing the top of tall cliffs with commanding views to the south and east. Climb the hills in early autumn and the vivid crimson-colored woods may convince you to make this trek an annual event.

From the parking lot, cross Route 31 to a wide, well-marked trail entering the woods. Within 100 feet, the trail turns sharply to the southwest (left), then swings north (right) and climbs steeply to the base of cliffs, 100 feet high in places. The trail then diverges north and south, with both branches looping up to the cliff tops. You can hike the loop in either direction; this description leads to the north (for a counterclockwise loop). Walk below the cliff to where stones arranged in steps lead steeply uphill to a junction with the Midstate Trail, marked by yellow triangular blazes. Turn south (left), carefully following the trail atop the cliffs past several spots that offer sweeping views; the best views are at the far end of the cliffs. Wachusett Mountain, with its ski slopes, is visible to the southwest.

As you explore the cliffs, take care not to kick any loose stones or wander near the cliff's edge as there are often rock climbers and hikers below. From the last open ledges, the Midstate Trail swings to the southwest, entering the woods again and continuing about 75 yards, then turning southeast (left) and descending a steep, rocky gully. At its bottom, turn north (left) and, diverging from the Midstate, walk the trail around the base of the cliffs to this loop's beginning. Turn east (right) with the trail to descend to the parking lot.

technical climbers at the base of the Crow Hills cliff face

© HEIDI J. BROWN

Options

The Crow Hills cliff face is one of the more popular rock climbing spots in the state. Technical climbers are required to obtain a permit (free of charge) at park headquarters before heading out to the cliffs.

Directions

The hike begins from a large parking lot at the Crow Hills Pond Picnic Area along Route 31 on the Westminster/Princeton line, 2.2 miles south of the junction of Routes 31 and 2 and 1.5 miles north of the junction of Routes 31 and 140.
GPS Coordinates: 42.5351 N, 71.8541 W

Contact

A $5 parking fee is collected May–October; a season pass costs $35. Dogs on leash are allowed. A free, basic trail map of Leominster State Forest is available at the state forest headquarters or at the Massachusetts Division of State Parks and Recreation website. The *Mount Wachusett and Leominster State Forest Trail* map costs $4 from New England Cartographics (413/549-4124 or toll-free 888/995-6277, www.necartographics.com). For more information, contact Leominster State Forest, Rte. 31, Princeton, MA 01541, 978/874-2303. Massachusetts Division of State Parks and Recreation, 251 Causeway St., Suite 600, Boston, MA 02114-2104, 617/626-1250, www.state.ma.us.

6 LEOMINSTER FOREST ROADS LOOP

Leominster State Forest in Westminster, Princeton, and Leominster

Level: Moderate

Total Distance: 5.5 miles

Hiking Time: 2.5 hours

Elevation: 50 feet

Summary: Spot wildlife, enjoy the forest quiet, and get ready to ramble on this long, level loop through the woods.

Leominster State Forest is only a short drive from Boston, but this 5.5-mile loop hike through a seemingly endless forest will make you feel a world away from bustling Beantown. Leominster's woods are made up of towering pines, pockets of birch, ash, oak, elm, beech, and thick stands of mountain laurel. In other words: classic New England forest growth. This hike largely follows old forest roads through the southern half of Leominster State Forest, and though demanding in length, the terrain is relatively flat and the footing easy, making this an excellent longer

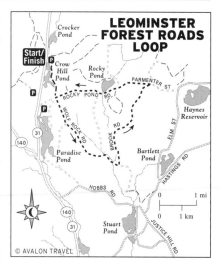

trek for novice hikers. Please note that though trail names have road names, they are not open to motor vehicle traffic, but they are open to mountain bikers. Take care when hiking to stay on the right side of the trail to avoid oncoming bikes.

From the parking lot, cross the picnic area and the earthen dike dividing the two halves of Crow Hills Pond. Across the dike, turn south (right), following the trail along the pond for about 0.7 mile. The pond's calm waters are a natural haven for waterfowl and it is common to spot heron, mallards, and Canada geese taking a swim here. As the pond gives way to a marshy southern shore, the trail reaches an intersection with the dirt Rocky Pond Road. Cross Rocky Pond Road onto Wolf Rock Road and continue about 0.5 mile.

Now deep in the woods, the road becomes coated with pine needles and sounds are muffled. With so much room, wildlife can be found abundantly here. If you're lucky, you might spot wild turkey taking a stroll or white-tailed deer darting among the shady groves of hemlock. Continue following Wolf Rock Road until you reach a fork (about 0.5 mile from Rocky Pond). Here, bear east (left) to stay on the road.

Continuing along through the woods, you descend a steep hill on the road before turning north (left) onto Brook Road. Follow Brook Road about 1.2 miles to Parmenter Road. Turn left (west), climbing a hill and crossing from Leominster into Princeton, where the road becomes Rocky Pond Road. From the road's high point, continue west for less than a mile to the junction of Rocky Pond Road, Wolf Rock Road, and the trail from Crow Hills Pond; turn north to return to this hike's start.

woods road, Leominster State Forest

© HEIDI J. BROWN

Options

Leominster is in the "snow belt" of Massachusetts, a section of northern Worcester County that sees some of the highest snowfall totals in the state. Snowshoeing this hike makes for a pleasant winter outing, but short sections of this loop that follow footpaths would be difficult under heavy snow. Snowshoers (or cross-country skiers) might instead begin this loop from the dirt parking area and gate where Rocky Pond Road crosses Route 31, 0.6 mile south of the main parking area.

Directions

The hike begins from a large parking lot at the Crow Hills Pond Picnic Area along Route 31 on the Westminster/Princeton line, 2.2 miles south of the junction of Routes 31 and 2 and 1.5 miles north of the junction of Routes 31 and 140.
GPS Coordinates: 42.5351 N, 71.8541 W

Contact

A $5 parking fee is collected May–October; a season pass costs $35. The parking lot may not always be plowed in winter; call the state forest headquarters before leaving for the trailhead. Dogs on leash are allowed. A free, basic trail map of Leominster State Forest is available at the state forest headquarters or at the Massachusetts Division of State Parks and Recreation website. The *Mount Wachusett and Leominster State Forest Trail* map costs $4 from New England Cartographics (413/549-4124 or toll-free 888/995-6277, www.necartographics.com). For more information, contact Leominster State Forest, Rte. 31, Princeton, MA 01541, 978/874-2303. Massachusetts Division of State Parks and Recreation, 251 Causeway St., Suite 600, Boston, MA 02114-2104, 617/626-1250, www.state.ma.us.

7 PINE HILL TRAIL

Wachusett Mountain State Reservation in Princeton

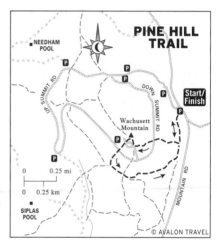

Level: Strenuous

Hiking Time: 1.5 hours

Total Distance: 2.0 miles

Elevation: 500 feet

Summary: A short, steep hop up to the top of the region's tallest peak, this former ski trail will test your skills at defying gravity.

A scant 40 miles from Boston, 2,006-foot Mount Wachusett, a great mound of a mountain whose name means "by the hill" in the Algonquin dialect, is the highest peak in the state between the Connecticut River valley and Atlantic Ocean. Wachusett may be better known for its downhill ski area (and the incessant commercials for the ski resort that have become a Boston media staple in winter). But the state reservation has a fairly extensive network of fine hiking trails, including a section of the long-distance Midstate Trail that passes over the summit. The shortest of the mountain's trails to reach the glorious views from the open Wachusett summit, the Pine Hill Trail is a steep, rocky climb that could be dangerous in snowy or icy conditions. Even on the loveliest of sunny days, this hike is a real leg stretcher.

From the visitors center parking lot, look for a dirt path leaving south from the visitor information center and marked with a large white sign for the Bicentennial Trail. Follow the Bicentennial Trail for only about 0.1 mile to the first trail branching off to the west (right), the Pine Hill Trail—actually an old ski trail that has since been reclaimed under the cover of a pine-laden forest. With pine needle duff underfoot and shady pine boughs overhead, the trail at first ascends at a moderate grade, heading due west up the mountain. After 0.2 mile, the trail crosses the Summit Road. Pay attention here to vehicle traffic; the Summit Road is open to cars April–mid-October.

Continuing on, the Pine Tree Trail gives way to rockier footing as its steepness intensifies. Still heading due west, the uphill climb reaches the summit in another 0.3 mile from the Summit Road. Picnic areas, observation decks, bathrooms, and

moss-covered rock on the Pine Hill Trail

a parking area await at the summit; expect crowds (who likely arrived by car or even tour bus) on most weekends through summer and early fall. It's no wonder so many flock here: the views are nothing short of amazing. Radiating out from the mountain, the vista stretches as far away as the Berkshires to the west and Boston and the Atlantic Ocean to the east.

After checking out the views from various spots on the broad summit, those with good knees, and who are prepared to possibly run down the mountain, are welcome to make the return trip on the Pine Hill Trail (but even very fit hikers should not attempt this in icy or wet conditions). For a more gentle descent and one with more scenic views, cross to the summit's southwest corner and look for the trail sign for the Harrington Trail. Descending the Harrington, you soon cross the paved summit road; after reentering the woods, take a short side path east (left) off the Harrington to enjoy a long view west over the sparsely populated hills and valleys of central Massachusetts. Backtrack and descend the Harrington to an intersection with the Link Trail. Turn east (left) at the sign for the Link Trail, follow less than 0.1 mile before turning slightly southeast to pick up the Mountain House Trail, marked with a sign. Descend briefly on the Mountain House Trail, and then bear east (left) onto the Loop Trail, which descends to the Bicentennial Trail. Turn north (left) to return to the visitors center in another 0.5 mile.

Options

For a fun side trip, pay a quick visit to Balanced Rock, a glacial-erratic boulder that lives up to its name. From the parking lot you passed about 0.5 mile before the parking lot for this hike, pick up the Midstate Trail's yellow triangular blazes heading west out of the lot. Here the trail is also known as the Balanced Rock Trail. Follow it, climbing gently, for 0.3 mile to Balanced Rock. Return the way you came.

Directions

From Route 140, 2.2 miles south of the junction of Routes 140 and 2 in Westminster and 1.8 miles north of the junction of Routes 140 and 31, turn onto Mile Hill Road, following signs to the Wachusett Mountain State Reservation Visitor Center.

GPS Coordinates: 42.5114 N, 71.8866 W

Contact

A daily parking fee of $2 is collected mid-May–mid-October. Dogs on leash are allowed. A free contour map of hiking trails is available at the visitors center and at the Massachusetts Division of State Parks and Recreation website. The Mount *Wachusett and Leominster State Forest Trail* map costs $4 from New England Cartographics (413/549-4124 or toll-free 888/995-6277, www.necartographics.com). For more information, contact Wachusett Mountain State Reservation, Mountain Rd., P.O. Box 248, Princeton, MA 01541, 978/464-2987. Massachusetts Division of State Parks and Recreation, 251 Causeway St., Suite 600, Boston, MA 02114-2104, 617/626-1250, www.state.ma.us.

8 WACHUSETT SUMMIT LOOP

Wachusett Mountain State Reservation in Princeton

Level: Strenuous

Total Distance: 5.0 miles

Hiking Time: 3. hours

Elevation: 700 feet

Summary: Take your time reaching the top of the largest peak in the region by first taking a woods walk to explore the mountain's old growth forest.

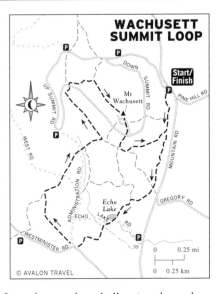

Because of its height and impractical use as farmland for 18th- and 19th-century New England farmers, large portions of 2,006-foot Mount Wachusett have been left with original old growth forest intact. Many of the oaks, maples, and ash trees on Mount Wachusett are thought to be more than 350 years old. This hike to the summit follows a circuitous, but enjoyable route up the largest mountain in central Massachusetts, taking advantage of the extensive trail network here and offering plenty of opportunities to explore the old growth forest. Rocky and steep for brief stretches, this hike ascends only about 700 feet in elevation and makes for a pleasant, but challenging day trek.

From the visitors center parking lot, follow the Bicentennial Trail for about a mile as it flows south and then west in a contour around the mountain's base, passing three trail junctions along the way. At the junction with High Meadow Trail, bear south (left) to follow the High Meadow Trail across an open, wildflower-filled meadow and then back into the woods again before reaching Echo Lake. Stay to the southeast (left) on the gravel road beside the lake for about 0.1 mile, turn south (left) on the Echo Lake Trail, and follow it less than 0.5 mile to a parking lot. Here, pick up the Stage Coach Trail at its trail sign on the northwestern edge of the parking area. At first climbing steadily up an old carriage road, the Stage Coach Trail narrows to a footpath, still heading uphill.

After more than 0.5 mile on the Stage Coach Trail, bear northeast (right) on the Harrington Trail. It crosses West Road, then the Administration Road, before suddenly growing much steeper as it makes a direct line for the summit. But

© HEIDI J. BROWN

Mount Wachusett

right before that steep part begins, turn northwest (left) on the Semuhenna Trail, staying on it for about 0.5 mile, and passing through a few nice stands of ancient oaks and maples. Cross the paved summit road, reenter the woods, and then immediately turn east (right) on the West Side Trail. You're on that path for less than 0.5 mile before turning south (right) on the Old Indian Trail, the steepest part of this hike. As you climb to the summit, you'll pass a ski area chairlift station right before reaching the top.

Enjoy the expansive views from the summit and then it's time to descend. Cross the summit to the paved auto road that heads down, follow it about 100 feet, and then bear south (right) into the woods on the Mountain House Trail. Descend about 0.25 mile, turn east with the trail to continue another 0.25 mile or less, and turn east (left) again to join the Loop Trail, descending over rocks to the Bicentennial Trail. Turn north (left) on the Bicentennial for the return to the visitors center.

Options

For a shorter trip to the summit that still takes you to various sites around the mountain, try the Jack Frost Trail. When you reach High Meadow Trail, turn north (instead of south) and follow it to an intersection with the Jack Frost Trail. Passing through dense hemlock forest, the Jack Frost Trail joins with the Mountain House Trail for a moderate 0.6 mile push to the summit. Descend from the summit by the route described in the main hike.

Directions

From Route 140, 2.2 miles south of the junction of Routes 140 and 2 in West-minster and 1.8 miles north of the junction of Routes 140 and 31, turn onto Mile Hill Road, following signs to the Wachusett Mountain State Reservation Visitor Center.

GPS Coordinates: 42.5114 N, 71.8866 W

Contact

A daily parking fee of $2 is collected mid-May–mid-October. Dogs on leash are allowed. A free contour map of hiking trails is available at the visitors center or at the Massachusetts Division of State Parks and Recreation website. The *Mount Wachusett and Leominster State Forest Trail* map costs $4 from New England Cartographics (413/549-4124 or toll-free 888/995-6277, www.necartographics.com). For more information, contact Wachusett Mountain State Reservation, Mountain Rd., P.O. Box 248, Princeton, MA 01541, 978/464-2987. Massachusetts Division of State Parks and Recreation, 251 Causeway St., Suite 600, Boston, MA 02114-2104, 617/626-1250, www.state.ma.us

9 MOUNT HOLYOKE

Skinner State Park in Hadley

Level: Moderate

Hiking Time: 2 hours

Total Distance: 3.2 miles

Elevation: 400 feet

Summary: Take a trip up the rocky ridge of Mount Holyoke to glorious views from the landmark Summit House, a former grand hotel.

Mount Holyoke is the westernmost summit of the Holyoke Range, a seven-mile long, five-peaked outcropping of metamorphic traprock. As it rises up from the Connecticut River and pushes to its terminus in Amherst, the range forms an almost unbroken ridgeline. At 878 feet, Mount Holyoke may be the most distinct of these summits, not just for its position towering above the Connecticut River and busy I-91, but also for the landmark Summit House that sits atop its western slope. (In the 1800s, the Summit House was a grand resort hotel, but today is operated by Skinner State Park and is open to the public.) This hike to the Summit House and the top of Mount Holyoke is one of the most popular climbs in the Pioneer Valley and for good reason; for not too much effort, the views west toward the Berkshires and south into Connecticut are simply stunning.

From the roadside pull-off, you will see a sign for the Metacomet-Monadnock (M&M) Trail at the entrance to a small footpath leaving east from the road. Follow the white blazes into the woods and immediately begin climbing a steep hillside. As tree cover begins to thin, the trail swings north and ascends the rocky ridge, reaching the first views in just over 0.5 mile.

Continuing to traverse the steplike traprock, at 1.6 miles, the trail passes by the historic Summit House; if you would like to duck inside for a bit of exploring, the Summit House is open weekends Memorial Day–Columbus Day for tours and programs. Picnic grounds also mark the top of Holyoke and numerous observation points offer unmatched views of the Connecticut Valley. An auto road also leads visitors to the top of Mount Holyoke and on most summer and fall weekends, the

© HEIDI J. BROWN

view from Mount Holyoke

place is packed with picnickers taking in the sights. If you crave solitude, be sure to come on a weekday when you just may have the summit to yourself.

You can return the way you came or continue over the summit, crossing the paved Mountain Road and turning right (south) in Taylor's Notch onto the red-blazed Dry Brook Trail. Follow it down the small valley, trending to the southwest and finally to the west and back to your vehicle.

Options
The long-distance Metacomet-Monadnock Trail stretches for 117 miles, from the blue-blazed Metacomet Trail on the Connecticut state line to Mount Monadnock in New Hampshire. The Holyoke Range ridgeline is considered one of the most scenic walks on the entire trail and very fit hikers could manage the 14-mile round-trip hike in one very long day on the trail. From the summit of Mount Holyoke, continue to follow the white blazes east, dropping and rising with the M&M trail to reach the summits of Mount Hitchcock (1,005 feet), Bare Mountain (1,010 feet), Mount Norwottuck (1,106 feet), and Long Mountain (920 feet).

Directions
From the junction of Routes 47 and 9 in Hadley, drive south on Route 47 for 4.9 miles (you'll see the Summit House on the Mount Holyoke ridge straight ahead). Across from the Hockanum Cemetery, turn left, continue 0.1 mile, and park at the roadside where the white blazes of the Metacomet-Monadnock Trail enter the

woods on the right. Or from the junction of Routes 47 and 116 in South Hadley, drive north on Route 47 for 2.7 miles, turn right at Hockanum Cemetery, and then continue 0.1 mile to the trailhead.

GPS Coordinates: 42.3084 N, 72.5896 W

Contact

Parking and access are free. Dogs on leash are allowed. A free trail map of Skinner State Park is available at the Halfway House on Mountain Road (off Route 47) when a staff person is there; at the Notch Visitor Center on Route 116, where the Metacomet-Monadnock Trail crosses the road and enters Holyoke Range State Park in Amherst; or at the Massachusetts Division of State Parks and Recreation website. The *Holyoke Range/Skinner State Park Trail* map (western section) costs $4 from New England Cartographics (413/549-4124 or toll-free 888/995-6277, www.necartographics.com). For more information, contact Skinner State Park, Rte. 47, Box 91, Hadley, MA 01035, 413/586-0350 or 413/253-2883. Massachusetts Division of State Parks and Recreation, 251 Causeway St., Suite 600, Boston, MA 02114-2104, 617/626-1250, www.state.ma.us.

10 RATTLESNAKE KNOB AND THE HORSE CAVES

BEST

Mount Holyoke Range State Park, Granby

Level: Easy/Moderate

Total Distance: 4.5 miles

Hiking Time: 2.5 hours

Elevation: 200 feet

Summary: Travel back in time as you explore the horse caves, the supposed hideout for Daniel Shays and his followers during the tax revolt event known as Shays' Rebellion.

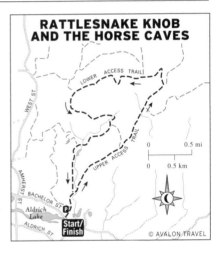

RATTLESNAKE KNOB AND THE HORSE CAVES

© AVALON TRAVEL

The highest point on the saddle between Mounts Long and Norwottuck, at an elevation of 813 feet, Rattlesnake Knob's relatively easy climb and excellent views make it a worthy destination along the ridgy Holyoke Range's eastern end. This hike also takes you to the Horse Caves, a large cleft in the rocks near the base of Mount Norwottuck. The caves are an interesting geological formation to explore, but are most well known for the supposed role they played as the hideout for Daniel Shays and his followers after their raid on the Springfield Arsenal in 1786, part of the tax revolt known as Shays' Rebellion. This is a great hike for bringing history class alive for kids and only comes with a modest few hundred feet in elevation gain.

From the parking area, reach the trailhead at a brown metal gate marked Main Entrance. On the other side of the gate, follow the well-worn path to a junction at 0.2 mile. Here, bear north (right) on the Upper Access Trail. For the next mile, the trail passes through a pleasant forest of oaks and hickory, stands of birch, and pine. Listen for the sound of woodpeckers and note their telltale drill holes in the bark of many of the trees along the route. At 0.9 mile, pass a rusted out old car (and make a guess as to how it ended up here) and then at 1.6 miles, bear east (right) onto the red-blazed Cliffside Trail. From here it's only a few feet to a left turn west onto the combined Robert Frost Trail (orange blazed) and Metacomet-Monadnock Trail (white blazed). At 1.7 miles, bear northwest at a fork (left) to stay with the orange and white blazes as the trail begins to climb the rocky hillside.

© HEIDI J. BROWN

Horse Caves

Reaching Rattlesnake Knob in another 0.1 mile, follow the sign marked To View-point. From the open ledge of Rattlesnake, Mount Long rises in a green mound to the east and to the north lies the village of Amherst and surrounding Pioneer Valley countryside.

Backtracking from the viewing area, follow the orange and white blazes again as they pass over the knob and drop quickly to reach a sign for the Horse Caves (at 2.1 miles). Bear north and follow the Horse Cave trail less than 0.5 mile to the caves. The rocky cliff overhangs are certainly large enough to have sheltered quite a few men and their horses, but most historians are doubtful this event ever took place, pointing to the large number of people in the Amherst community who sympathized with Daniel Shays and no doubt would have provided a place to hide. Or, perhaps it was one of these locals who recommended the caves as the perfect place to hide. Whatever the truth may be, the trek to see these unusual caves is worth the historical uncertainty.

Once you are done exploring, retrace your steps to the orange and white blazes and continue downhill. At the next junction, bear south onto the blue blazes of the Swamp Trail and follow 0.4 mile to turn west (right) onto the Southside Trail. At 3.2 miles, turn onto the trail marked Lower Access Trails to B-Street Gate. Follow past a large beaver dam and then bear south (right) at the last trail junction before returning to your car.

Options

Reaching the summit of Mount Norwottuck only adds another 0.6 mile to the hike and is well worth the effort for the stunning views from its open top. From the horse caves, the Robert Frost Trail/Metacomet-Monadnock Trail swings south and then hooks north for a short, steep push to the summit over rocky terrain. To return, return to the horse caves and then retrace your steps to the trailhead.

Directions

From Springfield, take I-91 north to Exit 19. From the exit, follow Route 9 east, soon crossing the Connecticut River. At 0.5 mile, turn right onto Bay Road, follow signs for Route 47 south. At 2.3 miles from the highway, turn left to remain on Bay Road and leave Route 47. At 5.2 miles, reach Atkins Farms Country Market and turn right onto Route 116 south. At 6.4 miles, turn left into the Notch Visitor Center for free maps and an interesting natural history center. Reach the trailhead by continuing south on Route 116, turning left onto Amherst Street at 7.5 miles (at a sign for Route 202 and Granby). At 7.9 miles, turn left onto Bachelor Street. Finally, at 8.6 miles, park on either shoulder of the road when you reach a brown metal gate on your left.

GPS Coordinates: 42.2811 N, 72.4938 W

Contact

Parking and access are free. Dogs are allowed. A free trail map and informational brochure are available at the park entrance at the Notch Visitor Center on Route 116, where the Metacomet-Monadnock Trail crosses the road and enters Holyoke Range State Park in Amherst; or at the Massachusetts Division of State Parks and Recreation website. The *Holyoke Range/Skinner State Park Trail* map (western section) costs $4 from New England Cartographics (413/549-4124 or toll-free 888/995-6277, www.necartographics.com). For more information, contact Mount Holyoke State Park, Rte. 116, Amherst, MA 01002, 413/586-0350. Massachusetts Division of State Parks and Recreation, 251 Causeway St., Suite 600, Boston, MA 02114-2104, 617/626-1250, www.state.ma.us.

11 QUABBIN RESERVOIR

BEST (

Belchertown

Level: Easy

Total Distance: 4.0 miles

Hiking Time: 2 hours

Elevation: 100 feet

Summary: Go bird-watching or simply take a pleasant woods walk as you explore the land surrounding the vast Quabbin Reservoir, Boston's main public water supply.

Created in the 1930s by the construction of two huge earthen dams along the Swift River, the vast Quabbin Reservoir is the main public water supply for the metro Boston area. As you stand on the shores and look out over this massive 39-square-mile body of water, it is almost impossible to imagine that 80 years ago, entire towns existed here. Though it is artificial, the Quabbin still qualifies as the largest inland body of water in Massachusetts.

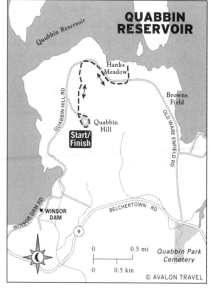

Surrounding the reservoir is Quabbin Park, managed by the state as a recreational area, with hiking and bike trails crisscrossing acres of woods and many low, rolling hills. This easy hike takes you from Quabbin Hill to the scenic Enfield Lookout for expansive views of the reservoir and surrounding Swift River valley. You should bring bug spray and be prepared to check for ticks after your hike (white-tailed deer are found in large populations here), but leave your swimsuit at home. Despite all the water, public water supply regulations make swimming and boating on the Quabbin strictly off-limits.

From the parking area near the top of Quabbin Hill, walk a few more feet uphill to the stone observation tower and views north toward the water. Backtracking to the parking area, the yellow-blazed trailhead is located on the eastern end of the lot. Follow the trail on a gentle descent through pleasant woods; frequent breaks in the tress offer glimpses of the reservoir off in the distance. After a mile of walking, cross through a grassy area (follow the yellow markers) to turn east (right) onto a dirt jeep road. After only a few yards, arrive at an intersection with a paved road. Turn east on the paved road to reach the Enfield Lookout, an upland bluff not far from the shoreline. This is an extremely popular perch for local bird-watchers. Soaring bald eagles and red-tail hawks are often spotted here, as well as great blue heron.

great blue heron, Quabbin Reservoir

To reach the water's edge, retrace your steps to the dirt road and take a right to head north, descending another 0.75 mile through thick stands of pine (known as the Pine Plantation) before reaching the shore. For the two-mile return trip to your car, follow the dirt road back to the hiking trail, climbing uphill to the parking lot.

Options

For a truly unique walk, the Dana Trail follows the old Petersham-Dana Road to the former town common of Dana. (Dana had to be vacated by residents because of its proximity to the reservoir). A flat walk surrounded by the reservoir's signature pine woods, the trail reaches a marker for the Dana town common at 1.8 miles. The foundation outlines can still be faintly seen of the hotel, stores, and several homes that once stood here. Retrace your steps on the return. Parking for the Dana Trailhead is found at Gate 40.

Directions

From the corner of West Street and Route 9/Main Street in downtown Ware, turn left on Main Street and follow for 4.7 miles to a right turn at a sign for the Quabbin Reservoir (as Route 9 leaves Ware, it is also called Belchertown Road). Follow the park access road for 0.3 mile to the parking area (almost at the top of Quabbin Hill).

GPS Coordinates: 42.2160 N, 71.9999 W

Contact

Parking and access are free. State regulations require visitors to enter and exit through gates or other designated areas only; no off-trail hiking or biking. Anything that could pollute the water supply system, such as litter or refuse of any sort, is prohibited. Direct water contact activities, such as swimming and wading, are strictly prohibited by regulation. Dogs and pets are not allowed on any property associated with Quabbin Reservoir.

A free trail map is available at the Quabbin Visitor Center. For more information, contact Quabbin Visitor Center, 485 Ware Rd. (Rte. 9), Belchertown, MA 01007, 413/323-7221. Massachusetts Division of State Parks and Recreation, 251 Causeway St., Suite 600, Boston, MA 02114-2104, 617/626-1250, www. state.ma.us.

12 HOWE POND
Spencer

Summary: Bridle trails take you on a tour of the former estate grounds of Elias Howe, the inventor of the sewing machine.

Level: Easy

Total Distance: 1.0 mile

Hiking Time: 30 minutes

Elevation: 10 feet

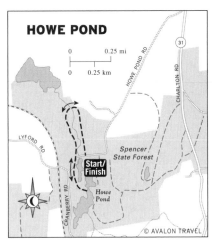

At almost 1,000 acres, Spencer State Forest is a landscape of hilly terrain, creeks, wetlands, and a beautiful transitional forest of oak, hickory, ash, and birch. The forest's most notable feature is the Howe Pond parcel, an estate formerly belonging to Elias Howe, the inventor of the sewing machine. Though the remains of the estate are limited to the old mill pond as well as a winding system of bridle trails constructed by the inventor, their peaceful setting in the Spencer woods still makes for a pleasant, and relatively flat, forest ramble. This gentle one-mile stroll is a perfect outing for small children.

From the parking area, first take in the beauty of the woods by crossing the road and heading north along the old bridle trail. A loop of about 0.5 mile, the trail takes you by the upper reaches of the Cranberry River, an especially pleasing stroll in autumn, when the wetlands here are a little less mosquito infested. Because trails see relatively light traffic from human visitors, even in summer (most visitors just head to the pond for swimming), wildlife feel quite at home in the Spencer woods. Just steps from the parking, don't be surprised to find frogs and garter snakes sharing the path with you, or perhaps a wild turkey wobbling along the trail.

Crossing over the river, the trail brings you back to the parking area. Next, head south past the picnic area to reach the Howe Pond. The trail passes over the dam and then hugs the shore of the Mill Pond, a popular swimming hole in summer. There is no loop around the pond, but it is possible to walk to the end of the trail about halfway around the water's edge. Farther away from the swimming area, the pond is a good place to spot ducks, wild geese, and sometimes a heron or two stopping by for a visit. From this spot, retrace your steps back to your car.

Howe Pond

Options

Spencer State Forest is unusual among Massachusetts State park offerings because it is divided into three parcels, each with its own hiking trails and entrance points, and each one divided from the other by a major road (and very much providing the sense of being a park within a park.) If more exploration of Spencer State Forest is desired, try the northernmost parcel, notable for its pleasant mix of woods and wetlands—and for the segment of the long-distance Midstate Trail crossing through its northeast quadrant.

Directions

From the center of Spencer, head east on Main Street toward Maple Street. Take the first right onto Maple Street and follow for one mile to a right turn onto Howe Road. Follow Howe Road for one mile to the forest entrance; keep following the road a short distance to the parking and picnic area.

GPS Coordinates: 42.2158 N, 71.9990 W

Contact

Parking and access are free. Dogs on leash are allowed. A free trail map is available near the picnic/parking area or online from the Massachusetts Division of State Parks and Recreation. For more information, contact Spencer State Forest, Howe Rd., Spencer, MA, 01562, 508/886-6333. Massachusetts Division of State Parks and Recreation, 251 Causeway St., Suite 600, Boston, MA 02114-2104, 617/626-1250, www.state.ma.us.

13 CARPENTER ROCKS
Wells State Park in Sturbridge

Level: Easy

Total Distance: 2.5 miles

Hiking Time: 1.5 hours

Elevation: 50 feet

Summary: Visit a picturesque wetland and explore glacially carved cliffs in this quiet patch of woods near Sturbridge Village.

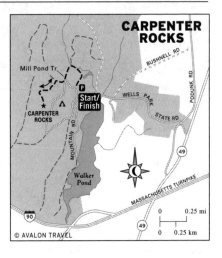

If your travels have led you to Sturbridge Village, the landmark living history museum that portrays an authentic New England village, circa 1800, why not enhance your outing with a side trip to explore the area's rich geological history? Nearby in Sturbridge, the 1,400-acre Wells State Park serves as a good example of how the last Ice Age affected New England. This hike takes you through a forest floor choked with giant glacial erratic boulders on the way to the massive cliff face of Carpenter Rocks, a great outcropping of metamorphic rock that was scraped clean of any soil cover by the massive ice sheets. A low-elevation walk in the woods until a final scramble to the top of the cliffs, this trail also takes you to Mill Pond, a picturesque wetland that serves as a favorite hangout for local waterfowl.

From the parking area, follow the markers for the Mill Pond Trail, a universally accessible trail. A little more than 0.25 mile in length, the level path takes you to the shore of Mill Pond, a serene little pool of water that's home to ducks, Canada geese, and beaver, before ambling off for a pleasant route through the woods. At the end of the trail, continue straight ahead onto the North Trail footpath (wheelchair users should double back to the trailhead from this point for a complete trip of 0.5 mile). Now heading north, the woods here are simply stunning. As forest cover closes in overhead, you will suddenly find yourself in a classic New England woods of eastern white pine and mixed groves of ash, beech, birch, and oak. An understory of mountain laurel along both sides of the trail makes this a worthy trip in June to take in the white blooms of the wild rhododendron.

In a very short distance, North Trail crosses a stream and reaches a trail junction.

upper end of Mill Pond

Here, turn east (left) on the smaller footpath, this is the trail that will lead you to Carpenter Rocks. Continue on for another 0.5 mile through a mix of hardwood forest and wetland. As you come upon the cliff, the trail suddenly grows much more rugged and steep and, almost without knowing it, you are on the cliff tops taking in a sweeping vista of nearby Walker Pond (the state park's swimming pond) and the surrounding wooded valley. Return the way you came.

Options

For a more watery end to your day in Sturbridge, leave from the parking area on campground road, heading due south to hug the shore of Walker Pond. Stop for a swim or a quick picnic (or make it a weekend by camping in the state park campground) and then continue on to the southern tip of the lake. Now on the Mountain Road Trail, the footpath hooks west and then north to ascend a ridge that treads high above the lake for an equally scenic return to the parking area, a total round-trip of about 1.2 miles.

Directions

Follow the Massachusetts Turnpike (I-90) to Exit 9 (Sturbridge). After the toll booths, follow Route 20 east less than a mile to the intersection with Route 49. Turn left onto Route 49 north. The park entrance is the third left off Route 49. **GPS Coordinates:** 42.1425 N, 72.0408 W

CAPE COD

© HEIDI J. BROWN

BEST HIKES

❰ Coastal Hikes
Province Lands Trail, **page 250**
Great Island Trail, **page 256**

❰ Wheelchair Access
Cape Cod Rail Trail, **page 268**

Henry David Thoreau once wrote that Cape Cod

is a place, "where a man can put all of America behind him." Standing on one of Cape Cod's windswept beaches, staring out into the vastness of the Atlantic, it's easy to understand that Thoreau wasn't just talking about the location of the Cape as one of the easternmost points in the United States

Across the Cape Cod canal, a completely different geography awaits. Created approximately 20,000 years ago, Cape Cod represents the approximate terminus of the massive ice sheet that once covered North America, and the region's unique landscape owes itself to the large deposits of glacial moraine that gradually built up into a distinctly shaped peninsula. Winds and vegetation also transformed the Cape and today, covering this 413-square-mile spit of land, jutting like a bent arm off the Massachusetts mainland, is a surprising mix of terrain, from sandy beaches, hilly scrub forest, and fresh water kettle ponds to coastal swamps, bogs, and dune-top meadows.

Cape Cod's natural features have also been influenced by human activity. Once populated by the Wampanoag, Native Americans who primarily fished, hunted, and took part in small scale farming, English colonists and early Americans who settled here almost succeeded in completely deforesting Cape Cod in their pursuit of lumber and cleared farmland. Though forest cover has rebounded, the types of trees have changed. Pockets of native Atlantic white cedar remain (and a hike to the Atlantic White Cedar Swamp will take you through one of these groves), but most of Cape Cod's forest cover is now pitch pine and scrub oak.

As forest growth has increased in recent years, so has the number of wild animals living on the Cape. Forest hikes in the area will usually offer glimpses of such creatures as box turtles, red fox, raccoons, opossums, and flying squirrels. Closer to the water, hikes to Cape beaches such as Race Point may take you in sight of humpback whales off the coast or seals sunning themselves near the shore. Coastal bird species on Cape Cod include the endangered piping plover and least tern.

It really does live up to the hype; Cape Cod truly feels like no place else on earth. And helping Cape Cod retain this wild maritime flavor is the Cape Cod National Seashore, a federally protected preserve occupying over 40 miles of pristine sandy beach, marshes, ponds, and forested uplands. A true glimpse of Cape Cod's past and continuing ways of life, covered boardwalk trails lead through terrain with a still-untouched feel. Highlights here include the Great Island Trail, an unforgettable place to watch the sunset over Cape Cod Bay, and the Province Lands Trail, taking you all the way to Race Point beach at the very tip of Cape Cod. Other hiking terrain on the Cape takes place in state parks and locally controlled land reserves.

Winter weather is erratic on Cape Cod, but generally milder in this area than much of New England, opening up opportunities for visiting many of these places year-round without having to deal with snow or extreme cold. More commonly, visitors must deal with wind and, in certain seasons, biting insects and traffic. Cape Cod sees more rain than snow in winter; if the weather is dry, and the winds calm, hiking here often extends into early December and starts again in early spring. No matter what time of year you take to the trails, your best bet is to dress in layers for changing conditions.

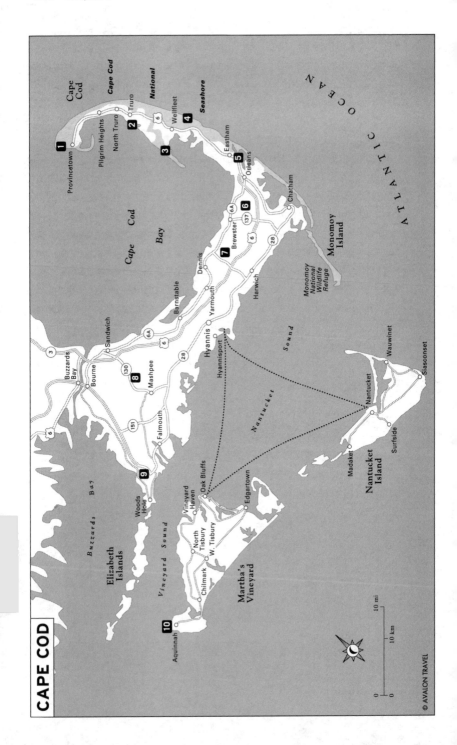

CAPE COD

© AVALON TRAVEL

TRAIL NAME	LEVEL	DISTANCE	TIME	ELEVATION	FEATURES	PAGE
1 Province Lands Trail	Easy/Moderate	6.0 mi	3 hr	50 ft		250
2 Ryder Beach and Atwood-Higgins House	Easy/Moderate	4.0 mi	2 hr	20 ft		253
3 Great Island Trail	Easy/Moderate	6.0 mi	3.5 hr	20 ft		256
4 Atlantic White Cedar Swamp	Easy	1.2 mi	30 min	15 ft		259
5 Nauset Marsh	Easy	1.2 mi	45 min	10 ft		262
6 Nickerson Kettle Ponds	Moderate	4.0 mi	2 hr	0 ft		265
7 Cape Cod Rail Trail	Easy	10.0 mi	5 hr	20 ft		268
8 Lowell Holly Reservation	Easy	3.0 mi	1.5 hr	0 ft		271
9 Beebe Woods and Punch Bowl	Easy	1.5 mi	1 hr	10 ft		273
10 Aquinnah	Easy	3.0 mi	1.5 hr	0 ft		276

1 PROVINCE LANDS TRAIL

BEST ◖

Cape Cod National Seashore in Provincetown

Level: Easy/Moderate

Total Distance: 6.0 miles

Hiking Time: 3 hours

Elevation: 50 feet

Summary: A paved bike path takes you deep into one of the last wild places on Cape Cod.

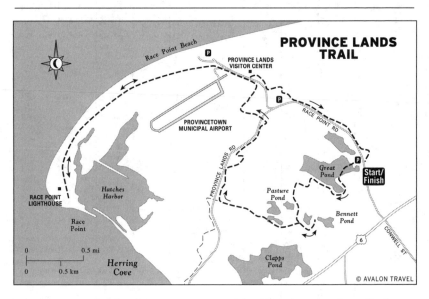

The barren spectacle of the Province Lands' rolling dunes and small, almost stranded-looking forests of scrub oak and bayberry were created thanks to the over-settlement of the Cape in the 18th century. As the once-thick forest covering even this most remote tip of Cape Cod was harvested for housing and fuel, top soil quickly eroded, leaving only windswept sand and the vegetation that could take hold in such a harsh environment.

Making a circuitous loop through forest, past ponds, and over sprawling sand dunes, the paved path that cuts through the Province Lands is popular with bikers, hikers, runners, inline skaters both young and old, and it's good for wheelchairs, too. Be sure to take the spur path 0.5 mile out to Race Point (included in the mileage), which is near the very tip of Massachusetts and a great place for whale-watching during the seasonal migrations, when the whales often swim close to shore. Because the trail is such a popular destination, heed the center dividing line on this path, especially around its many blind corners.

Province Lands Trail

Pick up the bike path from the Beech Forest parking lot at the marked trail sign, just steps away from the picnic area. Beech Forest itself is a serene land preserve known for its excellent bird-watching, especially in spring and early fall when the marshy forest lands serve as a major resting stop for semi-annual shore and seabird migrations along the Great North–South American Flyway. If you visit at these times, you will want to bring along your binoculars. And because there are birds here, don't be surprised if you spot a fox or two darting about trying to secure supper.

Following the bike path as it winds west and southwest, the trail passes stands of some of the last few remaining native hardwood trees in this outer region of the National Seashore. After approximately one mile, a spur trail leaves to the left (south) heading to Bennett Pond, one of the Province Lands' kettle ponds. (If you decide to explore the pond, this will add another 0.5 mile to the hike.) Continuing on, the still-forested path swings to the northwest, taking you within view of a few smaller kettle ponds. Reaching a trail junction in another 0.5 mile, here turn east (right) with the path. For the next mile, the path grows hilly as forest cover gives way to undulating sand dunes. Your legs will probably feel the burn as you continuously ascend and descend, but reaching the crest of each hill offers the reward of sweeping views of ocean, rippling grasses and even the Pilgrim monument in downtown Provincetown.

As the path turns north again, you will find yourself walking almost parallel to Race Point Road. In another 0.5 mile, you will reach Race Point Beach, a ribbon of sand that signifies the end of Cape Cod. From here, turn west (left) to leave the paved path and follow the shoreline as it continues out to Race Point Light, in another mile. Soak in the scenery from this majestic place before retracing your steps back to the paved path. On the return trip, note that the trail splits approximately halfway down Race Point Road. Here, take the paved path to the left (leaving east) to reach the Province Lands Visitor Center; a sign at the trail split will point toward the visitors center. Learn more about the geography and natural history of the Province Lands before continuing on the path to return about 0.5 mile to the Beech Forest parking area.

Options

Up for exploring another breathtaking Cape beach? Reaching the trail junction after passing the smaller kettle ponds (approximately 1.5 miles into this hike), head northwest (left) and follow the paved path another mile to reach the shores of Herring Cove Beach, one of the Cape's quieter beaches. Return the way you came, turning east (left) at the junction to continue on with the rest of the hike.

Directions

Drive U.S. 6 east to Provincetown. At the traffic lights on U.S. 6, turn right onto Race Point Road. Continue to the Beech Forest parking area on the left; the Province Lands Visitor Center is a short distance farther on the right.
GPS Coordinates: 42.0600 N, 70.1906 W

Contact

Parking and access are free. Dogs on leash are allowed. Paper trail maps are available at the Province Lands and Salt Pond Visitor Centers in Eastham. Or get the waterproof *Cape Cod National Seashore Map #250* for $2 from Trails Illustrated (800/962-1643, www.natgeomaps.com). For more information, contact Cape Cod National Seashore, 99 Marconi Station Site Rd., Wellfleet, MA 02667, 508/349-3785, www.nps.gov/caco/index.htm. Salt Pond Visitor Center, corner of Nauset Road and U.S. 6, Eastham, 508/255-3421. Province Lands Visitor Center, 508/487-1256.

☑ RYDER BEACH AND ATWOOD-HIGGINS HOUSE

Wellfleet and Truro

🗗 🎇 🏊 🏕 🐕 👫

Level: Easy/Moderate

Hiking Time: 2 hours

Total Distance: 4.0 miles

Elevation: 20 feet

Summary: Visit the grounds of a restored 18th-century Cape Cod home and a young dune habitat on the way to Cape Cod Bay.

Cape Cod may have the reputation of being packed end to end with tourists all summer long, but here's one more beautiful spot that no one else seems to have discovered. As you walk the shore of Ryder Beach, don't be surprised if the cawing gulls are your only companion.

This relatively flat, sandy hike, a long loop to the beach and back, kicks off with a bit of history. From the parking area, the hike first takes you on a visit to the Atwood-Higgins House. Built in 1730 on the banks of what was once a lush tidal waterway, the Atwood-Hig-

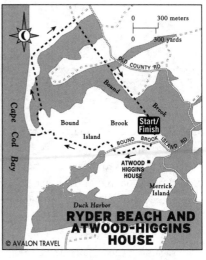

RYDER BEACH AND ATWOOD-HIGGINS HOUSE

© AVALON TRAVEL

gins House is a restored saltbox house, a good visual for those who have ever wondered where the distinctive Cape Cod–style home originated. The National Parks Service–administered land also contains farm fields and other outbuildings, all free for you to roam about and investigate; the house itself is open for tours on select dates.

Once you've gotten your fill of Cape Cod's colonial past, find the trail to Ryder Beach just north of the house property, marked by a sign. It's a relatively level walk for the next 1.5 miles out to the beach, passing through what looks to be just another garden variety Cape Cod freshwater wetland, complete with wild cranberry bogs and thickets of wild beach rose and sea lavender mixed in with the marsh grasses. But there's some history here, too. The land you are treading on was once a tide-fed estuary of Cape Cod Bay, but tidal action and shifting sand deposits created dunes along this portion of Cape Cod Bay that eventually cut off the opening to the bay. The anemic waters of the Herring River were no

young sand dunes on Ryder Beach

match for the dunes, so instead the marshes were formed as a way to mark the river's terminus.

Coming closer to the beach, a boardwalk helps you over the dunes. Turn north (right) once you are on the beach and follow the shoreline, with excellent views north toward Provincetown. If you have kids in tow, at low tide, this stretch is a great place for beachcombing and seashell collecting. For the next 0.5 mile, you will likely share the beach with only herring gulls and the plovers and terns who congregate on these more desolate shores. As you near the public parking area on the northern end of the beach, however, other human beachgoers will almost certainly be present, though still not in the numbers found at the more popular Cape beaches. At the parking area, the trail turns east again, linking up with the Old Colony Bike Path in one mile. From here, the trail heads southeast for the last mile back to the parking area, passing on the way another dune-choked wetland that was once water that ran freely to the sea.

Options

To explore more of the marshland, numerous side paths wander out into the vegetation to explore cranberry bogs, stands of beach plum, and patches of wild blueberry. With most plants found here lying relatively low to the ground, and the dunes of Ryder Beach an omnipresent landmark, there's really no way you can become lost. A nice side loop starts about 0.25 mile after leaving the Atwood-Higgins house, winding in a mile-long loop on the north side of the trail to Ryder

Beach. Where the loop rejoins the main path, you still have about a mile to go before reaching the dunes.

Directions

From Route 6 in Wellfleet, turn left onto Pamet Point Road (the last road in Wellfleet before reaching Truro). Follow Pamet Road for 1.5 miles to an intersection with Old County Road. Turn left and continue until the National Park Service sign for the Atwood-Higgins House appears at a right turn onto Brook Island Road. Parking is 0.25 mile ahead on the left.

Contact

Parking and access are free. Dogs on leash are allowed. Maps and information about the national seashore are available at area visitors centers. Or get the waterproof *Cape Cod National Seashore Map #250* for $12 from Trails Illustrated (800/962-1643, www.natgeomaps.coml). For more information, contact Cape Cod National Seashore, 99 Marconi Station Site Rd., Wellfleet, MA 02667, 508/349-3785, www.nps.gov. Salt Pond Visitor Center (corner of Nauset Road and U.S. 6, Eastham), 508/255-3421. Province Lands Visitor Center, 508/487-1256.

3 GREAT ISLAND TRAIL   BEST 【

Cape Cod National Seashore in Wellfleet

Level: Easy/Moderate   **Total Distance:** 6.0 miles

Hiking Time: 3.5 hours   **Elevation:** 20 feet

Summary: A stroll down this barrier beach at sunset offers breathtaking views over Cape Cod Bay.

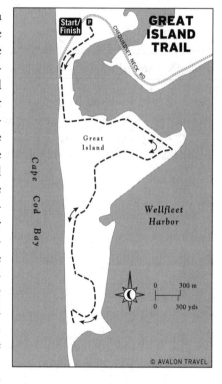

The sinking sun ignites the dunes a vivid yellow, tiny crabs scatter in the growing shadows, and the shoreline takes on a bluish hue to blend perfectly with the purple-indigo of Cape Cod Bay. Great Island, the narrow barrier peninsula separating Wellfleet Harbor from Cape Cod Bay, is simply the best place to take in the sunset on Cape Cod, both for the majestic views as well as the sense of solitude. Even in the middle of a crowded Cape Cod summer, come here toward dusk and your only company may be a lone sea kayaker paddling the glassy waters of the bay far offshore. Worried about getting lost if you stay out past sunset? This trek, to the tip of Great Island and back, does follow a well-defined path, but still bring along a flashlight in case your hike back is in the dark.

From the parking lot, find the trailhead near the National Park Service kiosk at the southern edge of the parking area (near the salt marsh). The wide, well-worn path briefly edges the marsh before bringing you within sight of a line of dunes that front Cape Cod Bay. Just when it looks like you will start ascending the grassy dunescape, the path turns sharply to the left, heading south on a narrow strip of land that is the entrance to the Great Island peninsula (this area is called "The Gut" by locals). Staying on the east side of The Gut, the trail also brings you back within view of Wellfleet Harbor. The terrain is easy footing on a packed dirt

a side path leading to Wellfleet Harbor

and sand path and the scenery of passing pleasure boats and diving gulls is classic Cape Cod.

Continuing south, at 0.75 mile, the trail reaches a junction marked by a boulder and sign pointing the way to the former site of a Colonial-era tavern. (There are no remains of the tavern left.) At one mile, the trail passes another junction and then begins pushing southwest toward the center of the island, passing through small patches of tree cover before entering a pine and hardwood forest at two miles. Now straightening out to again head due south, the path becomes a wide forest road as it rises slightly to crest Great Beech Hill (no views). Descending the other side of the hill, forest cover quickly gives way to grasslands, and then dunes, before ending at the beach on Cape Cod Bay (at three miles). Enjoy the sunset and retrace your steps on the return.

Options

From the beach, a sandy spit brings you all the way out to the southern tip of Jeremy Point, with splendid views across Cape Cod Bay to the west and Wellfleet Harbor to the east. At low tide, the walk is normally another 0.75 mile to reach the end of land (adding another 1.5 miles to this hike). But be aware that this spit disappears under the ocean when the tide rises. Do not attempt this hike when the tide is rising. Likewise, if you don't know when the next high tide will begin, do not attempt this walk.

Directions

From the Salt Pond Visitor Center at the Doane Road exit in Eastham, drive U.S. 6 east for 8.2 miles. Turn left at the sign for Wellfleet Center and Harbor. Drive 0.4 mile and turn left at the sign for Blue Harbor. In another 0.6 mile you reach the marina; turn right, following the road (with the water on your left) for 2.5 miles to the Great Island parking lot on the left.

GPS Coordinates: 41.9351 N, 70.0682 W

Contact

Parking and access are free. Trails are open to the public 6 A.M.–midnight. The Salt Pond Visitor Center is open 9 A.M.–4:30 P.M. daily. Dogs are not allowed. An information board is at the trailhead, and trail information is available at the Salt Pond Visitor Center. Or get the waterproof *Cape Cod National Seashore Map #250* for $12 from Trails Illustrated (800/962-1643, www.natgeomaps.com). For more information, contact Cape Cod National Seashore, 99 Marconi Station Site Rd., Wellfleet, MA 02667, 508/349-3785, www.nps.gov. Salt Pond Visitor Center (corner of Nauset Road and U.S. 6, Eastham), 508/255-3421. Province Lands Visitor Center, 508/487-1256.

4 ATLANTIC WHITE CEDAR SWAMP

Cape Cod National Seashore in South Wellfleet

🏕 🛫 ⚓ 🎨 👫 ♿

Level: Easy

Total Distance: 1.2 miles

Hiking Time: 30 minutes

Elevation: 15 feet

Summary: A short, easy walk takes you deep into one of the Cape's last remaining Atlantic White Cedar swamps.

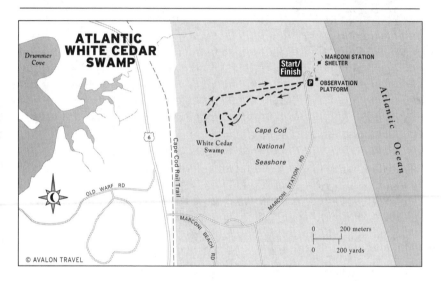

This is one of the true highlights of the Cape Cod National Seashore, as much for the site's historic significance as for the short, but uniquely beautiful walk through an old-growth swamp. It was from this spot, on January 18, 1903, that the Italian Guglielmo Marconi transmitted the first two-way transoceanic communication and first wireless telegram between America and Europe. The four huge towers that once stood here are long gone; in fact, more than half the land where they stood has since eroded into the sea.

But what does remain here is one of the last remaining old-growth Atlantic White Cedar swamps on Cape Cod. These forested wetlands were once abundant on the Cape, springing up within dune systems and in low-lying land depressions. Changes in water flow, deforestation, and even leaf litter that prevented tree germination made the swamps all but disappear. It's only a very short walk through this rare Cape Cod microenvironment, but as you quickly find yourself deep in the swamp, you will probably agree this hike has a feel like no other on the Cape.

From the parking lot, two trails leave the lot heading west to the swamp; take the

© HEIDI J. BROWN

A winding boardwalk leads through the swamp.

one to the left, heading into a forest of stunted oak and pine trees. As the landscape descends at a very gentle grade, the trees grow taller; they are more protected from the harsh ocean climate in this hollow of sorts. Even the sounds here are different, as the screeching of gulls, a noise heard almost everywhere on the outer Cape, is suddenly traded for the sounds (and sight) of forest-dwelling birds.

Continuing on, the trail reaches the swamp's distinct groves of white cedar, tall poles—some 70–80 feet tall—covered in shaggy, peeling bark. Pitch pine, black and white oak, golden beach-heather, and broom crowberry also thrive here, though many are still twisted in the manner characteristic of someplace buffeted by almost constant winds. The swamp itself is an eerie depression formed, like other kettles on the Cape, by a melting glacial ice block. Crossing on a boardwalk, cedars crowd in from both sides, some leaning over it, creating an almost overwhelming sense of intimacy in this odd little forest. The trail abruptly emerges from the swamp onto a sandy, tree-bordered road (marked on maps as Old Wireless Road) that leads back to the parking lot. To access the beach, take the access path leaving east from the lot, heading past the observation tower and Marconi Comfort Station.

Options

After touring the cedar swamp, take time to climb the observation tower located on the former Marconi Station site. From here, views extend from the dramatic, clifflike dunes to a sweeping ocean vista. On a clear day, it may also be possible to spot Eastham (to the south) and northward to Truro. Access to the beach can be found by continuing east from the observation platform.

Directions

Drive U.S. 6 east to Eastham. Five miles beyond the Doane Road exit for the Salt Pond Visitor Center, turn right at signs for the Marconi station and continue to the parking lot. The Marconi station, which has historical displays, is between the lot and the beach. The trail begins at the parking lot.
GPS Coordinates: 41.9044 N, 69.9843 W

Contact

Parking and access are free. Trails are open to the public 6 A.M.– midnight. The Salt Pond Visitor Center is open 9 A.M.–4:30 P.M. daily. Dogs are not allowed. The Marconi station is wheelchair accessible. A paper map and interpretive trail guide is available at the trailhead. Or get the waterproof *Cape Cod National Seashore Map #250* for $12 from Trails Illustrated (800/962-1643, www.natgeomaps. com). For more information, contact Cape Cod National Seashore, 99 Marconi Station Site Rd., Wellfleet, MA 02667, 508/349-3785, www.nps.gov. Salt Pond Visitor Center (corner of Nauset Road and U.S. 6, Eastham), 508/255-3421. Province Lands Visitor Center, 508/487-1256.

5 NAUSET MARSH

Cape Cod National Seashore in Eastham

🏕️ 🦌 ✈️ 👥 ♿

Level: Easy   **Total Distance:** 1.2 miles

Hiking Time: 45 minutes   **Elevation:** 10 feet

Summary: Explore the rich marine environment of the Nauset Marsh and enjoy some of the best birding the Cape has to offer.

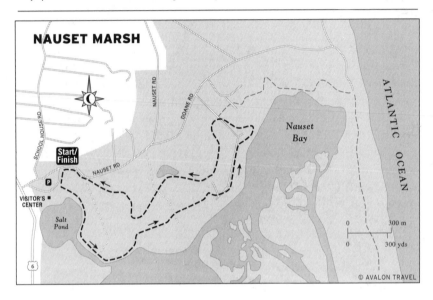

Teeming with marine life and a bird-watcher's paradise, the calm, tidal waters and sea grasses of Nauset Marsh create a lush home for shorebirds and migratory waterfowl, crabs, snails, fish, and even the occasional seal. If your trip to the Cape has led you to the Salt Pond Visitor Center, don't overlook this hike—the easy-to-follow loop trail has numerous interpretive signs with information about its abundant flora and a good view of Nauset Marsh. Kids (and grown ups) will love exploring the marsh as welcome relief from all that infamous Cape traffic you just endured. Plus, if it's a convenience you're looking for, the trailhead is located just outside the visitors center back door.

The trail to Nauset Marsh begins as a boardwalk leaving from the visitors center, with the first few hundred feet coinciding with the Buttonbush Trail for the Blind. (If you are starting out from parking lot, walk toward the visitors center and look for the boardwalk on the east—left—side of the building.) The Buttonbush Trail soon branches off to follow its own route, but the Nauset Trail, now

swans taking a swim in Nauset Marsh

a level dirt path, bears south to hug the shore of Salt Pond, a kettle pond created when a glacier receded and left behind enormous salt blocks, which eventually melted. Next turning east, the trail treads above the marsh, occasionally ducking through groves of pitch pine, black cherry, and eastern red cedar trees. It was here on this upland that the Nauset tribe once lived in their distinctive beehive-shaped homes, living for centuries off the bounty found within the shimmering waters and grasses of the marsh.

For bird-watchers, the open overlook above Nauset Marsh reached at the hike's halfway point is a good place to stop—piping plovers nest on islands in the marsh and migratory waterfowl make the place a routine stop on their spring and fall layovers. Leaving the overlook, the trail turns north and enters a forest of red cedar and bayberry. Passing two more kettle ponds, the trail soon loops backs to the Buttonbush Trail and the visitors center.

Options

The Buttonbush Trail for the Blind is completely wheelchair accessible; instead of taking a right onto the Nauset Marsh Trail, wheelchair users can stay on the Buttonbush for a short, scenic loop back to the visitors center. Or, if you would like a longer hike, a side path at the one-mile mark of this hike leads for another mile to a good view of the marsh next to the Doane Memorial, a plaque paying tribute to a family that once owned land here.

Directions

Drive U.S. 6 east to Eastham. Take the exit for Doane Road, following signs for national seashore information to the Salt Pond Visitor Center.
GPS Coordinates: 41.8404 N, 69.9616 W

Contact

Parking and access are free. Trails are open to the public 6 A.M.–midnight. The Salt Pond Visitor Center is open 9 A.M.–4:30 P.M. daily. Dogs are not allowed. A paper map and interpretive trail guide is available in a box at the trailhead, and maps and information about the national seashore are available in the visitors center. Or get the waterproof *Cape Cod National Seashore Map #250* for $12 from Trails Illustrated (800/962-1643, www.natgeomaps.com). For more information, contact Cape Cod National Seashore, 99 Marconi Station Site Rd., Wellfleet, MA 02667, 508/349-3785, www.nps.gov. Salt Pond Visitor Center (corner of Nauset Road and U.S. 6, Eastham), 508/255-3421. Province Lands Visitor Center, 508/487-1256.

6 NICKERSON KETTLE PONDS

Nickerson State Park in Brewster

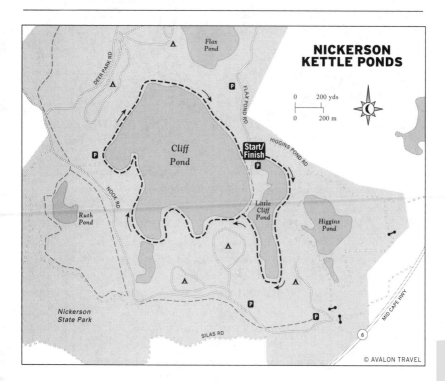

Level: Moderate

Hiking Time: 2 hours

Total Distance: 4.0 miles

Elevation: 0 feet

Summary: Explore the woods and kettle ponds in one of the Bay State's largest state parks.

One of the largest state parks in Massachusetts, Nickerson State Park was once a private estate and working farm on the outskirts of Brewster. Today, old cart paths and farm roads still lace the park, creating a network of trails that lead to piney woods, kettle ponds, uphill ridges and gently rolling hollows. The park is also home to one of the busiest campgrounds on the Cape, but with such a vast landscape to work with Nickerson maintains a sense of woodlands solitude.

This hike visits Little Cliff and Cliff Pond, two of a cluster of kettle ponds found in Nickerson. It's a relatively flat, kid-friendly trek to visit the ponds, and

the picnic area at Nickerson State Park

with picnic tables scattered at various points along the route, provides the ideal place for an afternoon of picnicking and swimming.

From the parking area near the Cliff Pond boat launch, amble south on the boat launch access road as it passes between Little Cliff Pond and Cliff Pond. After passing the trail for Higgins Pond and Eel Pond, a few feet later find the marked Little Cliff Pond Trail, a well-worn dirt footpath leaving to your left and heading west. For the next mile, the trail leads you in a clockwise direction around the shores of the finger-shaped Little Cliff Pond. With almost continuous water views, it's a good place for bird-watching. On a typical summer day, you will most likely find likely find large populations of swans, ducks, and geese skimming the placid waters, with sometimes a heron or two stopping by for a visit. Above your head, songbirds and kingfishers frolic in the upper reaches of the thick pine woods that surround much of the pond. Picnic tables about halfway around the loop make a shady spot for lunch, still in view of the water.

Taking you south and then back north, the Little Cliff Pond Trail links with the Cliff Pond Trail loop just before returning to the boat launch area. Taking you west and then north again, the Cliff Pond Trail continues the theme: views of water surrounded by pine woods. Only this time, the views are more expansive, reflecting the large, 200-acre size of Cliff Pond. There are ample places to swim along the pond's sandy shores and three picnic areas. In another three miles, the pleasant trek completes its loop around the pond, returning you to the boat access parking area.

Options

To visit two more kettle ponds, take the Eel Pond/Higgins Pond loop trail that starts near the boat access parking area. Using an old bridle path for its route, the trail hugs the eastern shore of Higgins Pond before looping around tiny Eel Pond on the return. Unlike the clear waters of Cliff Pond, both kettle ponds appear to be in the process of becoming marshes. Tall reeds and grasses may prevent you from taking a dip, but they do provide lots of room for spotting birds, frogs, and other marsh-loving creatures. And bugs love these two ponds, too. If you do decide to tackle this additional one-mile loop, be sure to bring along the bug spray.

Directions

From Route 6 in Orleans, take Exit 12. Turn left off the ramp onto Route 6A west toward Brewster. Continue for about two miles. The main entrance to Nickerson State Park is on the left. Once you've entered the park, bear left at the fork and continue to follow the access road for one more mile until its end at the boat launch access parking lot.

Contact

There is a fee of $5 per vehicle for day use. Dogs on leash are allowed. Maps are available at the park entrance or online from the Massachusetts Department of Conservation and Recreation. For more information, contact Nickerson State Park, Rte. 6A, Brewster, MA 02631, 508/896-3491, www.mass.gov.

7 CAPE COD RAIL TRAIL

BEST ◖

Dennis and Harwich

🐎 👫 ♿

Level: Easy	**Total Distance:** 10.0 miles
Hiking Time: 5 hours	**Elevation:** 20 feet

Summary: An easy, flat hike along a converted rail bed takes you within sight of cranberry bogs and kettle ponds.

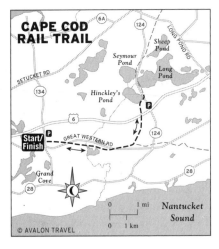

Following the bed of the former Old Colony railroad, the paved Cape Cod Rail Trail extends for 25 miles from Route 134 in South Dennis to Lecount Hollow Road in South Wellfleet, near the Cape Cod National Seashore's Marconi Visitor Center. The mostly flat, paved trail crosses cranberry bogs, forests, and several roads, providing numerous access and egress points. The rail trail is very much a citizen's path—busy in the summer tourist months with cyclists, inline skaters, walkers, wheelchair users, and adults and kids of all ages. This walk takes you to Dennis and Harwich, two of the first towns connected by this rail-bed-turned-recreation-path in 1978.

From the parking lot, the well-marked trail leaves to the east, at first heading past a few old factory sites and boat storage facilities. It's not the most pleasant scenery to look at while hiking, but still serves as a good reminder that the path you are walking on was once an important transportation route for moving goods on and off the Cape. And you don't have to look at it for long. Within a mile, the path dips into a pleasant forest of oak and pine. At two miles, it takes you within sight of vast cranberry bogs on both sides of the path. Continuing through more groves of scrub pine and oak, the trail reaches a rotary at just over three miles into the hike. It's a good place to stop for a rest, but as you leave, make sure to stay with the Cape Cod Rail Trail as it turns north. Another trail, the Old Colony Rail Trail continues east from the rotary (created from a separate spoke of the former railway). Both trails are well marked.

Leaving from the rotary, the Rail Trail pushes north along the arguably most lovely section in this Dennis-Harwich area, passing the Hacker Wildlife Sanctuary,

Cape Cod Rail Trail

an eight-acre wetland preserve. Continuing on, a bridge crossing takes you over bustling Route 6 and then it is one more mile to the shores of Hinckley's Pond, a good example of one of the Cape's many kettle ponds—clear, deep, and almost perfectly round pools formed by glacial action. To return, retrace your steps.

Options

Rail Trail hikers are welcome to visit the Hacker Wildlife Sanctuary. Use the marked entry on the trail (if traveling by bike, you are asked to leave it in the racks provided). Trails within the sanctuary take you to woodlands, wetlands, and 600 feet of shoreline on Katie's Pond. If miles of hiking on the hard, flat surface of the Rail Trail leaves you longing for some pine needle duff underfoot, this short detour is worth the added mileage (about one mile to Katie's Pond and back).

Directions

To reach the trail's western end, from U.S. 6 in Dennis, take Exit 9 onto Route 134 south. Proceed through two traffic signals to a large parking lot on the left for the Cape Cod Rail Trail. The eastern terminus is at Lecount Hollow Road in South Wellfleet, near the Cape Cod National Seashore's Marconi Visitor Center and off U.S. 6. The trail can be accessed at numerous points along its path.
GPS Coordinates: 41.9176 N, 69.9864 W

8 LOWELL HOLLY RESERVATION
Mashpee and Sandwich

Level: Easy

Hiking Time: 1.5 hours

Total Distance: 3.0 miles

Elevation: 0 feet

Summary: Take a hike – and then take a dip – on this pleasant, holly-lined peninsula bordering two freshwater ponds.

This pretty piece of conservation land is owned by the Trustees of the Reservation, a private land preservation society that administers scenic recreation properties throughout the state. Lowell Holly is named for former Harvard University president Abbott Lawrence Lowell, who once owned the land. Lowell, a hobby agriculturist, began planting wild rhododendron here in the early 1900s. Later, 50 varieties of American holly were introduced on the property, quickly becoming the dominant vegetation edging the preserve's crisscrossing paths.

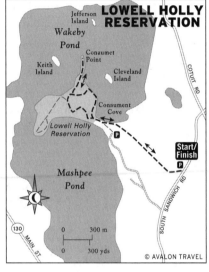

Before Lowell, however, the Wampanoag made extensive use of the ponds and peninsula as a fishing grounds. Today, the angling is still good in Mashpee and Wakeby ponds and makes the place a popular spot for freshwater fishing on Cape Cod. And even if you don't bring your fishing pole along on this loop hike to explore the sandy shores of Lowell Holly, you'll appreciate why the area was once called Conaumet, from the Wampanoag word kuwunut, meaning beach. The calm, warm waters of the ponds are just too inviting not to take a dip.

From the year-round parking area, an access path leads just under 0.5 mile through the woods to the entrance of the peninsula. If you parked in the pay/seasonal lot, a short access path heads northwest toward the peninsula; the two paths then merge. From here, the trail pushes west to reach a junction. Bear southwest (to the left) to begin the loop in a clockwise direction. Within the next 0.5 mile, the trail briefly touches the waters of Mashpee Pond before turning north and heading toward the center of the peninsula and an extensive wetlands field.

From here, the trail zigzags slightly before reaching another junction. Here, bear right (north) to stay on the path as it takes you to the shores of Wakeby Pond. A spur trail that leads all the way out to Conaumet Point and back is worth checking out and figured in the total distance of this hike (0.5 mile round-trip). Returning from the point, the trail edges the wetland again before returning to the shore of Wakeby Pond and then back to where the trail splits for the return to the parking areas.

Options

Want more Mashpee Pond? From the trail junction reached after you pass through the wetlands at the beginning of this hike, bear south (left) at the junction to walk out to a point jutting far out into Mashpee's calm, clear waters. Take a dip, stop for a picnic, and then return, adding only 0.5 mile to your total mileage.

Wakeby Pond

© HEIDI J. BROWN

Directions

From Route 6 in Sandwich, take Exit 2 onto Route 130 south. Follow for 1.5 miles and then turn left on Cotuit Road. Follow Cotuit Road for 3.4 miles to a right turn onto South Sandwich Road. Follow 0.2 mile to the free year-round parking area. In summer, continue to follow the road another 0.5 mile to a seasonal parking area where you will need to pay a fee.

Contact

From Memorial Day through Labor Day, nonmembers pay $6 per car at the seasonal parking lot; Trustees of the Reservation members park for free. Dogs on leash are allowed. Maps are available at the trailhead and online from the Trustees' website. For more information, contact Trustees of the Reservation, Southeast Region (Westport Field Office), A Main Road, Westport, MA 02790, 508/636-4693, www.thetrustees.org

9 BEEBE WOODS AND PUNCH BOWL
Falmouth

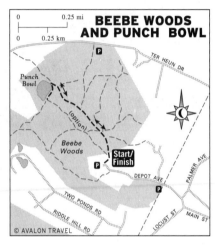

Level: Easy

Total Distance: 1.5 miles

Hiking Time: 1 hour

Elevation: 10 feet

Summary: Off the beaten path, this pleasant, wooded walk leads to a clear, deep kettle pond swimming hole.

Falmouth, on the southwestern edge of the upper Cape, more closely resembles the pine forest and pond-dotted mainland of southern New England than it does the sandy stretches of the lower Cape and Cape Cod National Seashore, just a few miles up the road. Once a farm, but now covered in dense new-growth pine, the Beebe Woods is a 383-acre, public land preserve of woods, wetlands, and kettle ponds located on the outskirts of town. And while it's true that a hike here won't take you to dunes or ocean surf—or really to any place that gives much of a hint that the roiling waters of the Atlantic are even remotely nearby, what makes the Beebe Woods so irresistable is the true sense of solitude the forest provides, a quality that can be hard to come by in the midst of one of the most popular vacation destinations in the United States.

This short hike quickly takes you deep into the woods before reaching the picturesque kettle pond known as the Punch Bowl. Pack a picnic for a pond-side lunch and don't forget your bathing suit! When it comes to swimming holes, the Punch Bowl may just be the Cape's best-kept secret.

From the parking area at the Cape Cod Conservatory, the unmarked trail leaves to the north of the lot. Follow the footpath as it bears northwest, passing a side path a few feet into the trek. As the trail leads farther into the woods, you will soon be surrounded by a thick cover of oak and pine, providing ample opportunity to spot squirrels, deer, and other forest dwelling animals. Continue on, passing several side paths branching off to the right (east) until reaching the Punch Bowl at 0.5 mile.

Walking around the trails that encircle this 103-foot deep kettle pond, it's easy

the path to the kettle pond

to see where the Punch Bowl name came from. The pond is, to the naked eye, perfectly round, with steep sides truly making it feel like you're taking a dip in a giant bowl. Looking for the river or stream that feeds this summer swimming oasis? There isn't one, a testimony to the glacial formation of the pond. The Punch Bowl, as well as every other kettle pond on Cape Cod, was created at the end of the last Ice Age when retreating glaciers dropped large deposits of ice-encased salt chunks all over the landscape. Their weight made depressions in the ground and when the massive ice-salt cubes finally melted, these distinctively shaped ponds were left behind. Some kettle ponds may be fed by underground springs, but most rely on the local water table and rainfall to stay filled.

Once you've dried off, it's time to head back. Retrace your steps on the main path back to the parking area, or take the shorter access path that leaves from the southeastern end of the pond.

Options

Want to see more of the woods? From the Punch Bowl, follow the path that parallels the pond's southern shore as it heads southwest into the forest. Tread over ridges and down into hollows for the next mile until reaching the Ice House kettle pond (called Miles Pond on some maps). Retrace your steps back to the Punch Bowl and then back to the parking area on the return, adding two miles round-trip onto your hike.

Directions

From the corner of Locust Street and North Main Street in Falmouth, follow North Main Street a few hundred feet and then turn left on Depot Avenue. Follow Depot Avenue for another 0.4 mile as it turns into Highfield Drive and reaches the Cape Cod Conservatory. The parking area is on the right.

Contact

Parking and access are free. Dogs on leash are allowed. Maps are available from the Falmouth 300 Land Preservation Committee. For more information, contact 157 Locust Street, Falmouth, MA 02540, 508/540-0876, www.300committee.org.

10 AQUINNAH

Aquinnah on Martha's Vineyard

Level: Easy

Hiking Time: 1.5 hours

Total Distance: 3.0 miles

Elevation: 0 feet

Summary: Wander the beach on the way to visit the famous cliffs at this westernmost point of Martha's Vineyard.

At the westernmost point of Martha's Vineyard island, the Aquinnah cliffs, striated clay deposits over 200 hundred feet high, drop abruptly down to the sea. An impressive and eye-catching attraction at any time of day, the cliffs are particularly striking at sunset, when the sun's low, long rays bring out the layered browns, yellows, reds, whites, and deep grays of the clay. For the Aquinnah Wampanoag, the Native American tribe that still makes up over 30 percent of the population of Aquinnah, this is a spiritual place. The layered cliffs are thought to tell the story of the

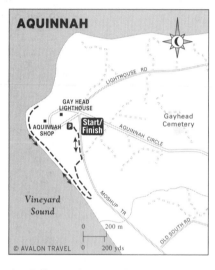

Wampanoag people and the land below the cliffs, Moshup Beach, where most of this hike takes place, is named for the giant the Aquinnah people believe created Noepe (the Wampanoag word for Martha's Vineyard). On weekends, a member of the tribe is often on hand at the cliffs to explain the land's significance.

It's an easy hike out to the cliffs along Moshup Beach, but does come with some warnings. Moshup Beach is a popular swimming beach and can be very crowded during the summer tourist season. It is also one of the few clothing-optional beaches in Massachusetts, with most nude sunbathers tending to congregate in the more secluded area of the beach near the cliffs. The cliffs themselves are protected by various conservation organizations. Not only is climbing on the cliffs prohibited, but it is also unlawful to take any clay that may have crumbled from the cliffs onto the beach (violators may be subject to a $100 fine). Lastly, if you have an older map of Martha's Vineyard, you may be confused about references to Gay Head. The name was officially replaced in 1998 when the town council decided to honor the original nameplace of the Aquinnah Wampanoag.

The lighthouse found atop the cliffs is often still referred to as Gay Head Light in tourist brochures and many locals still call the town Gay Head—important to know should you need to ask for directions!

From the parking lot, pick up the sandy trail at the sign for Moshup Beach. The trail to the beach parallels the road named Moshup Trail; the cliffs and Aquinnah lighthouse are visible from the start of this hike. Within minutes you are on the beach; turn northwest (right) and follow the beach for the rest of the way to the cliffs. Because there is so much clay found here, the terrain tends to be firm underfoot and easy on the legs for a beach hike. On the approach to the cliffs, take time to look out to sea to spot Cuttyhunk Island offshore to the north (right) and No Man's Island to the south (left). At high tide, you may have difficulty walking to the far end of the cliffs. Head back the way you came.

Options

To learn more about the history and cultural traditions of the Aquinnah Wampanoag tribe, visit the Vanderhoop Homestead, home of the Aquinnah Cultural Center of Tribal History. The building is easy to find just beyond the Aquinnah Cliffs at 35 South Road. Summer visitor hours are 9 A.M.–4:30 P.M. weekdays. For more information, call 508/645 9265.

Directions

The cliffs at Aquinnah are on Moshup Beach at the western tip of Martha's Vineyard, in the town of Aquinnah, and at the parking area located at the end of the State Road, which crosses the island from Vineyard Haven. Three seasonal ferry services make regular trips, May–October, to Vineyard Haven or Oak Bluffs from Falmouth (508/548-4800), and Hyannis on Cape Cod (508/778-2600), as well as from New Bedford, MA (508/997-1688). The Steamship Authority (508/477-8600) carries vehicles and passengers from Woods Hole on Cape Cod to Vineyard Haven year-round, and Woods Hole to Oak Bluffs May 15–October 15.
GPS Coordinates: 41.3877 N, 70.8348 W

Contact

A parking fee of $5 per hour or $15 maximum per day is charged Memorial Day weekend–mid-October, although cyclists, walkers, or anyone not parking a vehicle can access the beach for free. Dogs are not allowed. For more information and an area map, contact Martha's Vineyard Chamber of Commerce, P.O. Box 1698, Vineyard Haven, MA 02568, 508/693-0085, www.mvy.com.

RHODE ISLAND

© HEIDI J. BROWN

BEST HIKES

We all know good things come in small packages

and tiny Rhode Island doesn't disappoint. The country's smallest state and one of its flattest, Rhode Island is home to multiple wildlife and bird preserves, countless state recreation areas, and great big ocean views. There are no soaring peaks in the Ocean State, but hikes here can take you to very different heights – from Newport's famed Cliff Walk and its row of almost mountain-size Gilded Age mansions to the bluffs of Block Island, where hundreds of thousands of birds stop over during seasonal migrations. And like the rest of New England, hikes to waterfalls and hidden ponds, through lush forest and hilly terrain abound in Rhode Island, in numbers first-time visitors to the state might find surprising.

Most hiking trails in "Rhody" lie on either state park land or private preserves. Each state park's management creates regulations specific to its property, and many impose trail restrictions on bikes and require that dogs be leashed. The two premier public lands are the 3,489-acre George Washington Management Area, in the state's northwest corner, and the 14,000-acre Arcadia Management Area, in the southwest corner. Extensive forest, pond, and marsh habitats in both management areas provide for a rich mix of flora and fauna. Commonly spotted creatures include cottontail rabbits, wild turkey, ruffled grouse, woodcock, snowshoe hare, white-tailed deer, and a variety of waterfowl, including wood ducks, mallards, and black ducks. Trees range from hemlock to hickory, with enough deciduous forest cover to make autumn color burn brightly.

Several hikes covered in this chapter wind through Audubon-run bird sanctuaries or other preserves known to bird-watchers; the state's woods and waters around Narragansett Bay are a popular stop for migratory birds along the Atlantic Flyway. Private preserves are often open only to hikers (no pets of any kind), and some require a small fee for trail use. Though a visit to Block Island requires a ferry trip, trails on the island are free and open to the public.

Rhode Island's winters rarely see enough snow for cross-country skiing or snowshoeing and slushy, muddy winter trail conditions can make cold weather hiking a bit tricky. But many public lands, like the Arcadia Management Area, harbor a wealth of dirt roads perfect for winter pursuits when Mother Nature allows. And please note, hunting is generally allowed in season on any land that is not posted with signs specifically prohibiting it. The Arcadia Management Area requires all trail users, including hikers, to wear fluorescent orange during the hunting season.

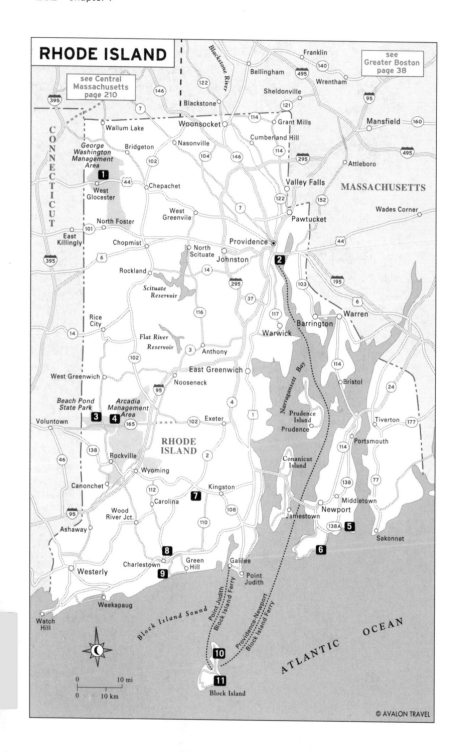

RHODE ISLAND

see Central
Massachusetts
page 210

see
Greater Boston
page 38

MASSACHUSETTS

CONNECTICUT

Franklin
Bellingham
Sheldonville
Wrentham
Mansfield
Blackstone
Woonsocket
Grant Mills
Wallum Lake
Bridgeton
Nasonville
Cumberland Hill
George
Washington
Management
Area
1
West
Glocester
Chepachet
West
Greenvile
Valley Falls
Attleboro
Wades Corner
North Foster
Pawtucket
East
Killingly
Chopmist
Providence
2
North
Scituate
Johnston
Rockland
Warren
Scituate
Reservoir
Rice
City
Barrington
Flat River
Reservoir
Warwick
Anthony
Bristol
West Greenwich
East Greenwich
Narragansett Bay
Beach Pond
State Park
Nooseneck
Prudence
Island
Prudence
Tiverton
Voluntown
3 **4**
Arcadia
Management
Area
Exeter
Portsmouth
RHODE
ISLAND
Conanicut
Island
Rockville
Wyoming
Middletown
Canonchet
Kingston
7
Newport
Carolina
Jamestown
5
Wood
River Jct.
Ashaway
6
Sakonnet
8
Galilee
Charlestown
Green
Hill
Westerly
9
Point
Judith
Weekapaug
Watch
Hill
Block Island Sound
Point Judith Block Island Ferry
Providence-Newport Block Island Ferry
ATLANTIC OCEAN
10
11
Block Island

0   10 mi
0   10 km

© AVALON TRAVEL

TRAIL NAME	LEVEL	DISTANCE	TIME	ELEVATION	FEATURES	PAGE
1 Walkabout Trail	Easy/Moderate	2–8 mi	1–4 hr	10 ft	🚶🏇	284
2 East Bay Bike Path	Easy	14.5 mi one-way	7 hr	10 ft	🏇♿	287
3 Stepstone Falls	Easy	3.4 mi	2.5 hr	20 ft		290
4 Penny Hill and Breakheart Pond Loop	Strenuous	6.0 mi	3 hr	200 ft		293
5 Norman Bird Sanctuary	Easy	2.0 mi	1 hr	50 ft		296
6 Newport Cliff Walk	Strenuous	6.0 mi	3 hr	100 ft		299
7 Great Swamp Management Area	Easy/Moderate	5.5 mi	2.5 hr	10 ft		302
8 Watchaug Pond Loop	Moderate	4.0 mi	2 hr	10 ft		305
9 Ninigret National Wildlife Refuge	Easy	3.0 mi	1.5 hr	0 ft		308
10 Clay Head Trail and the Maze	Easy	0.7 mi	45 min	0 ft		311
11 Rodman's Hollow	Easy	0.5 mi	45 min	20 ft		314

1 WALKABOUT TRAIL

George Washington Management Area in Chepachet

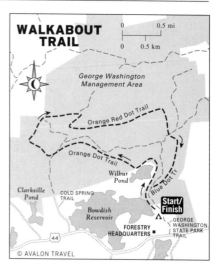

Level: Easy/Moderate

Hiking Time: 1-4 hours

Total Distance: 2-8 miles

Elevation: 10 feet

Summary: This wandering woods hike can be customized in length to explore a lot, or a little, of Rhode Island's remote northwest corner.

For such a small state, Rhode Island is home to a surprising mix of well-preserved wilderness areas, including the George Washington Management Area, a 3,489-acre landscape of forest, marshes, hidden ponds, and abundant wildlife tucked away in Rhody's remote northwest corner. There are no shortage of footpaths and dirt roads meandering through the management area, but one trail here is considered a can't-miss: the Walkabout.

Cut by Australian sailors holed up in the Ocean State waiting for their ship to be repaired, the Walkabout Trail is named for the Australian aborigine concept of walkabout—the sacred need to wander the landscape. The large, wooded loop really does wander as it winds along the shores of largely undeveloped ponds and through quiet woodlands punctuated by glacial-erratic boulders. Those ingenious Aussie trailblazers even gave hikers the ability to pick from three different loop lengths on this trail. Hikers can follow the entire orange-blazed trail for an eight-mile loop or take a red-blazed cut over to create a six-mile loop; for an even shorter hike, a blue-blazed cut through reduces the loop to a two-mile jaunt in the woods.

From the parking area, the orange, red, and blue blazes of the Walkabout Trail first lead you west to skirt the large Bowdish water reservoir. As you walk, it may seem as though trail blazers were a little too efficient in painting trees and rocks with small dots of color. If you take to the trail in summer, it may seem impossible to become lost here; but in winter, when deciduous tree cover no longer frames the path, the boundaries of the trail are much less defined—and can be very confusing.

Walkabout Trail

As the blazes turn north away from the reservoir, the trail continues on toward the shores of picturesque Wilbur Pond (at one mile). Here, the blue-blazed trail leaves to the right and heads east (away from the pond) to complete its loop. For those pushing on, the now orange- and red-blazed trail makes it way around the mountain laurel–ringed pond. Look for wood ducks, mallards, and black ducks floating on the quiet waters here. The trail reenters the woods and eventually heads west. In another mile, the red trail diverges south (to the left), cutting down to rejoin the main trail for the last few miles of its loop.

The orange trail heads next to the Pulaski Wildlife Marsh (a good spot for birding, but often very buggy) and then back into the forest. Rambling along for the next three miles under a mixed forest cover of pines, birch, and oak, you might find some unexpected trail partners as creatures ranging from ruffled grouse and wild turkey to cottontail rabbits and white-tailed deer roam about their woodland home. As the trail nears its completion, the orange blazes are joined first by red blazes and then blue blazes as the loop returns to the parking area.

Options

For those who want to turn their one day trip into an overnight back packing adventure in this wild little corner of Rhody, primitive tent and trailer campsites and two shelters in a wooded area overlooking Bowdish Reservoir are available. Call Management Area headquarters for reservations.

2 EAST BAY BIKE PATH

Providence

Level: Easy

Total Distance: 14.5 miles one-way

Hiking Time: 7 hours

Elevation: 10 feet

Summary: Rhode Island's premier bike path makes for easy, scenic hiking along the shores of Narragansett Bay.

There's no denying the overwhelming flatness of the Rhode Island landscape. But flat doesn't need to mean boring, as this stunning route along Narragansett Bay proves. From Providence to Bristol, this 14.5-mile, 10-foot wide ribbon of repurposed railroad line provides a scenic thoroughfare suitable for walking, inline skating, and cycling (the dominant form of recreation on the trail). Passing along or near the shore of the bay, the path connects eight parks: India Point Park in Providence, Bold Point and Squantum Woods in East Providence, Haines and Veteran's Memorial Park in Barrington, Burr Hill Park in Warren, and Colt State and Independence Parks in Bristol. The trail

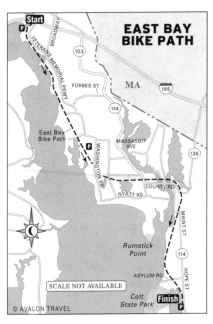

is completely wheelchair accessible and open year-round. It's a beautiful walk in summer, but may be even better in winter, when Rhode Island's milder temperatures (and almost no lasting snow cover) mean none of the ice and snow drifts that plague trails closer to Boston.

From the parking area at India Point Park, walk to the eastern end of the lot to find the sign and access ramp for the East Bay. The ramp takes you uphill to a bridge that runs alongside the highway as it crosses the Providence River. On the eastern bank of the river, the trail diverges from the highway and begins its southern journey. While the city of Providence is still very much alive and present to the east (your left), it's impossible not to focus your attention on the Providence River, growing wider with every step as it gives way to Narragansett Bay.

The trail eventually turns away from water views and, starting approximately

Just below the bike path, the rocky shore allows access to Narragansett Bay.

two miles into the hike, cuts east and then southeast through a leafy residential section of East Providence and eventually Barrington. Next passing by Laines Park and two pond natural areas on the way to a bridge crossing of the Barrington River, the trail reaches its halfway point. Crossing over first the Barrington River and a short distance later, the Warren River (both tributaries of Narragansett Bay), the path dips south again for the next seven miles to hug the shore of Narragansett Bay. Passing the entrance to Colt's Park, the trail finishes its run by briefly heading east away from the shore and then turning south again to reach scenic Independence Park on Bristol Bay.

Options

Multiple access points on the path provide for shorter or longer trips. For those interested in learning more about the abundant wildlife found along Narragansett Bay, a good entry point is the 28-acre McIntosh Wildlife Refuge, the grounds of the Audubon Society of Rhode Island's flagship Environmental Education Center. Located near Colt's Neck State Park at the southern end of the East Bay, parking at the refuge is free and its separate, wheelchair-accessible trail system provides for a lovely walk through old fields and salt marsh on the way to meet the access point for the bike path. Turn south (left) on the East Bay to continue on the Colt's Neck State Park or north (right) to hike toward Providence; views are lovely in either direction. For more information, contact Environmental Education Center,

Claire D. McIntosh Wildlife Refuge, 1401 Hope St. (Rte. 114), Bristol, RI 02809, 401/245-7500, www.asri.org.

Directions

To reach the bike path's Providence terminus, from Market Square in Providence, follow South Main Street north to the corner of College Street (the Rhode Island School of Design is here). Take a right, driving one block to the corner of Prospect Street. Turn left on Prospect and drive less than a block to a right turn on Waterman Street. Follow Waterman Street for several blocks, passing through the heart of the Brown University campus. Reaching an intersection with Gano Street, turn right and follow Gano Street for approximately 10 blocks. As it passes under the highway, Gano Street turns into India Street, the road leading to the park entrance and parking.

GPS Coordinates: 41.8175 N, 71.3907 W

Contact

Parking and access are free. Dogs on leash are allowed. A map of the East Bay Bike Path, part of the Guide to Bicycling in the Ocean State, is available free of charge from the Rhode Island Department of Transportation. Copies can be ordered by calling 401/222-4203, ext. 4033 (or downloaded at www.dot.state.ri.us/bikeri). For more information, contact East Coast Greenway Alliance, 27B North Rd., Wakefield, RI 02879, 401/789-4625, www.greenway.org.

3 STEPSTONE FALLS

Arcadia Management Area in Exeter

Level: Easy

Hiking Time: 2.5 hours

Total Distance: 3.4 miles

Elevation: 20 feet

Summary: This easy hike follows a rocky stream on the way to some of the prettiest waterfalls Rhody has to offer.

At over 14,000 acres, Arcadia Management Area is the state's largest recreation area, with mile after mile of crisscrossing trails cutting though a landscape of ponds, rivers, and low, forested hills. This kid-friendly hike, an out-and-back trek to the tumbling cascades of Stepstone Falls, ranks among Arcadia's most scenic. To save yourself from disappointment, however, save Stepstone Falls for a spring or early summer hike, when the waters of the Fall River roar and crash in awesome sight of rapids; come here at the end of a hot summer and you are likely to find only a slight trickle of water.

Beginning on the yellow-blazed Ben Utter Trail, marked by a sign at the back of the parking area, the route heads north, running parallel to the stone-littered brook known as Falls River and soon passing the site of a former gristmill to your right. At one mile, the trail reaches the Stepstone Falls camping area and a trail junction. Instead of following the Ben Utter Trail to the left, stay straight ahead on the white blazes of the Falls River Trail, crossing a footbridge to reach a vantage point above the falls in another 0.7 mile.

Dropping 10 feet over about 100 feet of distance, the falls are not the massive drops found elsewhere in the hillier states of New England, but in a state as low-lying as Rhode Island, it may be surprising to find even these peaceful little cascades. Tumbling over a series of granite ledges, the tallest drop measures only three feet, but forms a broad, flat and very picturesque curtain of water—proof that good things (and pretty waterfalls) can come in small packages.

rocky streambed on the Stepstone River

Anglers may want to take note that the Stepstone Falls area and surrounding rivers and tributaries are known for their prime trout fishing. Whether or not you decide to tote along your fishing rod, once you've soaked in the natural splendor, return the way you came.

Options

For those who prefer a one-way hike, the trail actually ends at the dirt Falls River Road, just beyond the falls, which is reached via Escoheag Hill Road; by shuttling cars, you could make this a 1.7-mile walk and not have to double back.

Directions

From the junction of Routes 3 and 165 in Exeter, drive west on Route 165 for about 5.5 miles and turn right onto the paved Escoheag Hill Road. Continue another mile and turn right onto the dirt Austin Farm Road. Two roads diverge here; take the left one, drive past a former ranger station, and pull into a parking area on the left, immediately before the bridge over Falls River. Austin Farm Road is closed to motor vehicles at Escoheag Hill Road during the winter. Other roads open to traffic in summer but closed in winter include Brook Trail, Barber Trail, and Blitzkrieg Trail.
GPS Coordinates: 41.5978 N, 71.7463 W

Contact

Parking and access are free. Dogs must be leashed March 1–August 15. Hunting

4 PENNY HILL AND BREAKHEART POND LOOP

Arcadia Management Area in Exeter

🦌 🐕 👫

Level: Strenuous

Hiking Time: 3 hours

Total Distance: 6.0 miles

Elevation: 200 feet

Summary: This trek through the Rhode Island wilderness leads to a forested summit and two backcountry ponds.

The perfect day outing for those seeking true wilderness adventure in Rhode Island, this six-mile loop through the woods of the Arcadia Management Area leads to the summit of 370-foot Penny Hill on the way to visit two backcountry ponds. Using the Breakheart Trail for much of its distance, a rocky and root-strewn path shaded by thick evergreen cover, the trek is one of the most rugged hikes Rhody has to offer. And with so many pines towering overhead, you might just feel like you are walking in the woods of Maine.

Although trees largely block any view from the 370-foot Penny Hill summit, the first stop on this hike offers an appealing walk through the woods to hilltop ledges that young kids would enjoy scrambling around on. From the parking area, cross the bridge over Falls River, ignoring the first yellow-blazed trail entering the woods to the south (right). About 75 feet past the bridge, turn south (right) into the woods on the yellow-blazed Breakheart Trail. The trail crosses a brook in an area that is often muddy, emerges from the woods within 0.5 mile of the start to cross Austin Farm Road again, and then ascends moderately to the craggy height of Penny Hill.

From Penny Hill, the Breakheart Trail descends to the northeast and flattens out into a rambling woods walk over the next two miles leading to Breakheart Pond. This is a good chance to spot native wildlife: populations of white-tailed deer, cottontail rabbits, fox, beaver, ruffled grouse, wild turkey, gray squirrel and a variety of other creatures of the northern forest all call this place home.

PENNY HILL AND BREAKHEART POND LOOP

SCALE NOT AVAILABLE

© AVALON TRAVEL

After two stream crossings over wooden bridges, the Breakheart Trail turns south to bring you to Breakheart Pond. At a junction at the pond's northern outlet, bear west (right) to hug the western bank of the pond, with decent water views. In 0.7 mile, reaching the southern end of the pond, you reach another junction of trails. Here, pick up the John Hudson trail, the first trail you reach that heads south from the pond. Following a stream bed for much of its course, the trail veers suddenly east and away from the stream to reach a junction. Here, turn west (right) with an unmarked trail that quickly takes you to Frosty Hollow Pond. Following the northern shoreline, the trail ends at a parking area next to the pond. Take the Shelter Trail, leaving to the northwest from the lot, following it for over a mile through the woods before reaching a junction with the Breakheart Trail. Turn west (left) on the Breakheart Trail for another mile of hiking back to the parking area.

Options

For a shorter hike that still provides a good introduction to hiking in Arcadia, try the 1.5-mile loop around scenic Breakheart Pond. From the parking area, pick up the Breakheart Trail—marked by a sign—and follow its yellow blazes counterclockwise around the pond to the eastern shore. Water views are few here, though you could bushwhack off the trail to the water's edge. Reaching the pond's north end in about 0.7 mile, turn left with the blazed trail, cross a brook on a wooden footbridge beside a small beaver dam, and reach a junction of trails. Turn left and you soon come upon the pond's west shore, with views of the pond's marshy inlets and calm, peaceful waters. The loop finishes in the parking area.

If you do go with this option for exploring Arcadia, be aware that driving directions for this hike are slightly different. To reach the trailhead, from the junction of Routes 3 and 165 in Exeter, drive west on Route 165 for 2.9 miles and turn right at the sign for Camp E-Hun-Tee onto the dirt Frosty Hollow Road. Follow that road for 1.6 miles and turn right onto the dirt Austin Farm Road. Continue another 0.5 mile to the road's end at Breakheart Pond. Park in the lot to the right.

Directions

From the junction of Routes 3 and 165 in Exeter, drive west on Route 165 for about 5.5 miles and turn right onto the paved Escoheag Hill Road. Continue another mile and turn right onto the dirt Austin Farm Road. Two roads diverge here; take the left one, drive past a former ranger station, and pull into a parking area on the left about a mile from Escoheag Hill Road, immediately before the bridge over Falls River. Austin Farm Road is closed to motor vehicles at Escoheag

Hill Road during the winter. Other roads open to traffic in summer but closed in winter include Brook Trail, Barber Trail, and Blitzkrieg Trail.

GPS Coordinates: 41.5978 N, 71.7463 W

Contact

Parking and access are free. Dogs must be leashed March 1–August 15. Hunting is allowed in season; all trail users are required to wear at least 200 square inches of fluorescent orange, as a cap and vest, during the hunting season (the second Saturday of October–the last day of February). A free trail map is available at the Arcadia headquarters and in various parking lots in the management area. For more information, contact Arcadia Management Area headquarters, 260 Arcadia Rd., Richmond, RI 02832, 401/539-1052. Rhode Island Division of Forest Environment, 1037 Hartford Pike, North Scituate, RI 02857, 401/647-1439, www.riparks.com/arcadia.htm.

5 NORMAN BIRD SANCTUARY

BEST ☾

Middletown

Level: Easy

Total Distance: 2.0 miles

Hiking Time: 1 hour

Elevation: 50 feet

Summary: Hike through bird-filled meadows on the way to an interesting cliff formation overlooking Narragansett Bay.

The Norman Bird Sanctuary lies along the major route of the Atlantic Flyway, and its advantage of being near the southern end of Aquidneck Island in Narragansett Bay means returning migrants often stop in the vicinity of the sanctuary as a refueling and rest stop. The months of March, April, and early May are the best times to observe warblers, swallows, and such shore birds as black-crowned night heron. September, October, and November are also busy migration months as birds head south to their seasonal destinations. For visitors to the sanctuary of the human va-

riety, the 450-acre sanctuary offers eight miles of trails through forests, old fields, pastures, and past red oak swamps. The most popular trail here is the Hanging Rock Trail, which traverses the narrow crest of a rock spine that seems wholly out of place rising 40–50 feet above the surrounding woods and marsh. Stunted trees, characteristic of high mountains, grow atop it. Although parts of the ridge are somewhat exposed, it's a fairly easy walk for kids and offers an excellent vantage point for birding.

From the parking lot, walk west past the visitors center (housed in a 125-year-old barn) onto the main path for a short distance. Reaching an area of low scrub growth, the trail reaches a junction. Here, turn south (left) onto the Quarry Trail. Birders will want to take their time on this relatively short trail as bird feeders placed among the low-lying bushes and wildflower-filled fields attract an ever-changing array of winged creatures. The Quarry Trail continues to flow south before turning sharply west. Passing a junction with the Indian Rock Trail, you will next reach a junction with the Blue Dot Trail. Turn south (left) on the Blue

the view from the rocky overlook, Norman Bird Sanctuary

Dot Trail, skirting a former slate quarry on the left, now filled with water. Turning west, the trail crosses a boardwalk and climbs a short hill past ledges before ending at a T junction.

Turning south (left) on the Hanging Rock Trail, views of Gardner Pond open as the trail turns sharply uphill onto the Hanging Rock ridge. Following the ridge of Hanging Rock to its knobby end, the trail terminates abruptly at a short cliff with nice views of Narragansett Bay. To return, stay with the Hanging Rock Trail, passing several junctions. When you reach a junction with the Woodland Trail, turn east (right) and follow the signs for a short walk back to the barn and parking area.

Options

Serious birders will want to check out the Warbler Meadows, located across Third Beach Road from the parking area and accessible via a 0.5-mile-long loop trail. According to Norman Sanctuary regulars, common yellowthroat, Wilson's warbler, and chestnut-sided warbler tend to congregate in the lower brushy growth; blackburnian and American redstart stay in the treetops edging the meadow; and northern waterthrush appear to prefer the meadow's low, wet areas.

Directions

From Route 114, at the Middletown-Portsmouth town line, turn east onto Mitchell's Lane at a small sign for the Norman Bird Sanctuary. At 1.4 miles, turn left at a stop sign. Drive 0.5 mile, then bear right at a fork and proceed another 0.3 mile to a four-way stop at a crossroads. Drive straight through the intersection and go another 0.8 mile to the sanctuary entrance on the right.

GPS Coordinates: 41.4997 N, 71.2500 W

Contact

There is a trail fee of $5 for adults and $2 for children 4–13. Sanctuary members and children under four are admitted free. Dogs and pets are prohibited. The sanctuary is open 9 A.M.–5 P.M. daily, except Thanksgiving and Christmas. A map and trail guide is available at the visitors center. For more information, contact the Norman Bird Sanctuary, 583 Third Beach Rd., Middletown, RI 02842, 401/846-2577, www.normanbirdsanctuary.org.

6 NEWPORT CLIFF WALK

BEST C

Newport

Level: Strenuous

Total Distance: 6.0 miles

Hiking Time: 3 hours

Elevation: 100 feet

Summary: This famous walk in view of the grand mansions of the Gilded Age is actually a challenging hike along a rugged stretch of coastline.

Come here during the height of the summer tourist season and the experience of your walk suffers from the crowds, which often form a conga line along the trail's length. But come here in the off-season—during the spring or fall—and you gain much more enjoyment from this scenic walk atop cliffs that fall away dramatically to the ocean. What is probably Rhode Island's most famous walk passes mansions built by some of the nation's wealthiest families in the late 19th and early 20th centuries—including Rosecliff, the house used in the filming of *The Great Gatsby.*

This hike brings you along the Cliff Walk and then up Bellevue Avenue for mansion views that are often better than the views from the Cliff Walk. From the Easton Beach parking, walk a short distance back up Memorial Boulevard to a large sign on the median strip indicating the start of the Cliff Walk (behind Cliff Walk Manor). Heading due south down the Newport coast, this first section of the

© HEIDI J. BROWN

An exciting add-on to the Newport Cliff Walk is a visit to Brenton Point.

walk is certainly its most tame, as the trail begins as a large, paved walkway edging along the fenced-off cliff tops. Reaching the corner of Narragansett Avenue, approximately 0.75 mile from the start of the walk, here you will encounter the famous 40 Steps, a staircase that drops steeply down the side of a cliff before ending in a platform balcony above the crashing surf.

The next 0.75 mile stretch passes the magnificent splendor of Salve Regina University, housed in four former mansions; immediately south of the university is The Breakers, the grand summer house built by Cornelius Vanderbilt. Passing an entrance to Ruggles Avenue, the walk suddenly begins to grow rockier and rugged. (For those uncomfortable with rocky footing, it's best to turn back here or exit via Ruggles Avenue.) It's another 2.5 miles from here to Ledge Road, with side paths leading to Rose Cliff, one of the mansions open to the public.

Continuing to pick your way along the rocks, the trail eventually turns west to reach Ledge Road. Here, turn north (right) and follow Ledge Road straight onto Bellevue Avenue. Walk north on Bellevue, past the front of the mansions, back to Memorial Boulevard, and then turn east (right) to return to Easton Beach.

Options

Another cliff walk of sorts in Newport can be found at Brenton Point State Park. Once the home to a lavish seaside

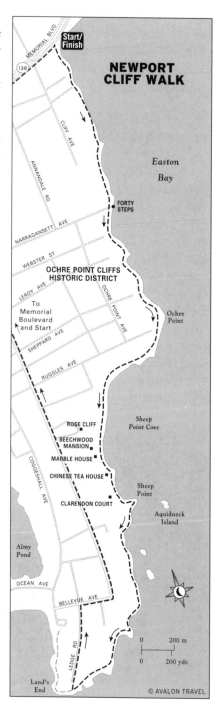

mansion (now gone), Brenton Point is now one of Newport's most scenic public lands, with lots of room to roam and wide-open views of Rhode Island Sound. The round-trip walk of about two miles hugs the shore and travels out into the sound atop a stone jetty. To reach the state park, from the corner of Memorial Boulevard and Bellevue Avenue in Newport, follow Bellevue Avenue south for 1.1 miles to a right turn onto Ruggles Avenue. Follow 0.5 mile to a left turn on Carroll Avenue. Follow this street for 0.5 mile to a right turn onto Ocean Boulevard. Brenton Point State Park lies 1.3 miles ahead on the left, with several places to park.

Directions
In Newport, follow Memorial Boulevard east to the Easton Beach parking area. **GPS Coordinates:** 41.4862 N, 71.2958 W

Contact
Parking and Cliff Walk access are free. The Cliff Walk is open to the public 6 A.M.–9 P.M. Dogs on leash are allowed. A Newport visitors' map is available from the Convention and Visitor Bureau. For more information, contact the Newport County Convention and Visitor Bureau, 23 America's Cup Ave., Newport, RI 02840, 401/849-8098 or 800/976-5122, www.gonewport.com.

7 GREAT SWAMP MANAGEMENT AREA
West Kingston

🦌 ✈ 🚣 🐎 👫

Level: Easy/Moderate

Hiking Time: 2.5 hours

Total Distance: 5.5 miles

Elevation: 10 feet

Summary: This long walk in the woods leads to the scenic shores of Worden Pond and the murky waters of the Great Swamp Impoundment.

The 3,349-acre Great Swamp Management Area, encompasses wildlife-friendly habitats ranging from freshwater wetlands to forest to its main feature, the Great Swamp, an artificially made marsh of more than 130 acres. Cottontail rabbit, white-tailed deer, fox, raccoon, coyote, mink, muskrat, wild turkey, grouse, and wood ducks all call this vast preserve home; the Great Swamp itself is a prime destination for bird-watchers. The best time for birding is during the spring migration in May when warblers, shore birds, and swallows pass through on their return

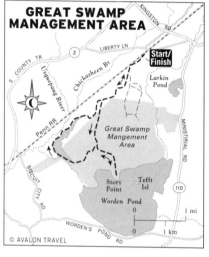

flight north. This loop to Worden Pond and around the Great Swamp follows mostly flat, wide woods roads that make for a pleasant forest ramble.

From the parking area, go around the gate and follow the woods road south (avoiding the side roads leading right) for just under a mile until you reach a footpath branching off the trail to your left, heading east. Pushing southeast through a mix of birch and ash, in just over 0.25 mile the path ends at Story Point, jutting out into the scenic Worden Pond. The pond—more the size of a lake—is a popular destination in the area for boaters, anglers, bird-watchers and those looking to take a dip on a hot summer day.

To next reach the Great Swamp, double back on the footpath to return to its junction with the woods road. Cross the woods road and walk west (straight) onto another dirt road, which in a very short distance ends at a T junction. Here, take the trail heading south (on your left). Momentarily leaving the woods to pass through fields, the trail eventually swings west to bring you to another junction. Bear to the southwest here to begin a clockwise loop around the Great Swamp

Moisture-loving ferns line the trail in Great Swamp Management Area.

© HEIDI J. BROWN

Impoundment. Edging northwest and then northeast to hug the perimeter of the swamp, breaks in the groves of red oak lining the marsh open to views of brackish, reed-choked waters. As the swamp narrows at its northern tip, the trail turns west away from the swamp and soon reaches its end at a T junction. Turn north (left) to follow the trail to a junction with the woods road this hike began on. Turn north (left) and follow the woods road 0.25 mile back to the parking area.

Options

If you have any interest in angling, you may want to bring your fishing pole along on this hike. Despite its size, Worden Pond's average depth of only four feet promotes heavy weed growth, and in turn, creates an ideal habitat for fish. Drawing anglers from all over New England, Worden Pond is known for largemouth bass populations and is also home to northern pike, perch, smallmouth bass, bluegill, chain pickerel, and sunfish. Even if you don't fish, it is an interesting sight to see anglers in their hip waders casting their lines far from shore.

Directions

From Route 138 in West Kingston, just west of the junction with Route 110, turn west onto Liberty Lane. Drive a mile to the road's end and then turn left onto the dirt Great Neck Road. Within a mile, you pass the headquarters on the right. The dirt road ends one mile from Liberty Lane, at a big parking area.

GPS Coordinates: 41.4773 N, 71.5754 W

8 WATCHAUG POND LOOP

Burlingame State Park in Charlestown

Level: Moderate

Hiking Time: 2 hours

Total Distance: 4.0 miles

Elevation: 10 feet

Summary: There's no better way to end this woods walk around the sparkling clear waters of Wachaug Pond than with a refreshing swim.

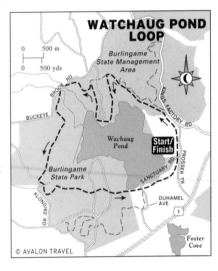

The soaring pine woods of Burlingame State Park are shady and lovely to walk through, but it's the giant Watchaug Pond that is the real attraction on this hike. A glacially formed kettle pond, the 573-acre Watchaug Pond is home to a variety of waterfowl and visiting migrant birds—and is also home to lots of human visitors during the summer months, taking advantage of the pond's swimming beach and large campground. This hike makes a big loop around Watchaug Pond using a series of connected footpaths, woods roads, and a short stretch of paved road; watch carefully for trail blazes on this hike. And though the terrain is mostly flat, you will also want to keep an eye out for rocks and exposed tree roots.

From the beach parking lot, look for the yellow blazes of the Vin Gormley Trail as it crosses the parking lot and heads north from the lot into the woods. Treading to the east of Watchaug Pond, the woods road crosses several brooks and boardwalks through boggy areas before reaching a junction, about one mile from the parking area. Here, bear northwest on a red-blazed footpath, now hiking near the northern shore of the pond. Passing a number of trail junctions in the next mile, at the sixth junction, turn south (left), still following the red blazes as this spur trail takes you out onto a point overlooking the pond. Take in the views from this lovely spot (or take a dip) and leave from the point using the blue-blazed trail that bears northwest. Follow the blue blazes back to the main red-blazed trail and turn west (left) to continue on through the woods.

Within another 0.5 mile you will be within view of a marshy inlet of Watchaug Pond; here the trail swings north before ending at a T junction with the yellow-blazed

Watchaug Pond

woods road. Bear southwest with the yellow blazes for a short distance before reaching a junction with another red-blazed path. Here, follow the red blazes due south through the woods for the next two miles—the pond is sometimes still visible through the trees to the east (your left). Eventually swinging to the east, the trail is paved in places as it skirts the southern section of the pond. Reaching another junction with the yellow-blazed Vin Gormley Trail, follow the yellow blazes, treading just above the beach on the way back to the parking area.

Options

The Vin Gormley Trail makes a big loop around Watchaug Pond, using the entire yellow-blazed trail and parts of the red-blazed trails for its circumference. (Signs at trail junctions will tell you which sections of red trail are part of the Vin Gormley). It's a trek measuring some eight miles in length, but a covered bridge with benches built across Perry Healy Brook at the four-mile mark makes a resting spot before continuing on your journey.

Directions

Take U.S. 1 to Charlestown and the exit for Burlingame State Park. Drive 0.6 mile to the park entrance on the left.

GPS Coordinates: 41.3606 N, 71.7021 W

Contact

Parking and access are free. Dogs and pets are not allowed. A map of the Vin Gormley Trail is available at the state park campground office off Klondike Road in Charlestown, which is open weekdays year-round, and at the picnic area off Prosser Trail, which is open Memorial Day–Labor Day. For more information, contact Burlingame State Park, Sanctuary Rd., Charlestown, RI 02813, 401/322-8910. Rhode Island Division of Parks and Recreation, 2321 Hartford Ave., Johnston, RI 02919-1719, 401/222-2632, www.riparks.com.

9 NINIGRET NATIONAL WILDLIFE REFUGE

Charlestown

BEST **◖**

Level: Easy

Total Distance: 3.0 miles

Hiking Time: 1.5 hours

Elevation: 0 feet

Summary: Explore and enjoy bird-watching as this walk takes you to the marshy shore of the state's largest saltwater pond.

Named after one of the original chiefs of the Narragansett Indians, the Ninigret refuge occupies 407 acres of shrublands, grasslands, barrier beach, salt marshes, and Ninigret Pond, the largest saltwater pond in Rhode Island. The refuge is a popular stopover for migrating birds and a wintering spot for some northern bird species; rangers at Ninigret estimate that over 250 bird species visit seasonally, and 70 species nest on the property. This hike, edging salt marshes and exploring the refuge's interpretive nature trails on the

way out to the shore of Ninigret Pond, is a good place to see herons, cormorants, geese, and migrating songbirds. If most trails in the refuge seem especially wide, it's because they were once the runways of a naval training site located here during World War II.

From the parking lot, follow the runway, a wide dirt trail bordered by brush and grasses, heading east. Not far from the trailhead, the start of the Grassy Point Nature Trail is marked by a kiosk with a map of the nature trail and interpretive panels. The nature trail itself consists of two loops totaling 1.4 miles. Take the shorter loop first, beginning north of the kiosk. Following arrows to stay on-trail, the path brings you briefly to the shore of Ninigret Pond before returning to the kiosk. The second loop begins south of the kiosk and travels only a short distance before reaching a junction. Here, swing to the southeast on a wide spur road out to Grassy Point, where an observation deck offers good views of Ninigret Pond and its birds.

Returning to the trail junction, take the trail to the northwest, a spur path that

A cormorant fishes for dinner in Ninigret National Wildlife Refuge.

takes you to the Cross Refuge Trail, a mile-long footpath that leads you through a flat landscape of pondlets and marshy wetlands—another good place for bird-watching, including sightings of heron and cormorants. Reaching the western end of the refuge, the trail ends at the beginning of the Foster Cove Loop, a footpath that winds by this deep inlet of Ninigret Pond. Walk straight onto the loop, heading west (ignoring the trail leading north) to hug the shore of Foster Cove. In less than 0.25 mile, the trail turns inland and soon reaches a parking area at the end of the end of the runway you drove down to reach the nature trail parking area. Turn east (right) on the runway to walk the 0.5 mile back to your car.

Options

Before or after your hike, it's worth the time to stop by the refuge's Kettle Pond Visitor Center and headquarters. Besides bathrooms, the facility contains interactive exhibits and displays about wildlife at Ninigret, lists of recently spotted birds, classes and demonstrations, nature-themed gift shop, and a number of rangers on hand to answer questions about the refuge.

Directions

Take U.S. 1 to Charlestown and the exit for Ninigret Park. Follow signs to the park, turn left into it, and then follow signs to the nature trails and a parking lot on an old runway.

GPS Coordinates: 41.3821 N, 71.6475 W

10 CLAY HEAD TRAIL AND THE MAZE
Clay Head Preserve, Block Island

Level: Easy

Hiking Time: 45 minutes

Total Distance: 0.7 mile

Elevation: 0 feet

Summary: Walk atop the dramatic Clay Head cliffs before testing your navigational skills in the aptly named Maze.

Block Island is a magnet for summer tourists, but in spring and fall, a different kind of visitor crowds the island's bluffs and beaches as hundreds of thousands of birds representing some 150 species descend on Block Island during their seasonal migrations. It's an awesome sight and has led the Nature Conservancy to dub Block Island as one of the earth's "last best places" and the Clay Head Preserve as one of the best spots in the Northeast to see migratory songbirds in autumn.

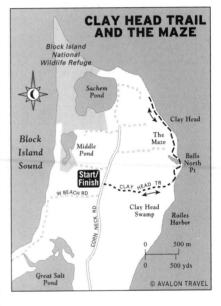

From the trail post, the Clay Head Trail follows a sandy, grass-strewn blufftop, passing Clay Head Swamp, the edge of the Littlefield Farm, and numerous views of the bluffs, seashore, and birds. At first, several trails leading west (left) into the dense scrub brush and forest are posted as private property. Once beyond these, however, you'll see many unmarked trails diverging off the Clay Head Trail and weaving through a cooked-spaghetti tangle of footpaths called the Maze. These trails are fun to explore, especially for kids, though they can get confusing—but getting lost and then unlost is part of the fun here. (And for those afraid of this more unstructured hike, consider that the sound—and often the sight—of the surf will be there to help you navigate.) Retrace your steps and return the way you came.

The best way to explore Block Island's trails is to ride a bicycle from the ferry landing in Old Harbor to the trailheads. This way you see more trails and enjoy some scenic cycling on country roads through a landscape of rolling hills and open

Clay Head cliffs

fields crisscrossed by an uncanny 2,042 miles of stone walls. Bikes can be brought over on the ferry or rented in Old Harbor when you get off the ferry.

Options

Also located on this end of the island is the Hodge Family Preserve, a 25-acre chunk of conserved land on the west side of Corn Neck Road. Marked by wandering dirt trails that lace grassy, wildflower-filled meadows, the area is home to many bird species and is a worthy stop for more island exploration. To reach the preserve's trailhead, travel north on Corn Neck Road 2.9 miles; on your left you will see a sign and parking area for the Hodge Family Wildlife Preserve.

Directions

The Interstate Navigation Company operates ferries year-round from Point Judith and during the summer from Newport. The Block Island Express Ferry operates between New London, Connecticut, and Block Island May–October. From the island's ferry landing in Old Harbor, turn right on Water Street along the waterfront strip, left on Dodge Street, and then right at the post office onto Corn Neck Road. Continue about 3.5 miles to a dirt road on the right marked by a post indicating the Clay Head Trail. Follow the dirt road about 0.5 mile to the trailhead (there is a bike rack).

GPS Coordinates: 41.1890 N, 71.5684 W

Contact

Access to hiking trails on the island is free. Dogs on leash are allowed. Get a basic map of the island and its hiking trails at the chamber of commerce, which operates an information booth at the ferry landing in Old Harbor and a visitors center around the corner on Water Street. Bike shops within walking distance of the ferry landing have maps of island roads. For more information, contact Block Island Chamber of Commerce, P.O. Box D, Block Island, RI 02807, 401/466-2982 or 800/383-2474, www.blockislandchamber.com. Block Island Tourism Council, Dept. B, 23 Water St., P.O. Box 356, Block Island, RI 02807, 800/383-2474, www.blockislandinfo.com. Interstate Navigation Company, 401/783-4613, www.blockislandferry.com. Block Island Express Ferry, 860/444-4624, www.longislandferry.com/bif.

11 RODMAN'S HOLLOW
Block Island

Level: Easy

Total Distance: 0.5 mile

Hiking Time: 45 minutes

Elevation: 20 feet

Summary: Take a Block Island walk on the wild side through this wild, brush-choked glacial depression – one of the island's first pieces of conservation lands.

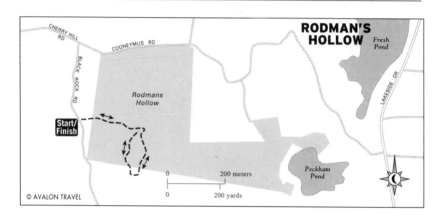

A depression left by a receding glacier, Rodman's Hollow is a wild little corner of the island overgrown with dense brush. A loop trail cuts through it, cresting one small hill with sweeping views of the homes and rolling hills at the southern end of the island. Rodman's Hollow was the inspiration for the 1970s conservation movement that helped protect a quarter of Block Island from development. It's also part of the Greenway, a network of interconnecting trail systems that includes the Enchanted Forest, Turnip Farm, and Fresh Swamp Preserve. The shadbush bloom in early- to mid-May is a beautiful sight.

From just beyond the turnstile, follow the loop trail to the east; a sign indicates a "short loop" and a "long loop," but it's all one trail. The trail crests a hill at a wooden bench. From here, the path forks; following the fork leading west brings you back to Black Rock Road, where you would turn north (right) to return to the trailhead. This hike follows the east-leading trail instead, bringing you through the hollow before winding back to the spot where the path first split. From here, return the way you came.

Bicycling from the ferry landing in Old Harbor to this and other Block Island trails in this chapter is recommended. Bikes can be brought over on the ferry or rented in Old Harbor when you get off the ferry.

Options

Two other interesting places worth exploring on this end of Block Island are Southeast Light and the Mohegan Bluffs. As you travel on Southeast Light Road to reach the trailhead for Rodman's Hollow, you will see a footpath on the left that leads a short distance to Southeast Lighthouse, sitting high above the Mohegan Bluffs (approximately two miles from the ferry landing). The lighthouse, built in 1873 on the eroding cliffs 150 feet above the sea, was moved back 200 feet in 1993 because the ocean had chewed away nearly all the land between it and the sea. Legend has it that in 1590 the island's first inhabitants, the Narragansett Indians—also known as the Manisses tribe—drove a party of invading Mohegan Indians over the cliffs here.

Southeast Light

© HEIDI J. BROWN

A short distance up the road is a trailhead (with a rack for parking bicycles) leading to a wooden staircase that drops steeply down to the rocky beach, a nice place to walk below the bluffs. Don't try scrambling around on the cliffs themselves, though—the soil and rocks are as loose as they appear and dangerous rockslides occur frequently.

Directions

The Interstate Navigation Company operates ferries year-round from Point Judith and during the summer from Newport. The Block Island Express Ferry operates between New London, Connecticut, and Block Island May–October. From the island's ferry landing in Old Harbor, turn left on Water Street and head straight through an intersection, passing the First Baptist Church on your left, onto Spring Street. The road becomes Mohegan Trail, then hooks right and becomes Lakeside Drive. About four miles from Old Harbor, turn left onto Cooneymus Road. The road doglegs left, then right, and then passes a stone wall and a sign on the left overlooking Rodman's Hollow. Just beyond that point, turn left onto the dirt Black Rock Road. A quarter mile farther is the trailhead, marked by a bike rack and a wooden turnstile. The road continues to a trail leading down to the beach.

GPS Coordinates: 41.1554 N, 71.5900 W

Contact

Access to hiking trails on the island is free. Dogs on leash are allowed. Get a basic map of the island and its hiking trails at the chamber of commerce, which operates an information booth at the ferry landing in Old Harbor and a visitors center around the corner on Water Street. Bike shops within walking distance of the ferry landing have maps of island roads. For more information, contact Block Island Chamber of Commerce, P.O. Box D, Block Island, RI 02807, 401/466-2982 or 800/383-2474, www.blockislandchamber.com. Block Island Tourism Council, Dept. B, 23 Water St., P.O. Box 356, Block Island, RI 02807, 800/383-2474, www.blockislandinfo.com. Interstate Navigation Company, 401/783-4613, www.blockislandferry.com. Block Island Express Ferry, 860/444-4624, www.longislandferry.com/bif.

RESOURCES

STATE PARKS
Blue Hills Reservation Headquarters
695 Hillside Street
Milton, MA 02186
617/698-1802
www.mass.gov

Maine Bureau of Parks and Lands
Department of Conservation
22 State House Station (mail)
18 Elkins Lane (AMHI Campus)
Augusta, ME 04333-0022
207/287-3821, fax 207/287-8111
www.maine.gov

Massachusetts Division of State Parks and Recreation
251 Causeway Street, Suite 600
Boston, MA 02114-2104
617/626-1250, fax 617/626-1351
www.state.ma.us
mass.parks@state.ma.us

New Hampshire Division of Parks and Recreation
P.O. Box 1856
172 Pembroke Road
Concord, NH 03302
603/271-3556, fax 603/271-2629
603/271-3628 (camping reservations)
www.nhstateparks.org
nhparks@dred.state.nh.us

Rhode Island Department of Environmental Management
Note: This department oversees the Division of Parks and Recreation and the Division of Forest Environment.
235 Promenade Street
Providence, RI 02908-5767
401/222-6800
www.dem.ri.gov

Rhode Island Division of Forest Environment
1037 Hartford Pike
North Scituate, RI 02857
401/647-4389 or 401/647-3367, fax 401/647-3590
www.dem.ri.gov

Rhode Island Division of Parks and Recreation
2321 Hartford Avenue
Johnston, RI 02919-1719
401/222-2635
www.riparks.com

NATIONAL PARKS
Boston Harbor Islands Partnership
408 Atlantic Avenue, Suite 228
Boston, MA 02110
617/223-8666
www.nps.gov/boha

Cape Cod National Seashore

99 Marconi Site Road
Wellfleet, MA 02667
508/771-2144, fax 508/349-9052
www.nps.gov/caco
CACO_Superintendent@nps.gov
also: Salt Pond Visitor Center
508/255-3421
also: Province Lands Visitor Center
508/487-1256

Minute Man National Historical Park

250 North Great Road
Lincoln MA, 01773
978/369-6993
www.nps.gov/mima

NATIONAL FORESTS AND WILDLIFE REFUGES
Great Meadows National Wildlife Refuge

73 Weir Hill Road
Sudbury, MA 01776
978/443-4661, fax 978/443-2898
www.fws.gov
fw5rw_emnwr@fws.gov

Parker River National Wildlife Refuge

6 Plum Island Turnpike
Newburyport, MA 01950
978/465-5753 or TDD 800/877-8339,
fax 978/465-2807
parkerriver.fws.gov

White Mountain National Forest Supervisor

719 North Main Street
Laconia, NH 03246
603/528-8721 or TDD 603/528-8722
www.fs.fed.us

MAP SOURCES
New England Cartographics

413/549-4124 or 888/995-6277
www.necartographics.com
info@necartographics.com

Rubel BikeMaps

P.O. Box 401035
Cambridge, MA 02140
www.bikemaps.com
info@bikemaps.com

Trails Illustrated

800/962-1643
www.natgeomaps.com

United States Geological Survey

Information Services
P.O. Box 25286
Denver, CO 80225
888/275-8747, fax 303/202-4693
www.usgs.gov

HIKING GEAR RETAILERS
Hilton's Tent City

272 Friend Street
Boston, MA 02114
617/227-9242
http://hiltonstentcity.com

Kittery Trading Post
301 U.S. 1
Kittery, ME 03904-5619
207/439-2700
www.kitterytradingpost.com
Orders@ktp.com

L.L.Bean
95 Main Street
Freeport, ME 04033
877/755-2326
www.llbean.com

Map & Book Store
Rte. 112
Lincoln, NH 03251
800/745-2707
www.mountainwanderer.com
info@mountainwanderer.com

Recreational Equipment, Inc.
401 Park Drive
Boston, MA 02215
617/236-0746
www.rei.com

TRAIL CLUBS AND ORGANIZATIONS
Appalachian Mountain Club
5 Joy Street
Boston, MA 02108
617/523-0636, fax 617/523-0722
www.outdoors.org
information@outdoors.org

Appalachian Trail Conservancy
799 Washington Street
P.O. Box 807
Harpers Ferry, WV 25425-0807
304/535-6331, fax 304/535-2667
www.appalachiantrail.org
info@appalachiantrail.org

Friends of the Blue Hills
P.O. Box 416
Milton, MA 02186
781/828-1805
www.friendsofthebluehills.org

The Friends of the Middlesex Fells Reservation
4 Woodland Road
Stoneham, MA 02180
781/662-2340
www.fells.org

Friends of the Wapack
P.O. Box 115
West Peterborough, NH 03468
www.wapack.org

The Trustees of Reservations
Long Hill
572 Essex Street
Beverly, MA 01915-1530
978/921-1944
www.thetrustees.org
information@ttor.org

Index

www.moon.com

DESTINATIONS | ACTIVITIES | BLOGS | MAPS | BOOKS

MOON.COM is ready to help plan your next trip! Filled with fresh trip ideas and strategies, author interviews, informative travel blogs, a detailed map library, and descriptions of all the Moon guidebooks, Moon.com is all you need to get out and explore the world—or even places in your own backyard. While at Moon.com, sign up for our monthly e-newsletter for updates on new releases, travel tips, and expert advice from our on-the-go Moon authors. As always, when you travel with Moon, expect an experience that is uncommon and truly unique.

MOON IS ON FACEBOOK—BECOME A FAN!
JOIN THE MOON PHOTO GROUP ON FLICKR

OUTDOORS

YOUR ADVENTURE STARTS HERE

MINNESOTA CAMPING
The Complete Guide to Tent and RV Camping

JAKE KULJU

CALIFORNIA HIKING
The Complete Guide to 1,000 of the Best Hikes in the Golden State

TOM STIENSTRA & ANN MARIE BROWN

OREGON FISHING

CRAIG SCHUHMANN

NEW ENGLAND BIKING
More Than 100 of the Best Rides for Road, Mountain, and Cyclocross Biking

CRAIG LERMAN

CALIFORNIA RECREATIONAL LAKES & RIVERS
The Complete Guide to Boating, Fishing, and Water Sports

TOM STIENSTRA

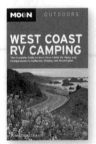

WEST COAST RV CAMPING
The Complete Guide to More Than 1,800 RV Parks and Campgrounds in California, Oregon, and Washington

TOM STIENSTRA

YELLOWSTONE & GRAND TETON CAMPING

BECKY LOMAX

TAKE A HIKE WASHINGTON DC
Hikes within Two Hours of the City

THERESA DOWELL BLACKINTON

For campers, hikers, cyclists, anglers, boaters, and for those that like the comforts of an RV, Moon Outdoors guides are written by outdoor experts who offer well-researched info and insider tips.

For a complete list of guidebooks, visit Moon.com/books.

Moon Outdoors guidebooks are available through online booksellers,

MOON TAKE A HIKE BOSTON

Avalon Travel
a member of the Perseus Books Group
1700 Fourth Street
Berkeley, CA 94710, USA
www.moon.com

Editor: Shaharazade Husain
Series Manager: Sabrina Young
Copy Editor: Emily Lunceford
Graphics Coordinator: Darren Alessi
Production Coordinator: Darren Alessi
Cover Designer: Darren Alessi
Interior Designer: Darren Alessi
Map Editor: Mike Morgenfeld
Cartographers: Chris Henrick, Kat Bennett,
 Kaitlin Jaffe, Andrea Butkoviz

ISBN: 978-1-59880-760-8
ISSN: 2160-8350

Printing History
1st Edition – June 2011
5 4 3 2 1

Text © 2011 by Jacqueline Tourville.
Maps © 2011 by Avalon Travel.
All rights reserved.

Front cover photo: © Frank Vetere / Alamy
Title page photo: © Heidi J. Brown
Frontmatter photos: page 3 © Heidi J. Brown;
page 4 © Jacqueline Tourville; page 5
© Jason Brown
Back cover photo: © Peter Cade / Getty Images

Printed in Canada by Friesens

Keeping Current

We are committed to making this book the most accurate and enjoyable hiking guide to the Boston area. You can rest assured that every trail in this book has been carefully reviewed in an effort to keep this book as up-to-date as possible. However, by the time you read this book, some of the fees listed herein may have changed and trails may have closed unexpectedly.

   If you have a favorite gem you'd like to see included in the next edition, or see anything that needs updating, clarification, or correction, please drop us a line. Send your comments via email to feedback@moon.com, or use the address above.